P9-DGE-882

Louisiana's Best Restaurant Recipes

Louisiana's *Best*

Restaurant Recipes

Compiled by John M. Bailey

Edited by Gwen McKee

QUAIL RIDGE PRESS

Preserving America's Food Heritage

To the people of Louisiana,
may God bless and protect you

To my wonderful wife Ann for her continued
love and support for my projects

Copyright ©2007 John M. Bailey

No part of this book may be reproduced or utilized in any form or by any means, including
photocopying and recording, or by any information storage and retrieval system without the
written permission of the author or publisher excepting brief quotations in connection with
reviews written specifically for inclusion in a magazine or newspaper.

Library of Congress Cataloging-in-Publication Data

Bailey, John M. 1936-
    Louisiana's best restaurant recipes / John M. Bailey
        p. cm.
    Originally published: Fine dining Louisiana style. 2003.
    ISBN-13: 978-1-893062-96-2
    ISBN-10: 1-893062-96-1
        1. Cookery, American--Louisiana style. 2. Restaurants--Louisiana--Guidebooks.
        I. Bailey, John M., 1936- Fine dining Louisiana style. II. Title.

    TX715.2.L68B345 2007
    641.59763--dc22   2007012295

ISBN-13: 978-1-893062-96-2 • ISBN-10: 1-893062-96-1

Photos by Greg Campbell.
Front cover: Seafood Gumbo, Mariner's Seafood and Steak House, Natchitoches.
Back cover: Sabayon Glacé, Maison Lacour, Baton Rouge.

Design by Cynthia Clark.
Pen and ink drawings by Bill Williams, Jr., AIA and Martha Miller Designs.

Printed in Canada

QUAIL RIDGE PRESS
P. O. Box 123 • Brandon, MS 39043 • 1-800-343-1583
email: info@quailridge.com • www.quailridge.com

Table of Contents

. . . .

Listing of Restaurants by Cities and Towns. . . . 7

Introduction 9

Acknowledgments, About the Author,
    About the Editor 10

New Orleans Metro 11

North Shore 109

Plantation Country. 137

Cajun Country 181

Crossroads. 265

Sportsman's Paradise. 295

Glossary. 356

Recipe Index 364

Restaurant Index 379

Listing of Restaurants by Cities and Towns

Abbeville
Dupuy's Oyster Shop 204
Alexandria
Cajun Landing 267
Basile
D.I.'s Cajun Food & Music 200
Bastrop
Slayden's Bar-B-Q 342
Baton Rouge
Brec's Magnolia Mound Plantation 139
Juban's Restaurant & Catering 148
Maison Lacour 152
Mansur's on the Boulevard 156
Primo's 172
Ralph and Kacoo's 175
Bayou Vista
Harbor Seafood Restaurant 226
Boyce
Tunk's Cypress Inn 290
Breaux Bridge
Café Des Amis 185
Broussard
Nash's Restaurant 237
Bunkie
The Magnolia Room 282
Charenton
Mr. Lester's Steakhouse 234
Clinton
Cajun Injector, Inc. 142
Covington
The Dakota Restaurant 118
Crowley
Fezzo's 207
Destrehan
Saia's Oak Plantation 178
Donaldsonville
The Grapevine Café and Gallery 218

Franklin
Hanson House 222
Franklinton
Main Street Restaurant 122
Gonzales
SNO'S Seafood and Steakhouse 253
Grand Cane
The Village Restaurant 350
Grand Coteau
Catahoula's 189
Hammond
Bella Rose Food and Spirits 115
Michabelle Inn and Restaurant 125
Tope Lá! 130
Trey Yuen 132
Houma
Cristiano's Ristorante 196
Jeanerette
Yellow Bowl Restaurant 262
Jennings
Walker's Cajun Dining 260
Jones
Ms. Lucy's Classic Cajun 336
Kenner
Le Parvenu 64
Lafayette
Blue Dog Café 183
Don's Seafood and Steakhouse 202
Lafayette's 228
Prejean's Restaurant 248
Thai Cuisine 257
Lake Charles
Pat's of Henderson 246
Pujo St. Café 251
Lecompte
Lea's Lunch Room 279

Listing of Restaurants by Cities and Towns (continued)

Livonia
Joe's Dreyfus Store Restaurant 145
Many
Cypress Bend 270
Minden
Country Place Restaurant 313
Monroe
Bountiful Foods Catering 300
Chef Hans' Gourmet Foods 306
Enoch's Café and Pub 319
The Brandy House Restaurant 303
Waterfront Grill 353
Natchitoches
Lasyone's Meat Pie Kitchen 276
Mariner's 288
The Landing Restaurant 273
New Iberia
Clementine Dining and Spirits 193
Landry's Restaurant 230
New Orleans
Bon Ton Café 13
Broussard's 19
Clancy's 25
Commander's Palace 28
Dickie Brennan's Steakhouse 30
Dooky Chase's 35
Emeril Lagasse's NOLA 37
Emeril's Delmonico 39
Emeril's Restaurant 42
Galatoire's Restaurant 45
GW Fins 50
Herbsaint 54
K-Paul's Louisiana Kitchen 57
Lilette Restaurant 69
Mr. B's Bistro 72
Palace Café 76
Peristyle 82
Ralph Brennan's BACCO 86
Ralph Brennan's Red Fish Grill 89

René Bistrot 93
Restaurant August 97
Restaurant Cuvée 101
Stella! 106
New Roads
Morel's 159
Opelousas
The Palace Café 242
Ponchatoula
A Taste of Bavaria 128
Rayne
Chef Roy's Frog City Café 191
Maison Daboval 232
Ruston
Follette Pottery 326
Shreveport
Bella Fresca Restaurant 297
Chianti Restaurant 311
Dominic's Italian Restaurant 316
Fertitta's 6301 Restaurant 321
Gerald Savoie's 329
Olive Street Bistro 339
Superior Grill 344
The Glenwood Village Tearoom 331
Slidell
Bealer's Restaurant 111
Thibodaux
Flanagan's 209
Fremin's 213
Vacherie
Oak Alley Plantation 167
White Castle
Nottoway Plantation 162
Winnfield
Uncle Earl's Pea Patch Café 348
Winnsboro
Jesse's Steak and Seafood 334

Introduction

. . . .

Because the release of this cookbook is close to the two-year anniversary of Hurricane Katrina's devastation of New Orleans and Hurricane Rita's impact on other parts of Louisiana, we want to remember those who were and continue to be affected by the storm. Progress has certainly been made, but Louisiana and her people are still recovering. And they are rising to new heights of historic and culinary excellence.

This cookbook showcases the fine chefs found across Louisiana, which is known for its music, great food, and the friendliness and warmth of its diverse culture. After spending many weeks in Louisiana researching this book, I can attest to that!

Louisiana has five distinctly different regions. Northern Louisiana is referred to as Sportsman's Paradise; Crossroads for the center of the state; Cajun Country for southern Louisiana; Plantation Country for the River Road area; and Greater New Orleans for the southeastern part of the state. The New Orleans area is further subdivided into the Metro and North Shore areas.

Please enjoy your culinary visit to Louisiana as much as I enjoyed working on this project. Use the book to guide you to the great chefs, the wonderful restaurants, and the delightful bed and breakfast inns across the state. The recipes have been tested over the years throughout Louisiana. Now enjoy them in your home, on the house, compliments of the chef!

Bon Appétit!
John M. Bailey

Acknowledgments

I would like to thank the following people:

- The chefs of Louisiana who contributed a sampling of their great recipes
- Gwen McKee and the editing staff at Quail Ridge Press
- The local chapters of the Louisiana Chamber of Commerce
- Bill Williams, Jr., AIA and Martha Miller Designs for the use of their wonderful pen and ink drawings
- The Louisiana Department of Tourism for the use of their historical information and descriptions
- My longtime friend Larry McIntire for showing me around New Orleans
- Tim and Ashley Francis for their hospitality and help
- I would also like to thank W. Jett Wilson, attorney, and Ed Neal, CPA.

JMB

About the Author

John Bailey, author of *Fine Dining Georgia Style*, *Fine Dining Mississippi Style*, *Fine Dining Tennessee Style*, and *Louisiana's Best Restaurant Recipes*, is a graduate of the University of Mississippi. He is a member of the Southern Foodways Alliance and a frequent judge at many culinary events. In his spare time, John enjoys photography, cooking, and collecting cookbooks. He and his wife Ann reside in Germantown, Tennessee.

About the Editor

Gwen McKee was born, raised, and educated (LSU) in Baton Rouge, and lends her knowledge of her favorite kind of cooking—Cajun and Creole—to editing this cookbook. Author of *The Little Gumbo Book* and *The Little New Orleans Cookbook*, she has edited over eighty cookbooks, including her Best of the Best State Cookbook Series and the Recipe Hall of Fame Collection.

New Orleans Metro

NEW ORLEANS METRO is a region so steeped in its history, so connected to its French and Spanish roots that visitors can't help but be overwhelmed with all there is to see and do here. The architecture will amaze you. From the hundred-year-old mansions and the French Quarter's colorful Creole cottages with their lacy iron balconies, to the Gothic spires of St. Louis Cathedral and the haunting marble tombs of the above-ground cemeteries, New Orleans reads like an epic novel, full of mystery and adventure.

The mystique of New Orleans only begins in the French Quarter—so let the rhythms carry you through the city as far as your imagination and sense of adventure will take you. The Warehouse District, the Garden District, Uptown, the West Bank, Chalmette—each area sports its own architecture, history, culture, and style.

New Orleans Metro Restaurants

Bon Ton Café 13

Broussard's 19

Clancy's 25

Commander's Palace 28

Dickie Brennan's Steakhouse 30

Dooky Chase's 35

Emeril Lagasse's NOLA 37

Emeril's Delmonico 39

Emeril's Restaurant 41

Galatoire's Restaurant 45

GW Fins 50

Herbsaint 54

K-Paul's Louisiana Kitchen 57

Le Parvenu 64

Lilette Restaurant 69

Mr. B's Bistro 72

Palace Café 76

Peristyle 82

Ralph Brennan's BACCO 86

Ralph Brennan's Red Fish Grill 89

René Bistrot 93

Restaurant August 97

Restaurant Cuvée 101

Stella! 106

Bon Ton Café

401 Magazine Street
New Orleans, LA 70130
(504) 524-3386

Wayne and Debbie Pierce
Chefs/Proprietors

Wayne and Debbie operate the oldest Cajun restaurant in New Orleans. Wayne, having grown up in southern Louisiana, was well aware of the wonderful lifestyle, culture, and cuisine of the Cajun people. Wayne's aunt and uncle first operated Bon Ton, and he has continued the tradition established by them. Contributing to his continued success is his ability to resist being influenced by new trends that alter the style of traditional Cajun cooking. Bon Ton Café received the 5 Star International Award of Excellence for its culinary accomplishments. On Sunday, July 19, 1998, Bon Ton Café hosted a private dinner party for former President William Jefferson Clinton.

Bon Ton Homemade Turtle Soup

. . . .

1 gallon water

2 cups tomato sauce

2 cups whole peeled tomatoes, cut up

2½ cups dried onions

5 bay leaves

2 cups all-purpose flour

2 cups vegetable oil

2½ pounds turtle meat, cut, almost diced, into small pieces, or may substitute beef such as brisket

6 eggs, hard-cooked and diced

1 lemon, cut into 5 to 7 slices

¼ cup whole cloves, wrapped in tightly sealed cloth

Salt and pepper to taste

1 cup chopped parsley

1 cup cooking sherry wine

Bring water to a boil in appropriate-size pot. Add tomato sauce, tomatoes, dried onions, and bay leaves; bring to a simmer.

In a separate skillet, make a roux by combining flour and oil; heat over low to medium flame, stirring often. Allow mixture to come to a golden brown color. Stir often to prevent burning of roux on bottom of skillet. You may have to add oil to keep the consistency of roux slightly loose. Once roux becomes golden brown, remove from heat. Add roux to simmering mixture and stir until thoroughly combined. Add turtle meat and simmer one hour. Add eggs, lemon slices, cloth with cloves, salt, and pepper. Continue to simmer ½ hour, stirring frequently to keep roux well dissolved and mixture evenly distributed. Turn off heat; add parsley and sherry, and sample for seasoning. Mixture may have to be reduced more to concentrate flavors or may be thinned by adding additional water, if desired. Makes 8 to 10 cups. (Double quantities if you want to freeze some for future use.)

Bon Ton Shrimp Rémoulade Salad

2 quarts water

1 package crab boil

Salt and pepper to taste

32 large Gulf shrimp, unpeeled

4 (4-ounce) jars Creole mustard

4 (4-ounce) jars Grey Poupon mustard

4 green onions with stems, chopped

2 cups olive oil

2 tablespoons sugar

1 tablespoon paprika

Romaine lettuce for 8 salads

4 ripe tomatoes, cut into wedges

Pour water into pot; add crab boil and salt and pepper to taste. Bring mixture to a boil; add shrimp. Bring back to a boil and cook 8 to 10 minutes or until shrimp are cooked. Strain and allow shrimp to cool. Peel and devein shrimp.

Make rémoulade sauce by combining both mustards with chopped onions, olive oil, sugar, and paprika. Mix together until blended to smoothness. (A small amount of water may have to be added to achieve this.) Place shrimp over bed of chopped lettuce and cover with rémoulade sauce. Garnish with fresh tomato wedges. Makes 8 servings.

Crabmeat Imperial

1 cup chopped green onions, including bulbs and stems

½ cup sliced mushrooms

1 cup olive oil

2 pounds jumbo lump crabmeat, fresh-picked

¼ cup diced pimento

½ cup sherry wine

Salt to taste

12 (4-inch) toasted French bread points

¼ cup chopped parsley

Sauté green onions and mushrooms in olive oil until clear or limp. Add crabmeat, pimento, and sherry and allow to marinate until warm throughout. Season with salt to taste. Place 3 toast points per serving on plate with wide ends of toast meeting in the middle and points facing out as a star. Mound crabmeat on top of toast. Sprinkle lightly with parsley. Makes 4 servings.

Oysters Alvin with Bouillon Rice

¾ quart frying oil

1 dozen oysters, freshly shucked

½ cup all-purpose flour

½ stick margarine

½ cup beef broth (bouillon)

¼ teaspoon salt, or to taste

½ teaspoon pepper, or to taste

Juice of ½ lemon

1 teaspoon paprika

1 teaspoon chopped parsley

Preheat oil to 350°. Dust oysters in flour. Deep-fry in oil until golden brown. Remove and drain.

Melt margarine in skillet. Add beef broth and simmer until mixture thickens slightly. Place fried oysters in mixture. (The bottom of the oysters become soaked while the tops remain crisp.) Season with salt, pepper, and lemon; sprinkle lightly with paprika. Place in broiler until oysters brown slightly. Sprinkle with parsley and serve around Bouillon Rice, adding sauce from oysters. Makes 1 serving.

BOUILLON RICE:

1 teaspoon margarine

¼ cup chopped onion

¼ cup beef bouillon

¼ cup chopped mushrooms

¼ teaspoon salt

¼ teaspoon pepper

1 cup cooked rice

Sauté margarine, onion, bouillon, mushrooms, salt, and pepper until onions are clear. Add to cooked rice and stir over low heat until rice absorbs the liquid. Mound rice onto plate, surround with Oysters Alvin, and serve.

Steak Cubed with Mushrooms in Cabernet Wine Sauce

4 (10-ounce) sirloin strip steaks, trimmed

Salt and pepper to taste

2 sticks margarine, divided

2 cups sliced mushrooms

1 cup beef broth

2 cups Cabernet (red wine)

1 teaspoon flour

4 cups cooked rice

Chopped parsley for garnish

Cut each sirloin into 5 equal cubes, making 20 pieces. Season with salt and pepper. In a large skillet, melt 1 stick of margarine over a high flame. Place steak cubes in hot margarine and brown on both sides. Add sliced mushrooms. (Use additional margarine if you feel it is needed.) Add beef broth and wine. Remove steak cubes when cooked to desired doneness. Add flour to sauce and stir until reduced to desired thickness. For each serving, place 5 steak cubes around rice pilaf. Spoon sauce with mushrooms onto steak and around rice. Sprinkle with chopped parsley and serve. Makes 4 servings.

Bon Ton Bread Pudding with Whiskey Sauce

BREAD PUDDING:

1 loaf French bread

1 quart milk

3 eggs, beaten

2 cups sugar

2 tablespoons vanilla

1 cup raisins

3 tablespoons margarine

Preheat oven to 350°. Soak bread in milk; crush with hands until well mixed. Add eggs, sugar, vanilla, and raisins; stir well. Melt margarine in thick baking pan, then add bread mixture to pan. Bake until slightly firm throughout and lightly browned on top. Allow to cool; cut into individual-sized servings. When ready to serve, heat, then pour Whiskey Sauce on top and place under broiler for a couple minutes to heat sauce. (Use as much sauce as individual likes.)

WHISKEY SAUCE:

2 cups sugar

2 eggs, beaten

2 sticks margarine

1 to 2 ounces Bourbon whiskey, or to taste

Cream sugar and eggs until well mixed. Melt margarine and add to creamed mixture. Add whiskey to taste, which should make sauce creamy smooth.

Broussard's

819 Rue Conti
New Orleans, LA 70112
(504) 581-3866
www.broussards.com

Gunter Preuss
Chef/Proprietor

Evelyn Preuss
Proprietress

Chef Preuss has been profiled in the PBS series *Great Chefs of New Orleans* and a recent recipient of the Millennium Chef International Award of Excellence as one of America's Top 100 Chefs.

A New Orleans Tradition Since 1920

Diners at Broussard's can enjoy their meal in the elegantly appointed dining rooms or the lush tropical courtyard. *New Orleans Magazine* calls the courtyard "the most beautiful in the French Quarter."

The Preuss family has made Broussard's a true family affair. Gunter, who supervises the kitchen, has been one of the city's most respected interpreters of classic Creole cuisine; proprietress Evelyn is always on hand to attend to patrons' needs, and the two have been joined by son Marc, who has been trained in a European hotel school and worked in luxury hotels such as the Ritz-Carlton in Houston and the Palace Hotel in Sun City, South Africa. Their efforts have been recognized by *Travel Holiday, Esquire* and *National Geographic Traveler*, as well as being awarded the coveted DiRoNA Award in 1998 and the prestigious Ivy Award in 2000. Broussard's was recently inducted into the Fine Dining Hall of Fame.

Crabmeat Broussard

- -

1 tablespoon butter

8 jumbo shrimp, peeled and butterflied

1 ounce olive oil

1 small onion, diced

2 artichoke hearts, chopped

1 clove garlic, minced

¼ cup all-purpose flour

¼ cup white wine

2 cups chicken stock

1 cup heavy cream

3 ounces Brie cheese

½ cup bread crumbs

1 tablespoon whole thyme leaves

3 tablespoons olive oil

¾ pound jumbo lump crabmeat

Preheat oven to 400°. In large skillet, melt butter and sauté shrimp. Set aside to cool. In heavy saucepan, heat olive oil. Sauté onion, artichoke, and garlic over medium heat until onion becomes limp. Sprinkle with flour and mix well. Deglaze with white wine; add stock. Reduce heat and simmer 3 minutes. Add heavy cream and simmer another 5 minutes. Remove from heat and let stand 2 to 3 minutes. Scrape off white "skin" from Brie and cut into small pieces. Add Brie to cream sauce and stir until all cheese is melted and mixed well. Let cool. Mix bread crumbs, thyme, and olive oil and set aside.

After cheese mixture has cooled, gently fold in crabmeat. Place 1 shrimp in the center of 2½-ounce oven-proof dish, so that it stands upright. If you have a problem, make butterfly cut deeper. Spoon crabmeat mixture around shrimp and sprinkle with bread crumb mixture. Repeat with remaining shrimp. Place dish on pan and heat in oven 15 to 20 minutes or until hot and bubbly. Makes 8.

Soft-Shell Crab Dorè

6 soft-shell crabs, cleaned
Salt and pepper to taste
Lemon juice
Butter

SAUCE DORÈ:

1 pound shrimp, cleaned
½ cup white wine
¼ cup chopped shallots
½ cup chopped green onions
1 cup sliced mushrooms
¼ cup lemon juice
½ teaspoon chopped garlic
½ cup heavy cream
¼ cup butter
Salt and pepper to taste
Chopped parsley
Lemon slice
Dill sprig

Sprinkle crabs with salt, pepper, and lemon juice. Sauté in butter until done or until crabs turn red. Set aside on a dish and keep warm.

Sauté shrimp in wine 2 to 3 minutes; add shallots, green onions, mushrooms, lemon juice, and garlic. Slowly cook 3 more minutes. Add heavy cream and butter. Cook until it becomes a sauce. Add salt and pepper to taste, and place sauce in the center of 6 warm plates. Top with warm crabs and garnish with chopped parsley, a lemon slice, and a fresh dill sprig. Makes 6 servings.

Spinach Salad Dressing

1 quart mayonnaise
2 tablespoons currant jelly
1½ tablespoons balsamic vinegar
Salt and black pepper to taste
½ tablespoon dried tarragon

Combine all ingredients in a mixer. Cover and place in a refrigerator for up to a week. Serve over your favorite spinach salad.

Shrimp and Crabmeat Cheesecake

• •

3 (¼-ounce) packets unflavored gelatin

¼ cup water

¼ cup cider vinegar

2 cups mayonnaise

2 cups sour cream

¼ cup fresh lemon juice

½ cup Dijon mustard

5 tablespoons chopped fresh dill, or 1 tablespoon dried dill, or to taste

2 teaspoons tarragon leaves, soaked 1 hour in white wine and drained

2 teaspoons minced, roasted garlic

1 cup sliced green onions

2 teaspoons paprika

¾ pound cooked shrimp, peeled and chopped

¼ pound jumbo lump crabmeat

PIMENTO SAUCE:

1 (12- to 14-ounce) can or jar whole red pimentos

½ cup heavy cream

1 (8-ounce) package cream cheese, softened

1 teaspoon salt

2 tablespoons chopped fresh dill

In a small, heavy saucepan, combine gelatin, water, and vinegar; set aside. In a large bowl, combine mayonnaise, sour cream, lemon juice, mustard, dill, tarragon, garlic, green onions, and paprika. Mix well. Fold in chopped shrimp. Place gelatin mixture over very low heat, stirring constantly until dissolved. Pour gelatin slowly into shrimp mixture and mix well. Quickly but gently fold in crabmeat. Pour into 8- or 9-inch springform pan. Cover and refrigerate overnight.

Drain pimentos and place in blender with heavy cream, cream cheese, and salt. Purée and pour into glass bowl; mix in the dill. Cover and refrigerate overnight.

(continued)

(Shrimp and Crabmeat Cheesecake continued)

PECAN MIXTURE:

2 tablespoons butter

1 cup chopped pecan pieces

½ teaspoon salt

Pinch of cayenne pepper

1 teaspoon Worcestershire sauce

Melt butter in skillet; add pecans, salt, cayenne pepper, and Worcestershire. Sauté 2 to 3 minutes, being careful not to burn. Cool; chop coarsely. Set aside, but do not refrigerate.

Remove side of springform pan from cheesecake and spread Pimento Sauce over top. Press Pecan Mixture into sides of cheesecake. Chill until ready to serve. Makes 15 servings.

Crêpes Broussard

1 (10-ounce) package frozen strawberries

¼ cup white sugar

¼ cup water

½ cup strawberry liqueur

12 medium fresh strawberries, hulled and halved

12 dessert crêpes

Purée frozen strawberries in blender. In saucepan, dissolve sugar in water and strawberry purée. Cool for 5 minutes. Add liqueur and cook until it becomes a thickened sauce. Use fresh strawberries to enhance the sauce. Using 12 pre-cooked crêpes, layer them flat on a work surface. Make the Filling.

FILLING:

¾ cup cream cheese

¼ cup whipping cream

2 tablespoons sugar

1 teaspoon lemon juice

½ cup chopped walnuts

Combine all ingredients except walnuts in a blender. Fold the walnuts in by hand. Pipe the Filling onto the crêpes; roll and heat in the strawberry sauce. Place 2 crêpes per person in a deep dish and serve. Makes 6 servings.

Pompano Napoleon

. . . .

1 tablespoon butter

1 tablespoon minced shallots

3 ounces capers, drained, liquid reserved

8 ounces whipping cream

3 ounces Creole mustard

Salt and pepper to taste

½ cup sweet paprika

1 tablespoon black pepper

1 teaspoon cayenne pepper

1 teaspoon granulated garlic

1 teaspoon dried oregano

1 teaspoon dried thyme

1 teaspoon dried basil

3 (6-ounce) pompano fillets

12 large dry-pack scallops

12 large shrimp, peeled, deveined

6 (3-inch) puff pastry rounds, baked

In heavy saucepan, melt butter; sauté shallots and capers. Deglaze pan with caper liquid; add cream. Bring to simmer; whisk in mustard. Season with salt and pepper. Keep warm. Combine paprika, black pepper, cayenne pepper, garlic, oregano, thyme, and basil to make Creole seasoning.

Slice fillets in half lengthwise; pound gently. Dust fillets, scallops, and shrimp with Creole seasoning; grill to desired doneness. Split pastry round in half; arrange bottom part on plate. Place fish on top followed by shrimp and scallops; spoon on sauce. Top with pastry round. Makes 6 servings.

Clancy's

6100 Annunciation Street
New Orleans, LA 70118
(504) 895-1111

Brian Larson
Owner

Brad Hollingsworth
Proprietor

Steve Manning
Executive Chef

Brad opened Clancy's in 1987 and since then, Clancy's has been dedicated to preserving the Creole tradition in a fine dining atmosphere. Clancy's has cultivated a strong local clientele that has made it one of the most popular restaurants in New Orleans as well as a "must go" for tourists and conventioneers. A few of the awards and ratings received are: 4 Stars by locally renowned restaurant critic Tom Fitzmorris, 4 Beans by the *Times Picayune Restaurant Guide*, Top Ten in Popularity by New York's *Zagat Survey*, Award of Excellence by *Wine Spectator Magazine* and Fodor's Choice by the 2001 *Fodor's New Orleans*.

Lemon Ice Box Pie

• •

CRUST:

4 ounces graham cracker crumbs

1 ounce white sugar

2 tablespoons brown sugar

1½ ounces fresh unsalted butter, melted

Preheat oven to 400°. Mix ingredients until well blended. Form mixture into ungreased 9-inch pie pan. Bake for 5 minutes until Crust is firm. Cool.

FILLING:

4 egg yolks

2 cups fresh-squeezed lemon juice

2½ (14-ounce) cans sweetened condensed milk

Blend and mix all ingredients. Pour mixture evenly into Crust. Freeze immediately. When frozen, cut and serve. Makes 1 pie.

Pan-Fried Louisiana Soft-Shell Crab, Sautéed Crawfish Tails, and Meunière Sauce

1 soft-shell crab
Salt and pepper to taste
Paprika
Cayenne pepper
Flour
Egg wash
Olive oil or clarified butter

Preheat oven to 350°. With a pair of kitchen shears, cut across the "face" of the crab, removing eyes and mouth. Raise "wings" of crab and cut out lungs. Turn crab on backside and remove paddle shaped "key." Season cleaned crab with salt, pepper, paprika, and cayenne. Dust crab thoroughly in white flour (under wings also). Immerse in beaten egg wash. Dust crab again in white flour. In a hot skillet over medium heat with oil or butter, lay crab on back side and sauté until golden brown, 2 to 3 minutes. Turn crab; place pan in oven 4 to 5 minutes.

SAUTÉED CRAWFISH TAILS:

1 pound crawfish tails
Salt and white pepper to taste
Cayenne pepper
Paprika
Whole butter
White wine
Pinch of sliced scallions

While crab is in oven, prepare cleaned crawfish tails. Season tails with salt, white and cayenne pepper, and paprika. Sauté tails in whole butter. Splash with white wine and add a pinch of sliced scallions; set aside. When tails are ready, prepare Meunière Sauce.

MEUNIÈRE SAUCE:

3 to 4 tablespoons butter
Pinch of chopped fresh parsley
1 teaspoon fresh lemon juice
5 to 6 dashes Worcestershire Sauce
Sautéed fresh asparagus
Roasted new potatoes

In a small skillet, melt butter. Allow butter to begin to brown, pull off heat, and immediately add parsley and lemon juice; add Worcestershire. Bring crab out of oven, having already assembled plate with sautéed fresh asparagus and roasted new potatoes (or your favorite starch and vegetable). Place crab on plate. Top with Sautéed Crawfish Tails and dress with sizzling Meunière Sauce. Serve immediately! Serves 2.

Commander's Palace

1403 Washington Avenue
New Orleans, LA 70130
(504) 899-8221
www.commanderspalace.com

Tory McPhail
Executive Chef

Chef Tory started his career at Commander's Palace in 1993 under legendary Chef Jamie Shannon. Since then Tory has honed his skills at the Breakers Hotel in Palm Beach, L'Escargot and the Piccasso Room, both in London, and has also lived in the Caribbean and Las Vegas. Since taking over as executive chef in 2002, Tory has appeared on the Food Network eight times and travels the country as a spokesperson for sustainable, regional food from Louisiana.

Commander's Palace, a turquoise and white Victorian fantasy of a building, complete with turrets, columns, and gingerbread, is nestled in the middle of the Garden District. Since 1880, it has been a New Orleans landmark known for the award-winning quality of its food, service, and commodious dining rooms. When Ella, Dottie, Dick, and John Brennan took over personal supervision of the restaurant in 1974, they began to give the splendid old landmark a new look. It was decided to design rooms and settings indoors that complemented and enhanced the lovely outdoor setting; so the décor was planned for a bright, casual airiness. Walls were torn out and replaced with walls of glass; trellises were handcrafted for the garden room to complement and accent this particular color and design.

Particular attention was paid to the heart and soul of the restaurant—the kitchen, and the dishes created there. Commander's cuisine reflects the best of the city and both Creole and American heritages.

Chef Tory's Seared Redfish and Chili Glazed Shrimp Salad

. . . .

MANGO VINAIGRETTE:

⅛ cup diced mango

2 lemons, juiced

⅛ cup Karo syrup

¼ cup vegetable oil

SHRIMP AND REDFISH:

1 tablespoon vegetable oil

⅛ teaspoon salt

2 jumbo shrimp, heads on

3 ounces medallion redfish, smoked

1½ tablespoons Commander's Creole Seasoning

2 ounces New Orleans rum

1 serrano chile, minced

¼ teaspoon red pepper flakes

⅛ cup Karo syrup

1½ cups baby greens

¼ cup thinly sliced hearts of palm

½ ounce shaved red onion

Brioche croutons

Salt and pepper to taste

⅛ cup diced mango

Make a vinaigrette by combining ⅛ cup mango, lemon juice, and Karo in a blender. Purée until smooth. When blending, slowly pour in ¼ cup vegetable oil in a steady stream to emulsify. Season with salt.

Heat a heavy bottom skillet over medium heat; add oil. While pan is heating, season shrimp and redfish on both sides with Commander's Creole Seasoning. Sear shrimp and redfish in pan for 1½ minutes on both sides. Remove redfish and shrimp and set aside. Deglaze pan with rum (make sure to remove pan from the flame while deglazing). Place pan back on stove and add chiles, pepper flakes, and remaining Karo. Reduce pepper mixture to sauce consistency. Add shrimp back to the pan and set aside.

Combine baby greens, hearts of palm, onion, croutons, and Mango Vinaigrette in a mixing bowl. Season with salt and pepper to taste. Place salad mixture on plate. Place the redfish on the greens. Place the glazed shrimp atop the redfish. Finish the plate with Mango Vinaigrette and garnish with mango. Serves 1.

Dickie Brennan's Steakhouse

716 Iberville Street
New Orleans, LA 70130
(504) 522-2467
www.dickiebrennanssteak
   house.com

Gus Martin
Executive Chef

In just three short years, Dickie Brennan's Steakhouse has received national accolades. In addition to receiving the Wine Spectator Award of Excellence, Dickie Brennan's Steakhouse has been named one of the Top Twelve Steakhouses in America by national food writer, John Mariani.

Dickie Brennan's Steakhouse features USDA Prime beef exclusively—a fact that sets it apart from other steakhouses. Straightforward USDA Prime steaks with a New Orleans touch, fresh seafood, and innovative Creole dishes define the cuisine.

Prime Beef Tenderloin

18 ounces beef tenderloin, seasoned

2 ounces oil

1 teaspoon chopped fresh garlic

4 ounces wild mushroom mix (shiitake, oyster, crimini), all sliced

1 red bell pepper, roasted, cooled, peeled, julienned

1 tablespoon brandy

9 ounces Brandy Cream Sauce

1 teaspoon Creole seasoning

2 quarts water

12 ounces capellini pasta

In large sauté pan over medium-high heat, blacken beef tenderloin to desired temperature, then remove and cool in refrigerator. In a sauté pan at medium heat, add oil, then garlic. Lightly toast the garlic; add wild mushroom mix. Add julienned roasted peppers; sauté until tender. Add sliced beef, then remove pan from fire and add brandy; carefully return to fire and flame it. Add the Brandy Cream Sauce and bring to a boil. Add Creole seasoning to season mixture.

In a large pot, bring 2 quarts water to a boil, and cook pasta al dente. Remove and drain. Plate the pasta, dividing it into 2-ounce portions. Spoon about 3 ounces of the beef mixture over the pasta. Serve immediately. Makes 8 to 10 ounces of sauce. Serves 6 appetizer portions.

BRANDY CREAM SAUCE:

2 tablespoons unsalted butter

2 tablespoons chopped fresh shallots

1 teaspoon chopped fresh garlic

1 tablespoon chopped celery, diced small

1 tablespoon chopped carrots, diced small

½ cup red wine

1 cup veal demi-glace

½ cup brandy

½ cup heavy cream

½ teaspoon salt

¼ teaspoon white pepper

In saucepan over medium heat, melt butter, then add shallots, garlic, celery, and carrots. Sauté all until tender. Add red wine; bring mixture to a boil; reduce by ¾ its volume. Add veal demi-glace and brandy; bring to a boil and reduce by ½ its volume. Add heavy cream; bring to a boil and reduce by ½ its volume. At this point the sauce has gone through a natural reduction and is ready to be seasoned with salt and white pepper to taste. Strain the sauce. Add sauce to sauté pan to be used in Prime Beef Tenderloin appetizer recipe.

House Filet

BÉCHAMEL SAUCE:

2 ounces unsalted butter
2 ounces all-purpose flour
1 cup whole milk
4 ounces chopped yellow onion
1 bay leaf
2 whole cloves
Kosher salt to taste
White pepper to taste

In medium-size pan, melt butter. Add flour and make a white roux by whisking thoroughly. In medium saucepot, combine milk, onion, bay leaf, cloves, salt, and pepper; bring to a simmer over low heat. Slowly add white roux by whisking it in, and allowing sauce to thicken. Strain sauce and set aside to cool. Serves 2.

CREAMED SPINACH:

1 tablespoon unsalted butter
3 ounces sliced yellow onion
12 ounces fresh spinach, picked clean
½ cup Béchamel Sauce
¼ cup heavy cream
Creole seasoning to taste

In sauté pan, melt butter. Add onions and fresh spinach; sauté until wilted. Add Béchamel Sauce and heavy cream; stir. Season to taste with Creole seasoning. Serve immediately in a dip dish. Serves 2.

BÉARNAISE SAUCE:

1 tablespoons chopped fresh tarragon
½ quart hollandaise sauce

Fold tarragon into hollandaise sauce; set aside.

(continued)

(House Filet continued)

PONTALBA POTATOES:

1 medium potato

3 cups vegetable oil

1½ tablespoons unsalted butter

1 ounce julienned yellow onion

1 ounce chopped tasso, diced small

½ tablespoon chopped fresh garlic

2 ounces wild mushroom mix (shiitake, crimini, oyster, etc.)

½ ounce finely chopped green onions

1 tablespoon brandy

Creole seasoning to taste

Preheat oven to 350°. Wash potato and bake for 40 minutes. Cool potato, peel, and cut into medium-size cubes (½x½-inch). In large pot, add oil and bring to 350°. Add potatoes and fry until golden brown (about 4 minutes). Strain and set aside over paper towels to absorb extra oil. In sauté pan, melt butter over medium heat, add onion, and cook until slightly brown. Add tasso and garlic; cook until garlic is lightly toasted. Add mushrooms and cook until tender. Add fried potatoes, green onions, brandy, and seasoning; toss to mix. Serves 1.

FILET:

8 ounces Creamed Spinach

4 ounces Pontalba Potatoes

1 (8-ounce) beef filet, cooked to desired temperature

1½ ounces Béarnaise Sauce

5 fresh oysters, fried golden brown

Spread Creamed Spinach in a circle across the entire bottom of a plate. Place Pontalba Potatoes in small circle in center of plate. Place filet on top of the potatoes. Ladle the Béarnaise Sauce over the filet. Place fried oysters around the filet. Serves 1.

Creole Onion Soup

· ·

1½ sticks unsalted butter

1½ pounds yellow onions, julienned

2 ounces all-purpose flour

1 quart chicken stock or broth

1 cup white wine

½ quart milk

½ quart heavy cream

2 bay leaves

2 tablespoons kosher salt

1 teaspoon freshly ground white pepper

4½ cups shredded Cheddar cheese

In large pot, melt butter over medium heat. Add onions and cook until translucent (do not brown). Add flour to pot, and cook 8 minutes, stirring constantly. Do NOT brown the flour! Add chicken stock or broth, white wine, milk, cream, and bay leaves; bring to a boil. Reduce to low heat and allow soup to simmer 20 minutes. Remove bay leaves; add salt and pepper. With hand mixer or blender, purée soup; add Cheddar cheese slowly until dissolved. Serve immediately. Makes 1 gallon.

Dooky Chase's

2301 Orleans Avenue
New Orleans, LA 70119
(504) 822-9506
www.dookychaserestaurant
.com

Leah Chase
Chef/Proprietor

Mrs. Leah Chase has worked in the food industry for more than fifty years creating down-home Creole dishes. Mrs. Chase has been recognized for her civic and culinary accomplishments by being the recipient of the Ella Brennan Savoir Faire Award from the Louisiana Restaurant Association, *The Times Picayune's* Loving Cup, and the Junior Achievement Hall of Fame Business Laureate.

Eggs New Orleans

. . . .

1 stick butter

2 tablespoons flour

2 cups evaporated milk

1 cup water

½ teaspoon salt

⅓ teaspoon cayenne pepper

1 teaspoon Worcestershire sauce

1 pound white crabmeat, thoroughly picked

6 hard-cooked eggs

1 tablespoon chopped parsley

Paprika and parsley for garnish

Preheat oven to 375°.   In a medium saucepan, melt butter. Add flour; stir well, and cook about 5 minutes. Add milk slowly, stirring constantly. Add water, cooking slowly until mixture thickens. Add salt, cayenne pepper, Worcestershire, and crab-meat. Cook 5 minutes. Pour into a greased glass baking dish. Cut the eggs in half and place eggs cut side up onto the crabmeat mixture. Sprinkle a little paprika and parsley over top. Bake 10 min-utes. Makes 6 to 8 servings.

Chicken Clemençeau

. . . .

3 (6-ounce) boneless, skinless chicken breasts, cut in cubes

Salt and pepper to taste

3 tablespoons butter

½ cup white wine

1 tablespoon chopped garlic

2 cups diced white potatoes

1 cup sliced mushrooms

½ cup cooked green peas

1 teaspoon chopped parsley

½ teaspoon paprika

White pepper

Season chicken with salt and pepper. In large fry-ing pan, melt butter; add chicken, and stir.   Let cook 5 minutes. Add wine, garlic, and potatoes. Cover and let cook another 5 minutes. Potatoes should be soft and wine just about cooked out. Uncover and add mushrooms, stirring well. Sauté until mushrooms begin to get soft. Add peas, parsley, and paprika. Cook until well blended, being careful not to mash vegetables. Add salt and white pepper to taste. Makes 4 servings.

Emeril Lagasse's NOLA

534 Rue St. Louis
New Orleans, LA 70130
(504) 522-6652
www.emerils.com

Michael Ruoss
Chef de Cuisine

NOLA is located in a four-story French Quarter warehouse. Emeril Lagasse's second restaurant features adaptations of classic Creole and Cajun cuisine. All fresh breads, desserts, ice creams, and sorbets are homemade on the premises. They also employ a full-time butcher to prepare sausages, bacon, and tasso. NOLA is extremely popular with tourists and locals alike. Chef de Cuisine Michael Ruoss oversees the daily activities of the kitchen.

Cedar Plank Fish with Citrus Horseradish Crust

¼ cup white wine

Juice from 1 lemon

8 peppercorns

1 bay leaf

½ teaspoon chopped fresh thyme

¼ cup heavy cream

8 ounces cold butter, cubed

Salt and pepper to taste

Zest and juice of 2 lemons

Zest and juice of 2 oranges

2 pounds horseradish, grated

4 tablespoons chopped cilantro

Kosher salt

Sugar to taste

2 (8-ounce) trout fillets, skin off

Drizzle of olive oil

Preheat the oven to 400°. In a saucepan, combine wine, lemon juice, peppercorns, bay leaf, thyme, and cream. Bring the liquid to a boil and reduce by half, about 2 to 3 minutes. Whisk in butter, a cube at a time, until all butter is incorporated. Season sauce with salt and pepper. Strain sauce through a fine mesh strainer and keep warm.

Bring a small pot of salted water to a boil. Blanch lemon and orange zest for one minute. Remove zest from water and shock in an ice bath. Remove zest from ice bath and pat dry. In a mixing bowl, combine horseradish, blanched zest, lemon juice, orange juice, and cilantro. Season it with kosher salt and sugar.

Rub the tops of 2 (10-inch) untreated cedar planks with olive oil. Place 1 fillet on each plank. Divide the horseradish mixture in half and cover the top of each fillet. Place the planks on a sheet pan and place in the oven. Bake the fillets for 12 to 15 minutes or until the crust is golden and the fish is flaky. Serve the planks with butter sauce. Makes 2 servings.

Emeril's Delmonico

Restaurant and Bar
1300 St. Charles Avenue
New Orleans, LA 70130
(504) 525-4937
www.emerils.com

Shane Pritchett
Chef de Cuisine

The Delmonico Restaurant had been in business since 1895 and closed its doors in February 1997. The restaurant re-opened in May 1998 under the ownership of Chef Emeril Lagasse. The building went through an extensive renovation under the direction of Trapolin Architects in New Orleans. The two-story structure, located in the Garden District, includes three main dining rooms, a bar, and private party rooms. The cuisine at Emeril's Delmonico is classic Creole. Chef de Cuisine Shane Pritchett oversees the kitchen operation.

Veal Marcelle

• •

6 tablespoons butter, divided

4 cups sliced exotic mushrooms

Salt and freshly ground black pepper

¼ cup chopped green onions

1 tablespoon minced garlic

4 egg yolks

1 lemon, juiced

1 tablespoon water

1 tablespoon Creole mustard

Salt and cayenne pepper to taste

16 spears fresh pencil asparagus, blanched

8 (2½-ounce) veal loin cutlets

1 cup all-purpose flour, seasoned with salt and pepper

½ pound butter, melted and warm

4 thin slices fresh lemon

1 tablespoon finely chopped fresh parsley leaves

In a large sauté pan over medium heat, melt 3 tablespoons butter. Add mushrooms. Season with salt and pepper. Sauté 2 minutes. Remove from heat and stir in green onions and garlic. Set aside and keep warm.

In a stainless steel bowl set over a pot of simmering water over medium heat, whisk the egg yolks with lemon juice, water, and mustard. Season with salt and cayenne. Whisk the mixture until pale yellow and slightly thick. Be careful not to let the bowl touch the water. Remove the bowl from the pot and, whisking vigorously, add butter, 1 teaspoon at a time, until 2 tablespoons are incorporated. Keep warm. In a large sauté pan, melt remaining 1 tablespoon butter. Add the asparagus. Season with salt and pepper. Sauté 2 minutes. Remove from heat and keep warm.

Place each piece of veal between a sheet of plastic wrap. Using a meat mallet, pound out very thin. Season both sides with salt and pepper. Dredge each piece of veal in seasoned flour, coating each side completely. In another large sauté pan over medium heat, melt ½ pound butter. Add the veal and pan-fry for 1 minute on each side. Remove from the heat. To serve, lay 2 pieces of the veal in the center of each plate. Spoon the Hollandaise over the veal. Lay 4 spears of asparagus over each plate of veal. Place a spoonful of the relish in the center of the asparagus. Garnish with lemon and parsley. Serves 4.

Emeril's Restaurant

800 Tchoupitoulas Street
New Orleans, LA 70130
(504) 528-9393
www.emerils.com

Christopher Lynch
Chef de Cuisine

Chef Emeril Lagasse opened Emeril's Restaurant in March 1990 in the Warehouse District. This highly successful restaurant uses only the freshest ingredients available. They are purchased from local farmers, ranchers, and fisherman. Lagasse refers to his food as "new New Orleans" cuisine. Chef de Cuisine Christopher Lynch oversees the daily operation of the kitchen. Emeril's was renovated by renowned New York design company, the Rockwell Group in 2000.

Banana Cream Pie with Caramel Drizzles and Chocolate Sauce

. . . .

There are a few secrets necessary to successfully making this pie, which, incidentally, has been on the menu at Emeril's since Day One, and continues to be one of the most requested desserts. First, the bananas, while ripe, need to be firm, so that they hold their shape when pushed into place. Second, the pastry cream needs to be very stiff, so that when sliced, the pie will not crumble or slide. It's also important to cover the bananas completely with the last layer of pastry cream to prevent them from discoloring. And while at Emeril's they pipe the whipped cream over each individual slice before serving . . . feel free to spread your whipped cream over the whole pie, if you'd prefer.

GRAHAM CRACKER CRUST:

1¼ cups graham cracker crumbs

¼ cup sugar

4 tablespoons unsalted butter, melted

Preheat the oven to 350°. Combine graham cracker crumbs and sugar in a medium bowl and mix well. Add butter and mix well. Press mixture into a 9-inch pie pan. Top with aluminum pie tin and with a circular motion, press the crust tightly into the pan. Bake until browned, about 25 minutes. Cool 10 to 15 minutes. Makes 1 (9-inch) crust.

CUSTARD:

4 cups heavy cream, divided

1½ cups whole milk

1½ cups plus 2 teaspoons granulated sugar, divided

1 vanilla bean, split in half lengthwise, seeds scraped and reserved

3 large egg yolks

2 large eggs

Combine 2 cups cream, milk, ½ cup sugar, vanilla bean, and vanilla seeds in a large heavy-bottom saucepan over medium heat. Bring to a gentle boil, whisking to dissolve the sugar. Remove from heat. Combine egg yolks, eggs, cornstarch, and 1 cup sugar in a medium bowl and whisk until pale yellow in color.

Whisk 1 cup hot cream mixture into egg yolks.

(continued)

(Banana Cream Pie with Caramel Drizzles and Chocolate Sauce continued)

CUSTARD: *(continued)*

½ cup cornstarch

3 pounds (about 9) firm but ripe bananas, peeled and cut cross-wise into ½-inch slices

½ teaspoon pure vanilla extract

Caramel Sauce

Chocolate Sauce

Shaved chocolate for garnish

Confectioner's sugar for garnish

Gradually add egg mixture to hot cream, whisking constantly. Bring to a simmer, stirring constantly with a large wooden spoon to cook out the corn-starch and allow the mixture to thicken, about 5 minutes. (The mixture may separate slightly. If so, remove from heat and beat with an electric mixer until thick and smooth.) Strain through a fine mesh strainer into a clean bowl. Cover with plastic wrap, pressing down against the surface to prevent a skin from forming. Chill in refrigerator about 4 hours.

To assemble, spread ½ cup Custard over bottom of prepared Crust, smoothing with the back of a large spoon or rubber spatula. Arrange enough banana slices (not quite ⅓) in a tight, tiled pattern over the custard, pressing down with your hands to pack them firmly. Repeat to build a second layer, using ¾ cup Custard and enough bananas to cover, smoothing down the layer evenly. For the third layer, spread ¾ cup Custard over the bananas and top with the remaining bananas, starting 1-inch from the outer edge and working toward the center. Spread 1 cup Custard evenly over the bananas to prevent discoloration. Cover with plastic wrap and chill for at least 4 hours or overnight.

In a medium bowl, whip the remaining cream until soft peaks form. Add the remaining sugar and vanilla, and whip until stiff peaks form.

Remove pie from refrigerator. With a sharp knife dipped in hot water, cut the pie into 10 equal slices. Transfer slices to dessert plates. Fill a pastry bag with the whipped cream and pipe onto

(continued)

(Banana Cream Pie with Caramel Drizzles and Chocolate Sauce continued)

CUSTARD: *(continued)*

each slice. (Alternately, spread the whipped cream evenly over the pie before cutting.) Drizzle each slice with the Caramel Sauce and Chocolate Sauce, sprinkle with the chocolate shavings and confectioners' sugar, and serve. Makes 1 (9-inch) pie, 10 servings

CARAMEL SAUCE:

¾ cup sugar

2 tablespoons water

½ teaspoon fresh lemon juice

½ cup heavy cream

2 tablespoons to ¼ cup whole milk

Combine sugar, water, and lemon juice in a medium, heavy saucepan over medium-high heat. Cook, stirring, until sugar dissolves. Let boil without stirring until mixture becomes a deep amber color, 2 to 3 minutes, watching it closely so it doesn't burn. Add cream, whisk to combine, and remove from heat. Add milk, 2 tablespoons at a time, until desired consistency is reached. Remove from heat and cool to room temperature before serving with the pie. (The sauce will thicken as it cools.) Makes a generous ¾ cup.

CHOCOLATE SAUCE:

¾ cup half-and-half

1 tablespoon unsalted butter

½ pound semisweet chocolate chips

¼ teaspoon pure vanilla extract

Scald the half-and-half and butter in a small, heavy saucepan over medium heat. Remove from heat. Place chocolate and vanilla in a medium, heat-proof bowl. Add hot half-and-half, and let sit for 2 minutes, then whisk until smooth. Serve slightly warm. (The sauce can be kept refrigerated in an airtight container for several days, but it must be returned to room temperature before serving.) Makes 1½ cups.

Galatoire's Restaurant

209 Bourbon Street
New Orleans, LA 70130
(504) 525-2021
www.galatoires.com

Brian Landry
Executive Chef

The grand dame of New Orleans' old-line restaurants, Galatoire's has remained committed to culinary excellence for more than a century. Under the guidance of the fourth generation of family ownership, it is her time-honored customs that still bind this renowned restaurant. Above all others, she has a rich tradition of serving authentic French Creole cuisine at a level that raises consistency to an art form. It is often said that the beauty of Galatoire's is that things never change. Even after 100 years, ageless New Orleans favorites grace her menu just as they did in 1905.

Crab Sardou

· ·

12 artichokes
2 pounds jumbo lump crabmeat
½ cup clarified butter

In a large pot, submerge artichokes in water and boil for approximately 30 minutes, until the stems are tender. Allow the artichokes to cool, and peel the leaves from the hearts. Using a spoon or your thumb, remove and discard the hearts, leaving the bottom of the artichokes. While waiting for the artichokes to cook and cool, prepare the Béchamel Sauce, Hollandaise Sauce, and Creamed Spinach, placing both of these items on the side.

Sauté the crabmeat in the clarified butter until hot, being careful not to break the lumps. Remove from heat. Arrange serving plates and spoon equal portions of the Creamed Spinach onto the plates. Place 2 peeled artichoke bottoms into the bed of spinach. Drain excess butter from the crabmeat, and spoon equal portions into the cavities of the bottoms. Finally, top with a generous portion of the Hollandaise Sauce. Serves 6.

BÉCHAMEL SAUCE:

1 cup milk
⅛ pound (½ stick) butter
¼ cup flour

Heat milk until it simmers. Melt butter and add flour to make roux. Continue whisking on a low heat to cook flour, but do not allow it to remain on the heat long enough to change from a blonde roux to a brown roux. Add ½ the heated milk to the roux while constantly whisking. This mixture will become thick like a paste. Add remaining milk and whisk until smooth.

(continued)

(Crab Sardou continued)

CREAMED SPINACH:

3 cups cooked spinach

1 cup Béchamel Sauce

Salt and pepper

In a sauté pan, fold the spinach and Béchamel Sauce together and simmer over low heat until heated through. Salt and pepper to taste. Serves 6.

HOLLANDAISE SAUCE:

6 egg yolks

7 tablespoons solid butter, cut into small pieces

Pinch of salt

Pinch of cayenne pepper

1 teaspoon lemon juice

1 teaspoon red wine vinegar

2 cups clarified butter

2 tablespoons cold water (optional)

In a double boiler, combine egg yolks with the butter, salt, cayenne, lemon juice, and vinegar. Over medium heat, whisk the ingredients continuously until the mixture increases in volume and achieves a consistency that adheres to the whisk. Using a ladle, slowly whisk the clarified butter into the mixture. If the sauce appears to be too thick, add a touch of the cold water to bring it back to a proper consistency. Makes 3 cups.

Chicken Clemençeau with Brabant Potatoes

. . . .

1 fryer chicken

Salt and white pepper to taste

2 Idaho potatoes

Vegetable oil for frying

1 pint jumbo button mushrooms, sliced

¼ cup clarified butter

3 tablespoons minced garlic

1 (15-ounce) can petit pois (English peas), drained

Preheat oven to 400°. Rinse chicken and cut into 4 quarters. Salt and pepper chicken and bake for approximately 30 minutes until golden brown. During the cook time for chicken, begin preparing Brabant Potatoes. Peel the potatoes and cut them into ¾-inch cubes. Deep-fry the potatoes in vegetable oil until golden brown and remove to a paper towel to drain.

In a large sauté pan, begin to sauté sliced mushrooms in clarified butter until tender. Add minced garlic, Brabant Potatoes, petit pois, salt, and pepper to taste. After checking seasoning, begin putting the chicken quarters into the sauté pan with the vegetables, and sauté an additional 3 to 5 minutes for the chicken to absorb the flavors. Place quartered chicken pieces onto a serving plate. Using a slotted spoon, drain the excess butter from the vegetables and top the chicken with equal portions.

Shrimp Rémoulade

1 bunch celery

1 bunch green onions

1 bunch parsley

½ large yellow onion

1 cup ketchup

1 cup tomato purée

1 cup Creole mustard

1 cup red wine vinegar

2 tablespoons horseradish, prepared

2 teaspoons Worcestershire sauce

½ cup oil

1½ ounces paprika

Jumbo shrimp, boiled and peeled

Place celery, green onions, parsley, and onion in a food processor and mince. Add ketchup, tomato purée, mustard, red wine vinegar, horseradish, Worcestershire, and oil to the vegetables. Mix all ingredients in the food processor, adding paprika last. Allow the sauce to stand refrigerated 6 to 8 hours and taste again before serving. Adjust horseradish, if necessary. Evenly coat shrimp with sauce in mixing bowl, and serve on a bed of lettuce. Serves 12.

GW Fins

808 Bienville Street
New Orleans, LA 70112
(504) 581-FINS (3467)
www.gwfins.com

Tenney Flynn
Executive Chef/Proprietor

Gary Wollerman
Managing Partner

GW Fins is a global seafood restaurant, which serves the highest quality seafood from every corner of the globe, every day. The menu changes daily, based on the freshest and best seafood that is available at that moment. The following are some of the seafood selections that you may find on GW Fins menu, along with their place of origin: Sea bass from Chile, scallops from New England, Dover sole from Holland, sockeye, king and coho salmon from Alaska, halibut from Alaska, snapper from Florida, speckled trout and pompano from the Gulf of Mexico, haddock and skate from New England, farm-raised catfish from Mississippi, and the list goes on and on!

Creole Tomato, Cucumber, and Vidalia Onion Salad

· ·

3 ounces Creole tomato slices, peeled and seeded

2 ounces cucumbers, peeled, seeded, cut on the bias, and macerated in seasoned rice vinegar

2 ounces Vidalia onions, cut in ³⁄₈-inch julienne

2 ounces Sherry Vinaigrette

1 ounce Maytag blue cheese, macerated in rice vinegar

1 sprig fresh basil

SHERRY VINAIGRETTE:

¹⁄₃ cup sherry vinegar

1⁷⁄₈ teaspoons Dijon mustard

1⁷⁄₈ teaspoons sugar

⁵⁄₈ teaspoon salt

⁵⁄₈ teaspoon freshly ground black pepper

⁷⁄₈ teaspoon combined herbs or choice of parsley, chervil, chives, thyme, etc.

½ cup olive oil

¹⁄₃ cup pomace oil

Toss together the tomato slices, marinated cucumbers, onions, and 2 tablespoons Sherry Vinaigrette. Place in a 4-inch salad ring. Top with blue cheese and basil sprig, and remove the ring. Spoon 1 tablespoon Sherry Vinaigrette around the salad. Makes 1 serving.

Note: Tomatoes should be held at room temperature unless very ripe.

Place all ingredients except oils in a large mixing bowl. Blend with a mixer and slowly add oils to emulsify. Makes 5 servings. Can be stored in a covered jar in the refrigerator.

Horseradish Crusted Drum

. . . .

½ cup Dijon mustard

½ cup prepared horseradish

2 cups panko (Japanese bread crumbs)

1 tablespoon dried parsley

Salt and pepper to taste

4 (7- to 8-ounce) drum fillets, or grouper, snapper, mahi, or redfish

2 tablespoons olive oil

1 tablespoon butter

Truffle oil

Mix mustard, horseradish, panko, parsley, salt, and pepper; coat the fillets. Preheat a large nonstick sauté pan. Add olive oil and butter, and place the prepared fillets crumb side down. Cook until golden brown, turn, and lower heat. Cook on low heat until done, 2 to 3 minutes. Ladle 2 ounces Truffled Potato Sauce on the side of the plate and place the drum fillet in the center. Mound ¼ cup Cripsy Fried Parsnips on top of the fish, drizzle a few drops of truffle oil on top of the sauce, and top with 3 Fried Baby Spinach leaves. Makes 4 servings.

TRUFFLED POTATO SAUCE:

2 large Idaho potatoes, peeled, cut in 2-inch cubes

2 ounces butter

8 ounces half-and-half, warmed, divided

Salt and pepper to taste

2 teaspoons truffle oil

Place potatoes in a saucepan and cover with cold water. Place on high heat and bring to a boil. Cook until fork-tender. Drain and leave in the hot pot to steam dry. Mash with a potato masher or fork removing all lumps before adding any liquid. Stir in butter and 4 ounces of warmed cream. Season to taste with salt and pepper. Thin with remaining warm cream; add truffle oil and strain through a sieve. Reserve and keep warm. Makes 4 servings.

(continued)

(Horseradish Crusted Drum continued)

CRISPY FRIED PARSNIPS:

4 large parsnips, peeled and cut in strips, using peeler

Ice water

Vegetable oil for frying

Peel the parsnips, place in ice water, then dry and fry in vegetable oil at 300° until crispy. Makes 4 servings.

FRIED BABY SPINACH:

12 perfectly shaped spinach leaves

2 cups vegetable oil for frying

Pick small washed spinach leaves (a few extra wouldn't hurt); wash and dry. Cut stems about 1 inch long. Heat oil to 300°, and place the leaves, one at a time, in the hot oil. Stir gently to separate the leaves and carefully remove them when they become translucent. Place on paper towel to drain. Reserve uncovered at room temperature. Makes 4 servings.

Mashed Sweet Potatoes with Bananas, Bourbon, and Vanilla

2 pounds sweet potatoes, peeled, cut in 2-inch cubes

1 cup heavy cream

2 tablespoons soft butter

½ tablespoon salt

1 vanilla bean, split and scraped

½ cup honey

½ cup brown sugar

½ cup freshly squeezed orange juice

2 ripe bananas, mashed

Place sweet potatoes in a thick-bottom saucepan; add cream, salt, and vanilla bean. Cover and cook on low heat until potatoes are soft, about 45 minutes. You may need to add 1 or 2 more tablespoons of cream, but the main thing is to cook at a bare simmer. Add honey, brown sugar, orange juice, and bananas. Increase the heat and cook, mashing all ingredients until somewhat smooth. Remove vanilla bean, then remove from heat. May be made in advance and reheated. Makes 6 servings.

Herbsaint

701 St. Charles Avenue
New Orleans, LA 70130
(504) 524-4114
www.herbsaint.com

Susan Spicer
Chef/Co-owner

Donald Link
Chef/Co-owner

Chef Susan Spicer of Bayona restaurant teams up with Chef Donald Link to offer French-American bistro fare at this sleek eatery. Entrées range from sautéed pork tenderloin with smothered greens to duck confit galette. Vegetarian dishes are available, as well as fine wines by the glass.

Shrimp and Green Chile Grits with Tasso Cream Sauce

GREEN CHILE GRITS:

4 cups chicken stock

1 cup quick-cooking grits

2 tablespoons butter

2 cups shredded Cheddar cheese

1 (4-ounce) can chopped green chiles

2 large eggs, beaten

TASSO CREAM SAUCE:

4 tablespoons whole butter, divided

½ cup diced onion

½ cup diced celery

½ cup diced tasso

1 tablespoon chopped fresh thyme

1½ teaspoons salt

1½ teaspoons black pepper

¾ teaspoon cayenne pepper

¾ teaspoon chopped garlic

4 tablespoons all-purpose flour

1 cup shrimp stock

1 cup heavy cream

Dash of lemon juice to finish

Dash of hot sauce to finish

2 pounds large shrimp (more or less, depending on whether this is an appetizer or entrée)

Preheat oven to 350°. In a 3-quart saucepan over high heat, bring chicken stock to a boil. Add grits, reduce heat to medium, and stir until stock is absorbed, 5 to 6 minutes. Stir in butter, cheese, and chiles. In a small bowl, whisk ½ cup of the cooked grits into the beaten eggs. When blended, stir this mixture back into the rest of the grits. Pour mixture into a buttered 2-quart baking dish. Bake 25 to 30 minutes, until just set

Melt 2 tablespoons butter in a saucepan over medium heat; add onion, celery, tasso, thyme, salt, pepper, cayenne, and garlic. Cook until vegetables are soft. Add remaining butter and melt into pan; add flour to blend in with vegetables in pan. Add shrimp stock and reduce by half; add cream and reduce again until a nice thick cream sauce has formed. Finish with the lemon juice and hot sauce. When sauce is done, set aside and cook shrimp in whatever oil or fat you desire for a couple of minutes on each side until they are almost all the way cooked; ladle sauce over shrimp and simmer 5 minutes. To serve, spoon over warm Green Chile Grits. Serves 4 to 6.

Tip: Whenever making sauce that has some sort of roux in the base, always add the liquids in stages so that sauce does not become too thin; sauce is always easier to thin out than thicken.

Shrimp Bisque

• •

1 cup chopped onion
½ cup chopped carrots
1 cup chopped celery
½ cup chopped scallions
1 tablespoon butter
1 teaspoon paprika
1 teaspoon salt
2 cups chopped tomatoes
5 whole shrimp, cut up with shells on
1 pint shrimp stock
1 pint water
¼ cup rice
1 sprig tarragon
Dash of brandy
Dash of Herbsaint
2 teaspoons salt
½ cup heavy cream
1 tablespoon butter
Dash of hot sauce (optional)

In a heavy-bottom saucepot, sauté onion, carrots, celery, and scallions in butter with spices, until soft. Add tomatoes and shrimp and cook until tomatoes break down, about 15 or 20 minutes. Add shrimp stock and water; simmer an additional 10 minutes, then add rice and cook another 15 minutes. Add tarragon about 5 minutes before removing soup to strain. Blend soup in a blender in small batches until smooth, then strain. Return to heat and finish with a dash of brandy and Herbsaint, salt, cream, and butter. A little hot sauce never hurts.

K-Paul's Louisiana Kitchen

416 Chartres Street
New Orleans, LA 70130
(504) 524-7394
www.kpauls.com

Paul Prudhomme
Chef/Proprietor

Paul Miller
Executive Chef

Magic Seasoning Blends
are available at most grocery
stores or by contacting:
Magic Seasoning Blends, Inc.
824 Distributors Row
New Orleans, LA 70183-0342
504-731-3590
504-731-3576
info@chefpaul.com

Born and reared on a farm near Opelousas in Louisiana's Acadiana country, Paul Prudhomme was the youngest of thirteen children. When the last girl left home, he was, at age seven, old enough to help his mother in the kitchen, and it was at her side that he learned the value of fresh, quality products.

From a very early age, Paul Prudhomme knew that he wanted to make preparing food his life's work. After completing school, he traveled for several years, working as a cook in all kinds of restaurants.

His wanderlust temporarily satisfied, Prudhomme came to New Orleans, a mere ninety miles from his home, where he honed his skills and built a following at a noted Garden District restaurant. Then, in 1979, he and his late wife, K. Hinrichs Prudhomme, opened K-Paul's Louisiana Kitchen. A small restaurant on Chartres Street in the French Quarter, it was originally envisioned as a casual eatery for local customers. Word soon spread of the magic being created in the little kitchen, and now he is one of this country's best-known chefs.

Chicken and Andouille Smoked Sausage Gumbo

- **1 (3- to 4-pound) chicken, cut up**
- **1 tablespoon plus 2 teaspoons Chef Paul Prudhomme's Meat Magic, divided**
- **1 cup finely chopped onions**
- **1 cup finely chopped green bell peppers**
- **¾ cup finely chopped celery**
- **1¼ cups all-purpose flour, divided**
- **Vegetable oil for deep frying**
- **About 7 cups chicken stock or water**
- **½ pound andouille smoked sausage, or any other good pure smoked sausage such as Polish sausage (Kielbasa), cut into ¼-inch cubes**
- **1 teaspoon minced garlic**
- **Hot cooked rice, preferably converted**

Remove excess fat from chicken pieces. Rub 2 teaspoons of Meat Magic on both sides of each piece, making sure each is evenly covered. Let stand at room temperature 30 minutes.

In a medium-size bowl combine onions, bell peppers, and celery; set aside. Thoroughly combine ¾ cup flour with 1 tablespoon Meat Magic in a paper or plastic bag. Add chicken and shake until pieces are well coated.

In a large skillet (preferably not a nonstick type), heat 1½ inches oil until very hot (375° to 400°). Fry chicken pieces until crust is brown on both sides, about 5 to 8 minutes per side; drain on paper towels. Carefully pour hot oil into a glass measuring cup, leaving as many browned particles in the pan as possible. Scrape pan bottom with a metal whisk to loosen any stuck particles, then return ½ cup hot oil to pan.

Place pan over high heat. Using a long handled metal whisk, gradually stir in remaining flour. Cook, whisking constantly, until roux is dark red-brown to black, about 3½ to 4 minutes, being careful not to let it scorch or splash on your skin. Remove from heat and immediately add reserved vegetable mixture, stirring constantly until roux stops getting darker. Return pan to low heat and cook until vegetables are soft, about 5 minutes,

(continued)

stirring constantly and scraping the pan bottom well. Set aside.

Place stock in a 5½-quart saucepan or large Dutch oven. Bring to a boil. Add roux mixture by spoonfuls to boiling stock, stirring until dissolved between additions. Add chicken pieces and return mixture to a boil, stirring and scraping pan bottom often. Reduce heat to a simmer and stir in andouille and garlic. Simmer uncovered until chicken is tender, about 1½ to 2 hours, stirring occasionally and more often toward the end of cooking time. When gumbo is almost cooked, adjust seasoning, if desired, with Meat Magic. Serve immediately over rice. Makes 6 main dish or 10 appetizer servings.

Traditional Potato Salad

• •

2 tablespoons plus 1 teaspoon Chef Paul Prudhomme's Vegetable Magic or Meat Magic

1 teaspoon salt

1½ cups salad dressing or mayonnaise

4 medium-size white potatoes, cooked, peeled, and diced into ½-inch cubes

6 hard-cooked eggs, peeled and finely chopped

¼ cup finely diced onions

¼ cup finely diced celery

¼ cup finely diced green bell pepper

Blend Chef Paul Prudhomme's Magic Seasoning Blend and salt into salad dressing or mayonnaise in a large bowl, then add remaining ingredients. Mix well and refrigerate until ready to serve. Makes 6 to 8 side dish servings.

Note: A suggested way to serve these two dishes is to put a scoop of potato salad into the bowl of gumbo and stir to blend.

Pasta Primavera

9 ounces uncooked pasta, your favorite

2 tablespoons olive oil

1 cup (about ¼ pound) thin strips prosciutto

2 cups cauliflower florets

2 cups sliced fresh mushrooms

½ cup diagonally sliced carrots

2 cups sliced zucchini

6 tablespoons unsalted butter

1 teaspoon minced fresh garlic

3 tablespoons plus 1 teaspoon Chef Paul Prudhomme's Pork and Veal Magic

1 cup asparagus tips, or ¾ cup snow peas

1 cup chopped green onions

3 cups heavy cream

Cook pasta according to package directions; drain and set aside. Heat oil in a 12-inch skillet over high heat. When oil is very hot, add prosciutto, cauliflower, mushrooms, carrots, and zucchini. Add butter and, as it melts, stir in garlic and Pork and Veal Magic. Stir in asparagus tips or snow peas and onions, mix well, and cook just until vegetables are crisp-tender, about 4 or 5 minutes. Stir in cream, and bring to a boil. Lower heat to medium and cook until sauce thickens a bit, about 3 minutes. Add drained pasta, toss well, and serve immediately. Makes 6 to 8 servings.

Vegetables in a Sweet Potato Cream with Pasta

· ·

The taste of the sweet potatoes is critical to the appeal of this dish, so choose carefully. We like to use the Burgundy variety, a delicious Louisiana product that is available in many markets across the country.

2 medium-size sweet potatoes, about 1¼ pounds total weight

2 tablespoons unsalted butter

1½ cups chopped onions, peeled, cut into ½-inch pieces, divided

1 cup chopped red bell peppers, cut into ½-inch pieces

1 cup chopped yellow bell peppers, cut into ½-inch pieces

1 cup chopped green bell peppers, cut into ½-inch pieces

1 cup chopped carrots, peeled, cut into ½-inch pieces

½ teaspoon chopped dill weed

5 teaspoons Chef Paul Prudhomme's Vegetable Magic

2 bay leaves

1 medium zucchini, peeled, cut into 6 equal wedges, then cut into ½-inch pieces (about 2 cups)

½ cup heavy cream

1½ cups vegetable, chicken, or beef stock, divided

3 cups chopped cabbage, cut into 1-inch pieces

Preheat oven to 350°. Place sweet potatoes on a sheet pan and bake until soft all the way through, 45 to 60 minutes. When cool enough to handle, peel and purée them in a food processor. If purée is stringy, force it through a strainer. Set aside.

Melt butter in a 14-inch nonstick skillet over high heat. When the butter sizzles, add 1 cup onions, and all peppers, and carrots. Stir well, then add dill weed, Vegetable Magic, and bay leaves. Cook, stirring frequently, until vegetables have a light golden coating from the seasoning, but are still bright in color, about 8 minutes.

Add the purée, and stir well; add zucchini and remaining onions. Cook, stirring frequently, until mixture makes large slow bubbles, about 4 minutes. Add cream and 1 cup stock and stir well until blended. Bring mixture to a boil and simmer, stirring frequently, until liquid is thickened and reduced, about 7 minutes.

Fold in cabbage and continue to cook, stirring frequently, until cabbage is cooked but still slightly crisp, about 6 minutes. Add remaining ½ cup stock. Stir well, then bring back just to a simmer and remove from heat. Makes 6 cups, enough for 6 side-dish servings.

Banana Bliss

• •

We developed this sauce for ice cream, but it's also great over pound cake, gingerbread, or pudding.

4 medium-size bananas, slightly ripe

½ cup roasted and coarsely chopped pecans

½ cup water

½ pound unsalted butter

1 cup lightly packed dark brown sugar

1 tablespoon Chef Paul Prudhomme's Sweetie Magic

½ teaspoon salt

½ teaspoon ground ginger

1 teaspoon vanilla

2 tablespoons crème de banana liqueur

2 tablespoons Bailey's Irish Cream liqueur

1 tablespoon cognac

1 teaspoon sesame oil

Vanilla ice cream

Peel bananas and cut them into diagonal slices about ½-inch thick. Set aside. In a small nonstick skillet over medium heat, roast pecans, stirring constantly, until they begin to darken and give off a rich toasted aroma. Remove from heat and set aside.

In a 10-inch skillet, whisk together water, butter, and sugar. When butter melts, add Sweetie Magic and bring to a boil, whisking frequently. Whisk in remaining ingredients, except ice cream; add reserved bananas and pecans. Continue to cook, stirring gently, 4 minutes. Remove from the heat and serve warm. Ladle ½ cup sauce over 2 large scoops vanilla ice cream. Be sure ice cream is very cold and sauce is still very warm. Makes about 4 cups sauce, enough for 8 servings.

Mango Lime Vinaigrette

・ ・

LIME SIMPLE SYRUP:

6 tablespoons sugar

¼ cup water

Zest of ½ lime

Combine all ingredients in a saucepan and bring to a boil, stirring constantly. Cool and set aside.

VINAIGRETTE:

½ mango, ripe, peeled, and seeded

1 cup vegetable oil

⅓ cup fresh lime juice

6 tablespoons Lime Simple Syrup

2 tablespoons minced shallot

1 teaspoon lime zest

¼ teaspoon white pepper

1 tablespoon salt

½ teaspoon pink peppercorns

2 tablespoons mirin (Japanese rice wine)

Purée mango in blender. Combine with remaining ingredients and whisk until ingredients are well mixed.

Le Parvenu

509 Williams Boulevard
Kenner, LA 70062
(504) 471-0534

Dennis Hutley
Chef/Proprietor

Chef Dennis is the Founding President of the ACF Junior Chapter (1976) and Sargeant at Arms of the New Orleans ACF Chapter (1978). He cooked for the Papal Entourage during Pope John Paul II's visit to New Orleans in 1987. Chef Dennis was featured in the Great Chefs Series "Louisiana New Guarde" in 1990 (three episodes), and was recognized in Gastronomy World Star in 1991.

Le Parvenu Restaurant was established in April 1996. Located very near the Mississippi River in the Historic District of Rivertown, it is a seventy-five-year-old house with four dining rooms and a small bar area. It is fronted by a white picket fence, large covered porch, and surrounded by a spacious yard and award-winning garden. The fare is award winning and labeled "Innovative American Creole Cuisine." It is fine dining in a business casual atmosphere.

Le Parvenu Restaurant has gotten a number of awards: Best New Restaurant–*New Orleans*, Top Ten in New Orleans–*Zagat Survey*, 4 Stars by local food writer Tom Fitzmorris, DiRoNA Award since 2002, Fodor's Choice–*Fodor's Travel Guide*, and AAA Recommended Dining–*Triple A Tour Book*.

Mirliton, Shrimp, and Crab Bisque

1 stick butter

¼ cup flour

⅓ cup (¼ inch) diced carrots

¼ cup (¼ inch) diced celery

¼ cup (¼ inch) diced onion

1 tablespoon minced garlic

2 medium bay leaves

2 medium mirlitons, peeled, seeded, and diced

1½ medium shrimp, peeled, deveined

3 cups crab, shrimp, and mirliton stock

2 cups cream, heated

¾ cup Sauternes (sweet wine)

¼ teaspoon liquid crab boil

1½ teaspoons salt

½ teaspoon white pepper

Boiled Shrimp

Louisiana jumbo lump crabmeat

½ cup freshly whipped cream

Paprika for garnish

Chopped parsley for garnish

Melt butter, then add flour; cook gently 2 to 3 minutes. Add carrots, celery, onion, garlic, and bay leaves, and cook 3 minutes without browning. Add mirlitons, mix well, and heat through. Whisk in strained stock, bring to a simmer, and cook about 5 minutes. Whisk in cream, simmer 5 minutes, then add wine and cook another 5 minutes. Season with salt and pepper; stir well. To serve, place boiled shrimp and lump crabmeat in soup cups or bowls and ladle in soup; garnish with a dollop of freshly whipped cream, paprika, and parsley, and serve. Makes 2 quarts.

Toasted Garlic Dressing

. . . .

GARLIC VINEGAR:

2 to 3 whole bulbs garlic

1 cup white vinegar

Put whole cloves of peeled, regular garlic on a sheet pan or cookie sheet; "toast" gently under the broiler, tossing and mixing as they brown. Chill well, put in a jar, and cover amply with white vinegar. Allow to "steep" about 2 weeks before using.

DRESSING:

6 egg yolks

1 teaspoon mustard powder

1 teaspoon Worcestershire sauce

½ teaspoon ground black pepper

1 cup garlic vinegar

½ teaspoon salt

3 cups olive oil

1 cup fine julienned elephant garlic, toasted under a broiler, cooled

Whisk together the yolks, mustard powder, Worcestershire, pepper, vinegar, and salt. Put this mixture in a blender at high speed; add the olive oil slowly (as if making mayonnaise) to emulsify. Stir in elephant garlic; store in clean container and chill. Stir well before using.

Louisiana Crab Cakes

2 cups heavy cream

½ cup sliced green onions

1 tablespoon chopped garlic

¼ cup brandy

1 teaspoon liquid crab boil

1 pound jumbo lump crabmeat

Salt and white pepper to taste

2½ to 3 cups finely shredded
   French bread

In a skillet combine cream, green onions, garlic, brandy, and liquid crab boil; bring to a boil and cook 3 or 4 minutes. Add lump crabmeat with salt and pepper, and mix in very gently. When thoroughly heated, remove from heat and very carefully fold in shredded bread crumbs. Spread mixture on a pan and allow to cool slightly. Spoon or scoop into 16 equal portions and then shape into cakes, without pressing, to facilitate a light texture. Place on a lightly buttered or greased pan and broil under medium-high heat until browned. Serve with your favorite sauce and choice of vegetables.

Note: Add the bread carefully and in 2 steps if possible; it might take more or less to get the mixture just to where it will "form." Makes about 8 servings.

Classic Crème Brûlée

• •

7 egg yolks

4 ounces sugar

3 cups heavy cream

1 fresh vanilla bean, split and scraped into cream

Brown sugar

Preheat oven to 300°. Combine egg yolks and sugar; whip to ribbon stage. Heat cream with vanilla bean just to a boil. Gradually whisk hot cream into egg yolks and sugar; skim any foam that appears. Ladle mixture into 6 (4-ounce) ramekins; place ramekins in a shallow pan containing about a ½ inch of warm water. Place the pan in the oven and bake approximately 1½ hours, or until just set. Remove ramekins from water bath and chill in refrigerator. To serve, spread a thin layer of light brown sugar on top of the chilled cream and glaze under the broiler until caramelized and slightly burnt. Makes 6 servings.

Note: The secret is slow cooking.

Lilette Restaurant

3637 Magazine Street
New Orleans, LA 70115
(504) 895-1636
www.liletterestaurant.com

John Harris
Chef/Proprietor

Growing up with an Italian mother, Chef John Harris' fondest childhood memories are of the kitchen. Later while working his way through college in restaurants, Harris couldn't resist the lure of cooking school, which would lead him to stints at Café Allegro in Pittsburgh, and Spiaggia in Chicago. After moving to New Orleans, John began working as sous chef under Susan Spicer at Bayona Restaurant, who sent him to France to apprentice at Amphyclese and Le Pre Catalin, both Michelin-rated, 2-star restaurants. During his apprenticeship, John lived with the Mauri family, whose matriarch Lilette instilled in him a love of traditional cooking, and is also the namesake of the restaurant.

Upon returning from France, John planned to open his own restaurant.

In 2000, John fell in love with the intimate space at 3637 Magazine Street that would become his own distinctive offering . . . Lilette. Lilette has received numerous awards and accolades.

Marinated Anchovies with Basil Bruschetta and Stewed Vidalia Onions

· ·

2 cups extra virgin olive oil

4 cups julienned Vidalia onions

5 garlic cloves, smashed

Kosher salt

Freshly cracked black pepper

Put 2 cups extra virgin olive oil and onions in small saucepot. Bring to a boil, reduce heat, and simmer for 20 minutes. Add 5 smashed garlic cloves and simmer an additional 20 minutes. Season with salt and pepper. Let cool.

Note: Olive oil should be about halfway up the onions in the pot. After simmering, the liquid will cover the onions.

BASIL PURÉE:

4 ounces chopped fresh basil

¾ cup extra virgin olive oil

1 garlic clove, smashed

1 baguette

½ pound marinated Spanish anchovies

Freshly cracked black pepper

Pick basil leaves, rinse, and pat dry. Place in blender with olive oil and garlic. Pulse until blended but still bright green. (Color will dull if blended too long.)

Slice baguette on bias into long croutons. Spread liberally with basil purée and grill for 2 minutes on each side. Place 2 slices on a plate, scoop 2 tablespoons of room temperature stewed onions onto each slice of baguette. Arrange 6 anchovies (3 on each slice) and garnish with freshly cracked pepper. Makes 4 servings.

Grilled Beets with Goat's Cheese and Walnuts

6 large whole beets

Cover beets by 3 inches with cold water in a large saucepot. Bring water to a boil and simmer until paring knife slides out of beet when pricked. Strain and let cool. While running under water, rub beets with towel to remove skin. Slice beets into ½-inch rounds. Prepare Marinade.

MARINADE:

¼ teaspoon salt

¼ teaspoon black pepper

¼ teaspoon dry thyme leaves

¼ teaspoon paprika

¼ teaspoon dry basil leaves

⅛ teaspoon dry oregano

⅛ teaspoon onion powder

⅛ teaspoon garlic powder

Pinch of cayenne pepper

¾ cup vegetable oil

Combine all dry ingredients in large bowl. Mix well; add vegetable oil. Toss with sliced beets and set aside.

WALNUTS:

½ stick butter

1¼ cups chopped walnuts

Salt and pepper

Melt butter in a 10-inch skillet and add walnuts. Cook, stirring occasionally, for 5 minutes, and season well with salt and pepper. Reserve leftover butter.

VINAIGRETTE:

1½ ounces red wine vinegar

2 ounces pomace olive oil

1 ounce walnut oil

Salt and pepper to taste

½ pound goat cheese, softened

¼ cup chives, cut into matchsticks

Add all ingredients except cheese and chives, and the reserved walnut butter. Whisk well. To finish, grill beets in walnut butter on both sides 2 minutes and toss in Vinaigrette. Place 4 to 6 slices of beets on each plate and drizzle with Vinaigrette. Add 5 dollops of goat cheese (1 to 2 ounces) per serving; sprinkle with walnuts and chives. Makes 4 to 6 servings.

Mr. B's Bistro

201 Royal Street
New Orleans, LA 70130
(504) 523-2078
www.mrbsbistro.com

Cindy Brennan
Managing Partner

Michelle McRaney
Executive Chef

Nestled in the heart of the French Quarter, Mr. B's Bistro is located at the intersection of Royal Street and Iberville, one of New Orleans's most celebrated food corners. In 1979, Mr. B's Bistro opened at the historical location and beckoned the culinary world inside. Since 1979, Mr. B's has been an integral part of an ongoing process of redefining New Orleans cooking. The location and growth of New Orleans as a port city has allowed many cultures to harmoniously blend together, utilizing the foods of southern Louisiana to create a style of cooking referred to as "Creole Cuisine." Mr. B's kitchen has attempted to revive the distinct qualities of Louisiana's varied cultural influences—adapting and incorporating local and regional ingredients into innovative culinary creations. Quality and farm freshness predominate. Mr. B's has been named "Best Business Lunch" in *Gourmet* and *Food & Wine*.

Mr. B's Gumbo Ya Ya

. . . .

We were first introduced to this rich, dark-roux gumbo from one of our early chefs, Jimmy Smith, who grew up eating it in Cajun country. Its name is said to come from women who would cook the gumbo all day long while talking, or "ya-ya-ing." We love it, and would never dream of taking it off our menu. In fact, it's our #1-selling soup. It is so beloved that customers actually fly in to New Orleans just for it. We sell fifty gallons of gumbo ya-ya a week—now that's a lot of soup!

1 pound unsalted butter

3 cups all-purpose flour, divided

2 red bell peppers, medium-dice

2 green bell peppers, medium-dice

2 onions, medium-dice

2 stalks celery, medium-dice

1 gallon chicken stock

1 pound andouille sausage, cut into ¼-inch-thick slices

2 tablespoons Creole seasoning

2 tablespoons kosher salt

1 teaspoon ground black pepper

1 teaspoon dried hot red pepper flakes

1 teaspoon chili powder

1 teaspoon thyme

1 tablespoon chopped garlic

2 bay leaves

1 (3½-pound) whole chicken, roasted and deboned

Hot sauce to taste

Boiled rice as accompaniment

In a 12-quart stockpot, melt butter over low heat. Gradually add 1 cup flour, stirring constantly with a wooden spoon, and cook, stirring constantly, 30 seconds. Add 1 cup flour and stir constantly 30 seconds. Add remaining cup flour and stir constantly 30 seconds. Continue to cook roux, stirring constantly, until it is the color of dark mahogany, about 45 minutes to 1 hour.

Add bell peppers and stir constantly 30 seconds. Add onions and celery and stir constantly 30 seconds. Gradually add stock to roux, stirring constantly with a wooden spoon to prevent lumps. Add andouille, Creole seasoning, salt, black pepper, red pepper flakes, chili powder, thyme, garlic, and bay leaves and bring to a boil. Simmer gumbo, uncovered, 45 minutes, skimming off any fat and stirring occasionally. Add chicken meat and simmer 15 minutes. Adjust with salt and hot sauce. Serve over rice.

Mr. B's New Orleans Barbequed Shrimp

• •

Don't break out your grill for this dish. Here in New Orleans, barbecued shrimp means sautéed shrimp in Worcestershire-spiked butter sauce. We serve these shrimp with heads and tails on, so you need to dig in to enjoy. I highly recommend a bib.

We are famous for our barbecued shrimp, and with reason. The biggest trick to making this taste like ours is to not hold back on the butter. The three sticks called for are enough to scare you into cholesterol shock, but are key to the flavor and consistency of the sauce. Another tip to keep in mind: to emulsify the sauce, be sure to add a little butter at a time while stirring rapidly. And don't overcook the shrimp or they'll become tough and hard to peel.

16 jumbo shrimp (12 per pound, about 1½ pounds), with heads and unpeeled

½ cup Worcestershire sauce

2 tablespoons fresh lemon juice (about 2 lemons)

2 teaspoons ground black pepper

2 teaspoons cracked black pepper

2 teaspoons Creole seasoning

1 teaspoon minced garlic

3 sticks cold unsalted butter, cubed

French bread as accompaniment

In a large skillet combine shrimp, Worcestershire, lemon juice, black peppers, Creole seasoning, and garlic, and cook over moderately high heat until shrimp turn pink, about 1 minute on each side. Reduce heat to moderate and stir in butter, a few cubes at a time, stirring constantly and adding more only when butter is melted. Remove skillet from heat. Place shrimp in a bowl and pour sauce over top. Serve with French bread for dipping.

Mr. B's Bread Pudding with Irish Whiskey Sauce

. . . .

Forever thrifty in the kitchen, New Orleans cooks would never dream of wasting good, but stale French bread. Over the years, bread pudding has become our city's favorite dessert. It's on every menu in town and every restaurant makes it differently. Some add chocolate, some dried fruit and nuts, some soufflé them. But our is traditional and delicious.

New Orleans bread is light and airy with a very tender crust that softens in this bread pudding. We would recommend other breads, but the bread pudding won't be like the one we serve at Mr. B's. Different breads absorb custard differently—your final result could be more custard-y or drier.

BREAD PUDDING:

- ¾ pound light, airy French bread, cut into 1½-inch-thick slices
- 1 cup dark raisins
- 2 dozen large eggs
- 1½ quarts heavy cream
- 2½ cups sugar
- 1 tablespoon plus 1 teaspoon cinnamon
- 1 teaspoon ground nutmeg
- ½ stick unsalted butter, chopped

Preheat oven to 250°. Arrange half the bread in a 9x13-inch baking pan and sprinkle with raisins. Arrange remaining half of bread over top. In a large bowl whisk together eggs, cream, 2 cups sugar, 1 tablespoon cinnamon, and nutmeg until smooth. Pour half of custard over bread and gently press down bread. Let sit until bread soaks up custard, about 15 minutes (depending on bread). Pour remaining half of custard over bread and gently press down bread. In a small bowl combine remaining ½ cup sugar and teaspoon cinnamon and sprinkle over bread. Dot bread with butter and bake 1½–2 hours, or until custard is just set in the center. Serves 12.

IRISH WHISKEY SAUCE:

- 1 cup heavy cream
- 1 cup whole milk
- ½ cup sugar
- 7 large egg yolks
- ¼ cup Irish whiskey

In a medium saucepan bring cream and milk to a boil. In a medium bowl whisk together sugar and yolks until combined well and gradually whisk in hot milk mixture. Transfer mixture to a double boiler and cook over just simmering water, stirring gently but constantly until thick, about 12 miinutes. Pour sauce through a fine sieve and stir in whiskey. Serve sauce warm or cold.

Palace Café

605 Canal Street
New Orleans, LA 70130
(504) 523-8311
www.palacecafe.com

Darin Nesbit
Executive Chef

Palace Café has earned national critical acclaim since it opened in 1991 with Best New Restaurant award from *Esquire* magazine and *USA Today*. Since then, Palace Café won the prestigious Ivy Award from *Restaurants and Institutions Magazine*, naming the restaurant as one of the top dining experiences in the United States. *The New York Times*, *Food and Wine*, *Cooking Light*, *Fine Cooking*, *Travel and Leisure*, *Wine Spectator*, Food Network's *In Food Today*, and CNN's *On the Menu*, have also recognized the restaurant.

Palace Café's cookbook *Palace Café: The Flavor of New Orleans*, is available at Palace Café and select bookstores. This book of more than 170 home cook-friendly recipes offers an intimate look at one of New Orleans' best restaurants from the "first family of Creole." The restaurant's cookbook is a collaborative effort by Dickie Brennan, who tells the story of Palace Café, with recipes from Executive Chef Darin Nesbit.

76 · *Louisiana's Best Restaurant Recipes*

White Chocolate Bread Pudding

PUDDING:

6 cups heavy whipping cream

2 cups milk

1 cup sugar

20 ounces white chocolate, broken into small pieces

4 eggs

15 egg yolks

1 (24-inch) loaf stale French bread, or fresh French bread that has been sliced and dried in a 275° oven

Combine whipping cream, milk, and sugar in a large heavy saucepot and mix well. Bring to a boil, then remove from heat. Add white chocolate pieces and let stand until chocolate melts; stir until smooth. Whisk eggs and egg yolks in a large mixing bowl. Whisk in warm chocolate mixture in a slow steady stream.

Preheat oven to 350°. Place French bread slices in a 9x12-inch metal baking pan. Top with half the chocolate mixture, and let stand about 5 minutes. Press bread into chocolate mixture to saturate well. Pour remaining chocolate mixture over bread, and stir to mix well. Cover pan with foil, and bake 1 hour. Uncover and bake 30 minutes longer or until golden brown. Cool to room temperature and chill, covered, 6 to 8 hours or until set.

Loosen pudding from sides of pan and invert onto a work surface. Cut into squares, then cut diagonally into triangles. Place on a baking sheet and reheat at 275° for 15 minutes or until warm. To serve, place pudding triangles on serving plate and top with White Chocolate Ganache. Garnish with dark chocolate shavings. Makes 12.

WHITE CHOCOLATE GANACHE:

½ cup heavy whipping cream

8 ounces white chocolate, broken into small pieces

Bring whipping cream to a boil in a small saucepan. Remove from heat and add white chocolate pieces. Let stand until chocolate melts; stir until smooth.

Crabmeat Cheesecake with Pecan Crust

This recipe has some do-ahead steps.

CREOLE CREAM CHEESE:

8 cups (½ gallon) skim milk

12 drops liquid rennin, or ¼ rennin tablet

¼ cup buttermilk

Heat the skim milk to 80° to 90° in a saucepot, using a thermometer to determine the temperature. Stir the rennin into the buttermilk in a bowl; if using tablet rennin, stir until the tablet dissolves. Add buttermilk mixture to skim milk and mix well. Pour into a clean container and let stand to curdle, uncovered, in a place that is not in a direct flow of hot or cold air for 24 to 30 hours. Pour curds into a large strainer lined with cheesecloth and placed over a bowl. Place in the refrigerator to drain for 2 days or until liquid no longer drains from the curds; discard the liquid. Store Creole Cream Cheese in the refrigerator for up to 1 week.

PECAN CRUST:

¾ cup chopped pecans

1 cup all-purpose flour

¼ teaspoon salt

5 tablespoons butter, chilled

3 tablespoons ice water

Preheat oven to 350°. Grind pecans fine in a food processor. Add flour and salt, and process to mix. Remove to a large mixing bowl and cut in butter with 2 knives until mixture resembles small peas. Add ice water, and mix just until dough holds together. Roll dough ⅛-inch thick on a lightly floured surface. Press into a lightly greased 9-inch tart pan, starting with the side and then the bottom. Bake 20 minutes or until golden brown.

(continued)

CRABMEAT FILLING:

½ cup finely chopped onion

1 tablespoon butter

4 ounces crabmeat

1 (8-ounce) package cream cheese, softened

⅓ cup Creole Cream Cheese, or sour cream

2 eggs, beaten

1 tablespoon Crystal hot pepper sauce

Kosher salt to taste

White pepper to taste

Reduce oven temperature to 300°. Sauté onion in butter in a sauté pan until translucent. Add crabmeat and cook just until heated through; remove from heat. Beat cream cheese in a mixer fitted with a paddle (or with a wooden spoon) until smooth. Add Creole Cream Cheese and mix well. Mix in eggs one at a time. Fold in crabmeat mixture gently. Stir in pepper sauce and season with salt and pepper. Spoon filling into prepared crust and bake 30 to 40 minutes or until firm to the touch.

MEUNIÈRE SAUCE WITH MUSHROOMS:

1 lemon, peeled, cut into quarters

½ cup Worcestershire sauce

½ cup Crystal hot sauce

¼ cup heavy whipping cream

1 pound (4 sticks) butter, chopped

Kosher salt to taste

White pepper to taste

2 cups sliced mixed wild mushrooms

2 tablespoons butter

Crab claw fingers to garnish

Combine lemon, Worcestershire, and hot sauce in a heavy saucepot. Cook over medium heat until thick and syrupy, stirring constantly with a wire whisk. Whisk in cream. Reduce heat to low and add butter, one piece at a time, mixing until completely incorporated before adding more butter. Remove from heat and stir until very smooth. Season with salt and pepper. Strain through a fine strainer and keep warm.

Sauté mushrooms in 2 tablespoons butter in a skillet until the mushrooms are tender and moisture has completely evaporated; excess moisture from mushrooms may cause sauce to break when mushrooms are added. Stir mushrooms into sauce. To serve, slice cheesecake and place on serving plates. Top each serving with the warm Meunière Sauce and garnish with 3 sautéed crab claw fingers. Makes 8.

Andouille-Crusted Fish with Cayenne Butter Sauce

CHIVE AÏOLI:

¼ cup chopped garlic

⅔ cup blend of 80% vegetable oil and 20% olive oil

1 bunch chives

2 tablespoons chopped parsley

2 egg yolks

1 teaspoon Dijon mustard

Juice of 1 lemon

Salt to taste

Cook garlic in the oil blend in a saucepan over medium heat for 20 minutes, stirring frequently; do not brown. Strain into a bowl and cool. Reserving 8 chive pieces for garnish, purée remaining chives and parsley in a food processor. Add garlic oil gradually, processing constantly. Add Dijon mustard, lemon juice, and salt; mix, adding a small amount of water if necessary for a thin mayonnaise-like consistency. Spoon into a pastry tube or plastic squeeze bottle and chill for up to several days.

CAYENNE BUTTER SAUCE:

¾ cup Crystal hot pepper sauce

1 cup (2 sticks) butter, chopped, chilled

Cook the hot sauce in a small saucepan over medium heat until reduced by ⅓. Reduce heat to low and whisk in butter a few pieces at a time, mixing well after each addition. Keep warm.

(continued)

ANDOUILLE-CRUSTED FISH:

6 ounces andouille sausage, or smoked pork sausage, coarsely chopped

1 onion, coarsely chopped

5 tablespoons blend of 80% vegetable oil and 20% olive oil, divided

1 cup bread crumbs

4 (8-ounce) fish fillets, skinless and boneless

Kosher salt to taste

White pepper to taste

Preheat oven to 350°. Grind the andouille in a food processor. Sauté the ground andouille with onion in 2 tablespoons oil blend, in a skillet over medium heat until sausage is brown and onion is transparent. Purée the mixture in a food processor. Add bread crumbs and pulse until mixed. Coat fish with bread crumb mixture, then season on both sides with salt and pepper. Heat remaining oil blend in an oven-proof skillet over high heat. Add fish fillets and sear for 2 minutes or until fish flakes easily and crust is golden brown. Ladle Cayenne Butter Sauce onto each serving plate. Place 1 fish fillet on each plate, and drizzle the Chive Aïoli across the fish in a zigzag pattern. Top with the reserved chive pieces. Serves 4.

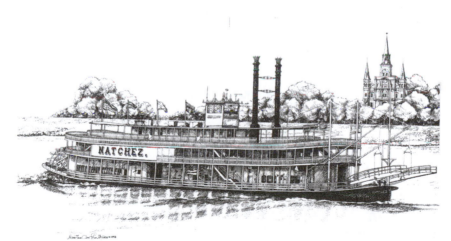

The Natchez
New Orleans, Louisiana

Peristyle

1041 Dumaine
New Orleans, LA 70116
(504) 593-9535
www.peristylerestaurant.com

Tom Wolfe
Executive Chef/Proprietor

With its burgundy-leather banquettes, multilevel seating and pitch-perfect service, this renovated drugstore makes for a relaxed, understated neighborhood bistro. Traveling foodies and French Quarter neighbors frequent the classy narrow bar. Arrive early for generously poured cocktails or offerings from one of the city's outstanding wine lists.

While not self-consciously Creole in its outlook, Peristyle's menu adheres to the cornerstone of French cuisine (use the freshest local ingredients), and emerges with combinations that border on perfection. Veal sweetbreads arrive gently sautéed and served with grilled artichoke and bacon lardons. A pan-seared Gulf drum in almond-brown butter sauce replaces the traditional pan-fried trout meunière. A confit heirloom tomato and aged balsamic vinaigrette raises a simple lemon and fresh herb roasted poussin to hearty perfection.

Arugula Salad with Apples, Ricotta Salata, and Poppy Seeds

· ·

2 Granny Smith apples
1 tablespoon light olive oil

Wash apples and cut into ¼-inch thick slices. Toss apples slices in olive oil and roast for 10 minutes on a sheet tray at 350°. Cool and slice into ¼-inch thick strips; discard seeds and core as you slice.

POPPY SEED DRESSING:

1 tablespoon white wine vinegar
1½ teaspoons Dijon mustard
Juice of ½ lemon
1 teaspoon white wine
1 tablespoon poppy seeds
1½ teaspoons diced shallots
1½ tablespoons sugar
½ cup peanut oil
1 tablespoon light olive oil
Salt and white pepper to taste

In a medium stainless steel mixing bowl, using a whisk, combine all ingredients, except oils. Mix well to break down sugar. While whisking, slowly add oils in a thin stream and whisk until uniform. Season with salt and pepper. This will keep up to 1 week, refrigerated.

SALAD:

1 pound arugula, picked free of stems, washed and air dried
1 tablespoon small diced shallots
1 ounce grated ricotta salata (firm Italian table cheese)

In a large salad bowl, gently toss arugula, shallots, and apples with ⅓ cup Poppy Seed Dressing. Season to your liking. Place arugula in the middle of 6 to 8 chilled salad plates, slightly mounding arugula in center of each plate. Sprinkle each salad with apples that may have fallen to the bottom of the bowl, then top with cheese.

Poached Oysters in a Saffron-Tomato Coulis

1 tablespoon vegetable oil

1 cup medium-dice yellow onions

½ cup medium-dice celery

½ cup medium-dice fennel bulb

1 tablespoon chopped garlic

2 cups white wine

1 bay leaf

⅛ teaspoon cayenne pepper

1½ teaspoons crushed saffron threads

4 cups chopped fresh tomatoes, save juices, or 1 (29-ounce) can diced tomatoes

60 large Louisiana oysters (preferably P&J), freshly shucked

2 tablespoons unsalted butter

Kosher salt and white pepper to taste

In a medium saucepot, heat oil, and gently sweat onions, celery, fennel, and garlic until very tender. Add white wine, bay leaf, cayenne, and saffron. Stirring occasionally, reduce wine until half remains; add tomatoes. Bring mixture to a boil, reduce heat, and simmer 15 minutes. Remove from heat and cool 20 minutes. Place mixture in a blender, pulsing blender off and on until mixture is very smooth (do this with extreme caution; it will still be hot). Set aside until needed. Refrigerate, if needed.

At service time, place sauce in a 6-quart saucepot and slowly bring it to a boil; add oysters, and stir to distribute. Cook oysters until they begin to firm up, about 2 minutes. Add butter, stir to incorporate, and adjust seasonings. You could serve this with boiled rice or even Brabant potatoes. Garnish and say "Yum!" Serves 6.

Note: Try garnishing this dish with sizzled leeks, crumbled bacon, grated cheese, chopped green onions, or your favorite herbs. Pick whatever looks best to you at the market that day.

Chilled Champagne-Strawberry Soup with Mint Ice Cream

- 4 cups Louisiana strawberries, hulled and quartered
- 1 (750 ml) bottle good quality champagne or California sparkling wine
- 2 cups unsweetened apple juice
- 1 cup spring water
- 1 cup sugar
- ½ vanilla bean, split
- Honey (optional)
- 2 tablespoons chiffonade fresh mint leaves
- 1 cup whipped cream, slightly sweetened
- 1 pint homemade mint ice cream, or your favorite mint ice cream
- 8 mint sprigs for garnish
- Powdered sugar to dust

In a medium nonreactive saucepot, combine first 6 ingredients and bring to a boil. Simmer 10 minutes. Remove vanilla bean and allow this mixture to cool 30 minutes. Purée in batches in a blender for 3 minutes until very smooth. Strain, then chill 2 hours. Adjust sweetness, if needed, using a little honey. Place a dollop of the whipped cream in center of each of 8 chilled, shallow soup bowls, top with a 2-ounce scoop of ice cream, garnish with mint, and ladle chilled soup around ice cream like a "moat." Dust with powdered sugar and serve on 8 plates used as liners for bowls.

Ralph Brennan's BACCO

310 Chartres Street
New Orleans, LA 70130
(504) 522-2426
www.bacco.com

Chris Montero
Executive Chef

BACCO'S Italian cooking offers guests a dining alternative to the Creole and Cajun food for which New Orleans is famous. BACCO has a delicious assortment of homemade pastas, wood-fired pizzas and fresh regional seafood selections for its guests. BACCO is housed in a historic building in the heart of the French Quarter on Chartres Street. *New Orleans Magazine* ranked BACCO Best Italian 1995. *Gambit Weekly*'s Reader's Poll rated BACCO with Best Ambiance. The *Zagat Survey* ranked BACCO One of New Orleans Best Italian Restaurants and One of New Orleans Most Romantic Restaurants, 1999. The *Times Picayune* gave BACCO its 4 Beans rating, and food critic Tom Fitzmorris gave BACCO 4 Stars. New Orleans' *Where Magazine* Visitor's Choice Poll voted BACCO Best Italian Restaurant 1998, 1999, and 2000.

Rosemary and Garlic Marinated Pork Tenderloin

ROSEMARY/GARLIC PASTE:

2 cups olive oil

6 ounces chopped garlic

8 ounces finely chopped rosemary

1 ounce cracked black pepper

Purée all ingredients in a food processor.

SWEET AND SOUR PRUNE SAUCE:

2⅔ cups water

1 pound sugar

½ bottle sherry vinegar

1 pound pitted prunes

Place all ingredients in a saucepan. Bring to a boil and remove from stove.

MARINATED PORK TENDERLOIN:

8 ounces pork tenderloin, cleaned

¾ ounce Rosemary/Garlic Paste

1 ounce Sweet and Sour Prune Sauce

5 prunes

½ ounce unsalted butter

3 ounces Wilted Escarole

4 ounces Garlic Mashed Potatoes

Rub pork tenderloin with Rosemary/Garlic Paste. Put tenderloin on grill or into oven at 350°. Roast until medium-rare or medium. Set aside to rest for 5 minutes and slice. In a saucepan, add 1 ounce of Sweet and Sour Prune Sauce and prunes; reduce by half. Add butter and mix well. Sauté escarole. Place sliced pork on Wilted Escarole and coat with Sweet and Sour Prune Sauce and prunes. Serve with Garlic Mashed Potatoes.

WILTED ESCAROLE:

½ ounce olive oil

½ ounce minced garlic

1 pinch crushed red pepper

3 ounces escarole, cleaned and cut

½ ounce unsalted butter

Over medium-high heat, add oil, garlic, and crushed red pepper. Add escarole and butter. Toss until escarole is wilted.

(continued)

(Rosemary and Garlic Marinated Pork Tenderloin continued)

GARLIC MASHED POTATOES:

8 russet potatoes, peeled

6 ounces unsalted butter

½ cup roasted garlic purée

Salt and pepper to taste

6 ounces scalded milk

Boil potatoes until tender, then drain and let dry for 5 to 8 minutes; place in mixer. Pulse at high speed for 30 seconds. Add butter, roasted garlic purée, salt, and pepper. Slowly add milk until smooth. Do not overwhip potatoes or they will become very sticky and gummy.

Fettuccine con Tartufi Nero
· · · · · · · Black Truffle Fettuccine · · · · · · · ·

4 ounces fresh fettucine

1 ounce black truffle purée

½ ounce extra virgin olive oil

½ ounce white truffle oil

½ ounce unsalted butter

Pinch of salt

1 ounce shaved Reggiano Parmigiano cheese

Pinch of minced parsley

Drop fettuccine into a large pot of boiling salted water. While pasta is cooking, mix all ingredients except Parmigiano and parsley in a mixing bowl. Drain pasta and toss with mixed ingredients. Empty contents from mixing bowl using a pasta fork to spin fettuccine into the center of a large hot pasta bowl. Top pasta with shaved cheese and sprinkle with minced parsley. This recipe is for 1 appetizer. For an entrée size, double all ingredients.

Ralph Brennan's Red Fish Grill

115 Bourbon Street
New Orleans, LA 70130
(504) 598-1200
www.redfishgrill.com

Haley Gabel
Corporate Executive Chef

Gregg Collier
Executive Chef

Casual New Orleans Seafood

Ralph Brennan's Red Fish Grill, under the culinary direction of the Executive Chef Robert Gregg Collier, boasts a variety of fresh seafood selections, including an abundant supply of fresh Gulf shellfish, fin fish, a raw oyster bar, and many other New Orleans classic seafood dishes.

A state-of-the-art kitchen has been installed and the focal point is the hickory wood-burning grill that will impart the signature rich, smoky flavor and taste to all of Red Fish Grill's grilled seafood, meat, and vegetable menu items.

The Red Fish Grill has won many awards and accolades: Best Seafood Restaurant, *Where New Orleans*, Best Grilled Fish, *New Orleans* magazine, and one of the Ten Most Architecturally Interesting Restuarants by Tom Fitzmorris.

Barbequed Oyster Po-Boys

• •

BBQ OYSTER SAUCE:

2½ tablespoons honey

3¼ tablespoons clarified butter

5 ounces Crystal hot sauce

Combine honey and butter, and warm to 100°. Using a mixer, add hot sauce in a steady stream. Sauce will emulsify. For serving, sauce should be warmed slowly but not heated or sauce will break.

BLUE CHEESE DRESSING:

5 ounces crumbled blue cheese

1 cup mayonnaise

1 ounce sour cream

2 tablespoons heavy cream

1 tablespoon white vinegar

2 tablespoons salad oil

½ teaspoon black pepper

½ teaspoon white pepper

Mix all ingredients and blend well.

OYSTERS:

6 oysters

Seasoned flour

2 ounces BBQ Oyster Sauce

1 teaspoon chopped parsley

1 (8-inch) po-boy loaf

1½ ounces Blue Cheese Dressing

½ ounce julienned lettuce

3 tomato slices

4 red onions, thinly sliced

Coat oysters in seasoned flour and fry until golden. Toss with BBQ Oyster Sauce and parsley. Dress po-boy with Blue Cheese Dressing, lettuce, tomato, and red onion.

Sweet Potato Catfish
with Andouille Cream Drizzle

SWEET POTATO CRUST:

1¼ pounds roasted sweet potato flesh

½ cup mayonnaise

¼ teaspoon salt

1 dash black pepper

2 teaspoons bread crumbs

⅜ teaspoon Creole seasoning

Roast sweet potatoes. Peel, then place sweet potato flesh and remaining ingredients in mixer and mix to incorporate. Reserve.

ANDOUILLE CREAM DRIZZLE:

¼ pound andouille sausage, ¼-inch dice

¾ ounce vegetable oil

1 tablespoon Creole seasoning

1½ ounces bourbon

1 tablespoon honey

½ quart heavy cream

1½ tablespoons blonde roux

Salt and pepper to taste

Sauté andouille in oil until lightly browned. Add Creole seasoning. Deglaze with bourbon. Reduce. Add honey and cream. Add roux and let simmer until flour taste is gone. Salt and pepper to taste.

CATFISH:

4 (8- to 9-ounce) catfish fillets, trimmed as needed

Salt to taste

1 teaspoon Creole seasoning

16 ounces Sweet Potato Crust

4 ounces clarified butter

12 ounces spinach, cleaned

Creole seasoning to taste

Pepper to taste

6 ounces Andouille Cream Drizzle

Sprinkle catfish with salt and Creole seasoning. Spread Sweet Potato Crust on top of fish. In a hot skillet, add clarified butter and fish, crust side up. Remove fish to sizzle skillet, and finish in salamander (or place under broiler to finish). When fish is done, crust should be nicely browned. Sauté spinach in clarified butter and season with Creole seasoning, salt, and pepper. Drain spinach and put in center of plate; lay catfish on top, allowing spinach to be seen on either side of fish. Drizzle Andouille Cream Drizzle around fish and spinach. Garnish fish with chopped green onions. Serves 4.

Chocolate Bread Pudding

- -

3 cups milk (do not use low-fat or skim)

3 cups whipping cream

1¾ cups sugar, divided

12 ounces semisweet chocolate, chopped

12 eggs, lightly beaten

1½ tablespoons vanilla extract

1½ pounds day-old bread cubes, cut in 1-inch pieces

½ cup chopped pecans

¼ pound butter, cut into pieces

Preheat oven to 250°. In a medium saucepan combine milk, cream, and 1½ cups sugar, and cook over medium-high heat, stirring until sugar dissolves and mixture comes to a boil. Remove from heat, add chocolate, and stir until smooth and completely melted. Beat eggs and vanilla in large bowl to blend. Gradually whisk in chocolate mixture; add bread cubes, and let stand until bread absorbs some of the custard, stirring occasionally, about 30 minutes. Stir in pecan pieces. Pour into baking dish and top with butter and remaining sugar. Bake 1 hour. Makes 8 servings.

René Bistrot

**Renaissance Pere
   Marquette Hotel
817 Common Street
New Orleans, LA 70130
(504) 412-2580
www.renebistrot.com**

René Bajeux

French Master Chef/
Proprietor

An Authentic French Bistrot

Chef René has opened his own bistro in the Central Business District to rave reviews! He is the former executive chef at the Grill Room in the Windsor Court Hotel. He was awarded the Master Chef of France in 1996, the Chef of the Year in Los Angeles that same year, and the Hotel Chef of the Year by the American Testing Institute for 2002. Chef Bajeux has been featured in Food and Wine, Zagat Survey, Food Network, Great Chefs of America, Esquire magazine, and Life of the Rich and Famous.

Tuna Pasteur

• •

KIM CHEE CABBAGE:

10 ounces diced Napa cabbage

4 tablespoons hot sauce

1 tablespoon puréed garlic

3 tablespoons chopped chives

8 ounces fish sauce

Place all ingredients in a nonreactive crock and mix well. Place in refrigerator for at least a week.

SPRING ROLL:

1 package glass noodles

10 ounces diced smoked chicken

4 ounces julienned carrots

8 ounces julienned snow peas

4 tablespoons soy sauce

1 ounce crushed peanuts

8 pieces spring roll wrappers

Egg yolk

2 quarts peanut oil for frying

Soak glass noodles until soft. Drain and add the smoked chicken, carrots, snow peas, and Kim Chee Cabbage. Mix in the soy sauce and peanuts well. Then place a small amount of mixture in center of each spring roll wrapper. Fold in the 2 sides first, then fold in the side toward you and start rolling. Make sure you roll tightly. Brush the ends with egg yolk to seal; deep-fry until crispy brown.

ROUILLE:

1 ounce mayonnaise

½ ounce sun-dried tomatoes

Tabasco hot sauce to taste

Blend all ingredients in blender.

(continued)

(Tuna Pasteur continued)

VINAIGRETTE:

2 ounces olive oil

1 ounce diced carrots

¼ ounce basil

4 tablespoons puréed ginger

1 ounce champagne vinegar

Salt and pepper to taste

Mix all ingredients and whisk by hand. Season to taste.

TUNA:

6 pieces tuna

2 pounds potatoes, cooked and mashed

1 ounce puréed basil

Sear tuna on 4 sides in a cast-iron pan until desired temperature. Set aside at room temperature. Make the mashed potatoes and add the puréed basil; set aside. To serve, place mashed potatoes in center of plate, fan rare tuna on top of the potatoes. Place the Spring Roll that has been cut at an angle on the side of the plate. Drizzle the Vinaigrette around and place the Rouille near the tuna. Makes 8 servings.

Passion Fruit Crème Brûleé

• •

2 cups cream

2 cups milk

1 vanilla bean, split and scraped

11 ounces egg yolks

7 ounces sugar

2 tablespoons passion fruit compound

Boil cream, milk, and vanilla bean. Temper into beaten yolks and sugar. Add passion fruit compound. Strain through fine strainer. Pour into buttered crème brûleé dishes. Bake at 200° to 225° for 1 hour or until set. Cool.

Alligator Ragout
with Chipotle Creole Tomato Sauce

• •

1 ounce olive oil

4 ounces leeks, white and green parts

¼ cup chopped onion

2 pounds alligator meat, tenderized and diced to ¼-inch cubes

Salt and pepper to taste

1 ounce chopped garlic

6 ounces peeled and diced tomato

Zest of 2 oranges

¼ cup diced andouille sausage

1 ounce chipotle pepper, roasted

1 cup white wine

2 cups chicken stock

1 ounce roux (made with ½ ounce each flour and butter)

1 cup corn

In a medium-size stockpot, heat olive oil. When hot, brown leeks and onion. Add the alligator meat; season to taste with salt and pepper. Add garlic, diced tomatoes, and orange zest. After 3 minutes, add sausage and chipotle peppers. Deglaze with white wine and chicken stock; let boil. Add roux little by little and whisk. When thick, add rest of ingredients. Let stew 1 hour. Can be served with pasta or rice. Serves 8.

Restaurant August

301 Tchoupitoulas Street
New Orleans, LA 70130
(504) 299-9777
www.restaurantaugust.com

John Besh
Executive Chef

"The correlation between our cuisine of Nouvelle Orleans and that of southern France is intriguing," Besh says. "Our Creole food and culture are quite exotic to the French, yet familiar enough for them to enjoy."

Acclaimed chef John Besh grew up in southern Louisiana, learning at an early age the essentials of Louisiana's rich culinary traditions. Besh has set the benchmark for fine dining in New Orleans, one of the world's most esteemed restaurant cities—with four successful restaurants: Restaurant August, Besh Steak, Lüke, and La Provence. His talent and drive have earned Besh continuous kudos from the outset of his career: in 1999, *Food & Wine* named him one of the "Top 10 Best New Chefs in America." In 2003, *Gourmet* magazine included Restaurant August in its "Guide to America's Best Restaurants," and in 2006, it cited Restaurant August as one of America's Top 50 Restaurants. In 2005, Chef Besh received a nomination for a James Beard Award, and he won the Beard for Best Chef of the Southeast in 2006. Also that year, he defeated Chef Mario Batali on *Iron Chef America* on the Food Network. The 2007 *Zagat Guide* rates Restaurant August #1 in New Orleans for both Food and Service.

Salad of Dandelions, Crispy Seared Foie Gras, and Tempura Cèpes

TEMPURA CÈPE:

½ cup flour

¼ cup cornstarch

½ teaspoon onion powder

½ teaspoon garlic powder

2 dashes cayenne pepper

¼ teaspoon salt

1 cup ice water

12 slices fresh cèpe (porcini) mushrooms, cleaned

Peanut or canola oil for frying

Blend the flour, cornstarch, onion powder, garlic powder, cayenne, and salt. Add ice water to dry ingredients. Do not overmix the batter. Add water until just combined and reserve in the refrigerator until ready for use. Coat each slice of cèpe with tempura batter and deep-fry in oil; carefully turn each cèpe at least once until they become a uniform golden brown. Remove and reserve each slice on an absorbent paper towel.

FOIE GRAS:

6 ounces fresh foie gras, divided into 4 equal portions

Salt and freshly cracked black pepper to taste

Season each slice of foie gras and sear in a very hot, nonstick skillet for one minute before removing from heat.

DRIED CHERRY VINAIGRETTE:

6 tablespoons minced dried cherries

1 teaspoon minced shallot

2 tablespoon rice wine vinegar

3 tablespoons walnut oil

1 dash pumpkin seed oil

1 pinch sugar

Salt and freshly cracked black pepper to taste

1 teaspoon minced black truffle

Combine cherries, shallot, and wine vinegar in a food processor. While processing, slowly add walnut and pumpkin seed oils until well combined. Season with sugar, salt, and pepper to taste. Add minced truffle.

(continued)

SALAD:

4 (6-ounce) servings young dandelions (or baby arugula), well-cleaned

Toss the young dandelion greens in a bowl with the Dried Cherry Vinaigrette and place in a bed in center of each plate. Around the greens, place 3 slices of Tempura Cèpe. Place a seared medallion of Foie Gras on bed of greens. Serves 4.

Note: Any fresh wild mushroom will do if cèpes are out of season. Cèpes also go by the name porcini and steinpilzen. John Besh loves using chanterelles, black trumpets, and hedgehog mushrooms in this recipe as well. He often garnishes this salad with delicate chervil leaves and chive blossoms. Chef Besh likes to use a mixture of 3-inch greens, all of which are quite spicy, such as arugula, pepper cress, or any of the baby mustards.

Warm Strawberry Cobbler with Vanilla Ice Cream

4 tablespoons unsalted butter, diced

2 pints fresh strawberries

¼ cup sugar

2 whole eggs

Zest of 1 lemon

1 teaspoon vanilla

¼ cup flour, sifted with 2 teaspoons baking powder

6 tablespoons heavy cream

4 tablespoons powdered sugar

4 sprigs fresh mint, chiffonade

Vanilla ice cream (optional)

Preheat oven to 400°. Liberally butter a 2-quart earthenware dish. Add a layer of berries. In a mixing bowl, cream together remaining butter, sugar, eggs, lemon zest, and vanilla. Add flour mixture, and slowly add cream until well combined and without lumps. Pour mixture over berries and bake 25 minutes. Remove from oven and dust with powdered sugar and chiffonade of fresh mint. Can be served hot or cold, with or without ice cream. Serves 4.

Note: You may substitute any type of seasonal berries or fruit.

Gnocchi with Crab and Truffle

GNOCCHI:

2½ pounds Yukon gold pota-toes

3¼ ounces butter

5 egg yolks, beaten

7 ounces all-purpose flour

1½ teaspoons salt

Dash of freshly grated nutmeg

Preheat oven to 250°. Place potatoes in small pot covered with water. Cook over high heat until fork-tender. Strain and return to pot. Place in oven for 15 minutes. Force potatoes through ricer into a fine mesh drum sieve. Use spatula to press all potatoes through into clean bowl. Add butter and egg yolks. Mix well. Fold in flour, salt, and nutmeg until dough forms. Roll into 6 logs, about 1 inch in diameter. Cut dough in 1-inch pieces. With a gnocchi board (a grooved wooden board), roll cut dough using thumb so dough curls around thumb and grooved edges form on outside of dumpling. Drop into boiling water and poach for 30 seconds. Remove.

SAUCE:

2 cups dry vermouth

2 cups heavy cream

1 quart crab stock

3 shallots, minced

½ teaspoon cayenne pepper

2 sprigs marigold mint

½ pound unsalted butter

1 pound lump crabmeat

Salt and white pepper to taste

1 medium-size black truffle

¾ pound Reggiano Parmigiano, shaved

Combine vermouth, cream, and stock with shallots, cayenne, and mint in a saucepot, and bring to boil. Reduce by ⅔, then add butter. Add Gnocchi and crabmeat. Season and reserve. To assemble, spoon Gnocchi and crabmeat into bowl. Shave truffle over mixture and top with cheese. Serves 6.

Restaurant Cuvée

322 Rue Magazine
New Orleans, LA 70130
(504) 587-9001
www.restaurantcuvee.com

Robert Iacovone
Executive Chef

Robert Iacovone, thirty-two, assumed the position of executive chef at Cuvée on March 15, 2003.

As a 1991 graduate of the Culinary Institute of America at Hyde Park, New York, Chef Iacovone holds an Associate Degree in Culinary Arts. He also holds a first-level certificate from the Court of Sommeliers in London. A native of Worcester, Massachusetts, he began his culinary career in Florida, first at the PGA National Resort and Spa in Palm Beach Gardens, then as executive sous chef at the Booking Table. In 1999, during the pre-opening period at Cuvée, Iacovone was chosen as the restaurant's chef de cuisine, a post he held until his ascension to the restaurant's top kitchen position in March 2003.

He came to New Orleans in 1995 to join the kitchen staff of the Windsor Court Hotel's Grill Room. "I realized immediately what a great food town this city was," he says. "I knew that if I could make it here, I could make it anywhere." His affection for New Orleans, he says, stems from its "marrying of food cultures, the combinations of French and Spanish, the rich flavors, and the one-pot cooking. I think flavor counts down here more than it does anywhere else in the country."

Seared Wild Striped Bass, Potato Porcini, Risotto Fried Leeks, Tomato, Cognac Fumé

• •

4 cups finely diced potatoes

Olive oil

2 medium leeks (white and green parts)

6 ounces dried porcini mushrooms, soaked in water (may also use fresh)

2 cups chicken stock

4 pounds bass, or snapper fillets, deboned

½ ounce butter

¼ cup diced shallots

2 tomatoes, diced

1 cup fish stock

2 ounces cream

1½ ounces cognac

Cooked risotto

Wash and dry potatoes. In a saucepan, place olive oil and white parts of leeks. Let these sweat for a few minutes. Add mushrooms and potatoes. Sauté very gently; add chicken stock little by little. Cook about 8 minutes or until tender. Set aside until ready to use.

Portion and season the fish. Sear in a very hot pan about 4 minutes on each side, or until desired doneness is reached. In a saucepan, place butter, shallots, diced tomatoes, fish stock, and cream. Cook over low flame 15 minutes. Add cognac. Strain through fine sieve, then keep warm until ready to use.

Julienne the green parts of the leeks. Deep-fry them for 2 minutes. Place on paper towels to drain oil. To assemble, place risotto on one side of the plate, fish in center, sauce around, and leeks on top for garnish. Serves 8.

Pan-Roasted Seafood Bouillabaisse with a Tomato-Saffron Broth and Garlic Creamed Potatoes

....

BROTH:

2 tablespoons olive oil

¼ cup diced bell pepper

¼ cup diced onion

2 tablespoons diced fennel

2 tablespoons diced celery

2 tablespoons diced carrots

1 pinch saffron

1 to 2 tablespoons tomato paste

1 teaspoon minced garlic

Worcestershire sauce to taste

Crystal hot sauce to taste

⅓ cup white wine

1 quart fish or seafood stock

Salt and pepper to taste

1 teaspoon fresh thyme

Sauté onions, peppers, fennel, celery, carrots, and saffron in olive oil. Add tomato paste, garlic, Worcestershire, and hot sauce. Deglaze with white wine and add fish stock. Season with salt, pepper, and thyme. Simmer for about 10 minutes.

BOUILLABAISSE:

2 scallops

2 to 3 ounces fish pieces

3 shrimp

Salt and pepper to taste

½ cup diced tomatoes

2 tablespoons crawfish tails

Green onions for garnish

Roasted, garlic mashed potatoes

French bread croutons

Red pepper rouille

Season all of the seafood with salt and pepper. In a hot sauté pan, sear scallops, fish, and shrimp. Add diced tomatoes and crawfish. Add desired amount of Broth. Add green onions and season with salt and pepper. Place mashed potatoes in center of the bowl. Ladle stew around the potatoes. Garnish with the croutons and rouille. Serves 1.

Cajun Frittata with Tomato Horseradish and Boiled Shrimp

. . . .

2 ounces sausage

1 tablespoon chopped red bell pepper

1 tablespoon chopped yellow bell pepper

1 tablespoon chopped green bell pepper

1 tablespoon chopped green onion

1 tablespoon chopped onion

3 new potatoes, diced and blanched

4 whole eggs, whipped

1 ounce Pepper Jack cheese

2 ounces traditional cocktail sauce

2 jumbo shrimp, boiled

Preheat oven to 325°. Sauté sausage and vegetables in omelet pan till golden brown. Add eggs, stirring constantly until medium firmness. Fold in cheese. Bake until eggs are firm. Serve on pool of cocktail sauce. Garnish with boiled shrimp. Serves 1.

Duck Confit Wild Mushroom Potato Hash

1 medium bag regular Zapps Potato Chips

1 cup pulled duck confit

1½ cups sautéed wild mushrooms

1 to 2 tablespoons white truffle oil

½ bunch green onions, sliced

¼ cup grated Parmesan cheese, divided

Salt and pepper to taste

2 ounces demi-glace

Preheat oven to 300°. In a large bowl, toss potato chips with duck, mushrooms, truffle oil, green onions, and ½ the cheese. Season with salt and pepper and top with remaining cheese. Place in oven 1 to 2 minutes. Drizzle with the demi-glace. Serves 4.

Jackson Square / St. Louis Cathedral

Stella!

1032 Rue Chartres
New Orleans, LA 70116
(504) 587-0091
www.restaurantstella.com

· · · · · · · · · · · ·

Scott Boswell
Chef/Proprietor

Louisiana native Scott Boswell attended the Culinary Institute of America in Hyde Park, New York, where he graduated with high honors. He credits Chef Pascal Morel at L'Abbaye de Ste Croix (one Michelin star) in Salon de Provence, France, with teaching him many of the techniques and nuances that prevail in his food today.

His year in Provence was followed by another six months in Italy's famed Enoteca Pinchiorri (Michelin 2 Stars) in Florence. It was in this wonderful restaurant that Scott learned to make the pasta he is quickly becoming known for. It was also in this kitchen where Boswell worked at the side of and befriended Masahiko Kobe, now better known as "The Italian Iron Chef."

Stella! was opened on April 4, 2001. This lovely French Quarter restaurant is located just 2½ blocks from historic Jackson Square. Stella! serves up polished European fare with Asian accents and bold Creole flavors. In its short time on the scene, Stella! has quickly become a favorite for locals. The small, intimate restaurant has the ambiance of a French country inn.

106 · Louisiana's Best Restaurant Recipes

My Good Friend Bob's Tomato Curry Purée with Cumin Grilled Shrimp

• • • • • • New Improved Version • • • • • • • • • • • • • • •

GARAM MASALA (MIXTURE OF GROUND SPICES):

1 tablespoon cumin

1 tablespoon coriander seed

1 tablespoon mustard seed

1 cinnamon stick

3 whole cloves

3 whole green cardamom

1 teaspoon whole black pepper-corns

3 bay leaves

Preheat oven to 350° and lightly toast all ingredients, adding the bay leaves toward the end. Cool spices and grind in a spice grinder; reserve for soup.

SOUP PURÉE:

⅓ cup chopped garlic

⅓ cup chopped ginger

3 tablespoons olive oil

6 pounds diced pear tomatoes

2 cups ketchup

2 cups chicken stock

2 tablespoons Vietnamese chile paste

Garam Masala to taste

2 cups heavy cream

3 tablespoons finely chopped methi leaves (fenugreek)

Chili powder

Salt and pepper to taste

Sugar to taste

Sauté garlic and ginger in olive oil until lightly brown. Add tomatoes, ketchup, and chicken stock. Slowly bring to a simmer and cook 15 minutes. Add chile paste and Garam Marsala to taste. Add heavy cream, methi leaves, and chili powder. Purée soup and adjust salt, pepper, and sugar. More Garam Masala may be added for stronger curry flavor.

Note: Garnish with a grilled shrimp dusted with cumin and fresh chopped chives.

Fresh Ricotta and Maine Lobster Ravioli

PASTA DOUGH:

½ **pound all-purpose flour**

2 **whole eggs**

⅛ **teaspoon salt**

½ **teaspoon extra virgin olive oil**

Place all ingredients in food processor and pulse until it forms a ball. You may have to add a little more flour or a touch of water if too dry or wet. Wrap dough in plastic wrap and rest for about an hour.

RICOTTA FILLING:

3 **cups ricotta cheese**

1 **whole egg**

1 **egg white**

1 **cup grated Parmesan cheese**

Salt and pepper to taste

1 **steamed Maine lobster**

Place ricotta cheese, whole egg, egg white, and Parmesan cheese into bowl and mix well. Salt and pepper to taste. Steam lobster about 4 to 5 minutes and set aside to cool. Cut into small medallions to fill ravioli.

Flour counter top to roll out Pasta Dough. Set pasta machine to highest number to start. Flatten out ball of Pasta Dough and flour both sides moderately. Roll through on highest setting and fold in half. Repeat this process 4 to 5 times to knead the dough. Lower your setting one number at a time and roll out dough to desired thickness. Take top section of ravioli press and measure rolled-out dough into sections. Flour base of ravioli press generously. Place one section of dough over ravioli base. Fill each section with Ricotta Filling (a pastry bag will make this easier). Place one medallion of lobster over each filling. Place another sheet of pasta over this and lightly press with hands to remove air. Use a rolling pin to roll over the ravioli press and cut the ravioli. Makes 10 portions of 3 ravioli.

North Shore

The **NEW ORLEANS NORTH SHORE** was once a resort region for wealthy New Orleanians, known as l'autre cote du lac (the other side of the lake). It is connected to New Orleans by a causeway across Lake Pontchartrain. Here you'll find beautiful countryside, winding waterways, gently rolling hills, piney forests, and small-town charm blending in a delightful way with many of the flavors and joys of New Orleans culture.

North Shore Restaurants

Bealer's Restaurant 111

Bella Rose Food and Spirits 115

The Dakota Restaurant 118

Main Street Restaurant 122

Michabelle Inn and Restaurant 125

A Taste of Bavaria 128

Tope Lá! 130

Trey Yuen 132

The R/B River Explorer

Bealer's Restaurant

348 Robert Boulevard
Slidell, LA 70458
(985) 649-1805

Floyd Bealer
Proprietor

Bealer's Restaurant (formerly Doug's Restaurant) has the distinction of being named Best Restaurant in Slidell by the *Times-Picayune* restaurant columnist Gene Bourg. Bealer's serves up delicious Creole dishes as well as grilled fish, seafood, lobster, and prime steaks. Bealer's is open for lunch Tuesday through Saturday from 11:00 a.m. until 2:00 p.m. with dinner from 5:00 p.m. until 10:00 p.m.

Turtle Soup

• •

1¼ cups unsalted butter, divided

¾ cup all-purpose flour

1 pound turtle meat, cut in ½-inch cubes

1 cup minced celery

1¼ cups minced onions

1½ teaspoons minced garlic

3 bay leaves

1 teaspoon oregano

½ teaspoon thyme

½ teaspoon ground black pepper

1½ cups tomato purée

1 quart beef stock

Salt and pepper to taste

½ cup lemon juice

5 hard-cooked eggs, chopped

1 tablespoon minced parsley

Dry sherry

Melt 1 cup (2 sticks) butter in a heavy saucepan. Add flour and cook over medium heat. Stir frequently until roux is light brown; set aside. In a 5-quart saucepan, melt remaining butter and add turtle meat. Cook over high heat until meat is brown. Add celery, onions, garlic, and seasonings, and cook until vegetables are transparent. Add tomato purée, lower heat, and simmer 10 minutes. Add stock and simmer 30 minutes. Add roux and cook over low heat, stirring until soup becomes smooth and thickens. Add salt and pepper to taste. Add lemon juice, eggs, and parsley. Remove from heat and serve. Serve with sherry to taste. Serves 6.

Corn and Crabmeat Bisque

CRAB STOCK:

Shells from 6 medium hard-shell crabs

2 quarts water

2 medium onions, quartered

Drop shells into water and add onions. Bring to a boil and simmer over low heat until liquid is reduced to 1 quart. Strain and set aside.

BISQUE:

½ pound unsalted butter

1 cup all-purpose flour

1 teaspoon liquid crab boil

Kernels from 4 ears of sweet corn

1½ cups heavy whipping cream

1 pound lump crabmeat

Salt and pepper to taste

1½ cups chopped green onions

Melt butter in a 5-quart saucepan. Add flour and cook, stirring until flour begins to stick to the pan. Add crab stock and crab boil. Bring to a boil, stirring constantly, and simmer 15 minutes. Add corn and simmer 15 additional minutes. Pour in cream and stir well. Gently add crabmeat. Remove from heat and let stand for 15 minutes so that the flavors may blend. Reheat gently to serving temperature. Add salt and pepper to taste. Before serving, add green onions. Makes 1 quart. Serves 8.

Note: To hold for serving or to reheat, use a double boiler to prevent scorching.

Bread Pudding with Bourbon Sauce

. . . .

1 cup sugar

8 tablespoons (1 stick) butter, softened

5 eggs, beaten

1 pint heavy cream

Dash of cinnamon

1 tablespoon vanilla extract

½ cup raisins

12 (1-inch-thick) slices fresh French bread

Preheat oven to 350°. In a large bowl, cream together sugar and butter. Add eggs, cream, cinnamon, vanilla, and raisins, mixing well. Pour into a 9x9-inch-square pan. Arrange bread slices flat in egg mixture and let stand 5 minutes to soak. Turn bread over and let stand 10 minutes longer. Then push bread down so that most of it is covered. Set pan in a larger pan filled with water ½ inch from the top. Cover with aluminum foil. Bake 45 to 50 minutes. Uncover pudding for the last 10 minutes to brown the top. When done, the custard should be soft not firm.

BOURBON SAUCE:

1 cup sugar

1 cup heavy cream

1 dash cinnamon

1 tablespoon unsalted butter

½ teaspoon cornstarch

¼ cup additional water

1 tablespoon bourbon

Combine sugar, cream, cinnamon, and butter. Bring to a boil. Add cornstarch mixed with ¼ cup water and cook, stirring, until sauce is clear. Remove from heat and stir in bourbon. Serves 8 to 10.

Bella Rose Food and Spirits

200 East Charles Street
Hammond, LA 70401
(985) 345-1538

Coy Mollega
Head Chef/Proprietor

Bella Rose Food and Spirits opened in March 2002. This restaurant features Italian and Mediterranean cuisine in a relaxed and casual environment.

Coy's Contemporary Cuisine is a full-service catering and event planning company. They can coordinate everything from food, wine, and liquor to venue selection, decoration, design, linens, china and silverware—every aspect of your event. The staff will design the perfect menu, specifically crafted for your occasion.

Coy Mollega, owner and head chef, has more than ten years of food service experience. A classically trained chef, he formalized his education at the Culinary Institute of America in New York. After graduating from the CIA, Coy returned to his roots in New Orleans. He worked with such renowned chefs as Kevin Graham of the Grille Room at the Windsor Court and Mike Fennelly, owner and head chef of Mike's on the Avenue. Coy also traveled across Europe to expand his knowledge of the culinary arts. He worked in some of Spain's finest restaurants as well as Barcelona's largest catering company.

Roasted Red Pepper Cream Soup

. . . .

4 red bell peppers

½ cup julienned Bermuda onion

1 tablespoon minced garlic

½ teaspoon thyme

1 teaspoon basil

1 cup white wine

Pinch of cayenne red pepper

1 teaspoon Spanish paprika

2 tablespoons olive oil

1 quart cream

Roast red peppers in oven at 450° for 10 minutes. Put peppers in paper bag for 15 minutes. Remove skins and purée. Sweat rest of ingredients except for the cream. Add wine and purée of peppers. Cook until mixture has reduced by ¼, then add cream and reduce by ¼. Salt and white pepper to taste.

Red Snapper with Roasted Garlic and Tomato Provençal

. . . .

Juice of 1 lemon

½ cup extra virgin olive oil

1 teaspoon coarsely ground black pepper

Fresh basil

2 teaspoons capers

8 garlic cloves, roasted

8 Roma tomatoes, seeded and diced small

Anchovies

Calamata olives

Red onions

Roasted red peppers

Salt and white pepper to taste

4 (8-ounce) snapper fillets, pan-seared

½ cup flour

To make the Provençal, put lemon juice, olive oil, pepper, and chopped basil in bowl. Dice all remaining ingredients except fish and flour and toss in bowl; season with salt and white pepper. Let stand for at least 2 hours. (Good for up to 2 days in refrigerator.)

Coat snapper fillets with flour and sauté in olive oil. Top pan-seared snapper with Provençal.

The Dakota Restaurant

629 North Highway 190
Covington, LA 70533
(985) 892-3712
www.thedakotarestaurant
  .com

Ken LaCour, Jr.
Kim Kringle, C.E.C
Owners

Since the opening of The Dakota Restaurant in 1990 with partner Kenneth LaCour, Chef Kim Kringlie has created an eclectic menu that marries global flavors with the zing of Louisiana accents. The food takes on characteristics from French, Southwestern, Asian, and other ethnic cuisine. The restaurant is located in Covington, across Lake Ponchartrain from New Orleans. Kim Kringlie was named Chef of the Year by *New Orleans* magazine, October 2000. The *New Orleans Times-Picayune* awarded Dakota its 4 Beans designation for outstanding food. The restaurant received the 5 Stars Award as one of the Top 5 New Orleans Restaurants by Tom Fitzmorris, *New Orleans City Business*. Dakota has received the *Wine Spectator's* Award of Excellence for eight years running!

Dakota's Lump Crabmeat and Brie Soup

2 pounds fresh Louisiana blue crabs

2 ounces olive oil

2 medium yellow onions, chopped

1 medium carrot, chopped

3 ribs celery, chopped

1 clove fresh garlic, chopped

2 bay leaves

¼ cup brandy

1 cup white wine

2 quarts water

½ cup unsalted butter

¾ cup flour

1 quart heavy whipping cream

8 ounces Brie cheese

1 teaspoon salt

1 teaspoon white pepper

1 teaspoon cayenne pepper

½ pound picked jumbo lump crabmeat

Using a meat mallet or hammer, crack open crab shells until meat is exposed. In a 1-gallon stockpot, heat olive oil; add cracked crabs, and sauté for 5 minutes. Add chopped vegetables and bay leaves; continue to sauté for an additional 5 minutes. Add brandy, white wine, and water, bring to a simmer over medium heat, and cook for 30 minutes. Using a skimmer, remove crabs and vegetables from stock.

In a separate small sauté skillet, melt butter, add flour, and blend with a wire whisk until smooth and creamy; simmer over low heat for one minute. Add flour and butter mixture to stock, using a wire whisk until all the roux is dissolved. Add heavy cream and simmer for 10 minutes. Remove outside rind from Brie and discard; cut Brie into 1-inch cubes. Add to stock while constantly stirring until all the cheese is completely dissolved. Season soup with salt, white pepper, and cayenne. Strain soup through a fine strainer, add jumbo lump crabmeat, and serve. Makes 3 quarts.

Potato and Parmesan Crusted Oysters with Saffron Barbecue Sauce

- -

CRUSTED OYSTERS:

3 cups instant potato flakes

1 cup grated Parmesan cheese

2 tablespoons cracked black pepper

1 egg

1 cup milk

20 large select oysters

2 cups flour

4 tablespoons olive oil

In a small pan, mix potato flakes, Parmesan, and pepper. In a separate pan, mix egg and milk. Lightly dust oysters in flour, then dip in egg wash, and coat with potato mixture. Heat oil in skillet until hot. Sauté oysters on both sides until golden brown. Place on napkin to drain excess oil. Prepare Sauce.

SAUCE:

2 tablespoons olive oil

2 tablespoons minced garlic

½ cup diced tomatoes

½ cup sliced mushrooms

½ cup chopped sweet peppers

¼ cup beer

4 dashes Worcestershire sauce

1 teaspoon fresh rosemary

1 teaspoon fresh basil

1 tram saffron threads

½ cup seafood stock

2 tablespoons lemon juice

2 ounces unsalted butter

¼ cup chopped green onions

Heat olive oil in a skillet and sauté garlic, tomatoes, mushrooms, and peppers until tender. Deglaze pan with beer, add Worcestershire, rosemary, basil, saffron, seafood stock, and lemon juice. Simmer until reduced by half. Slowly add butter and swirl into Sauce until dissolved; do not boil. Add green onions. Serve sauce on base of plate and garnish with crusted oysters. Serve with your favorite rice or pasta dish. Makes 4 portions.

Sesame Crusted Yellow-Fin with Asian Vinaigrette

. . . .

TUNA:

3 tablespoons sesame oil

16 ounces yellow-fin tuna loin, fresh, #1 grade

¼ cup sesame seeds

Heat oil in sauté pan until hot. Coat tuna with sesame seeds. Place tuna in hot oil and sear on all sides. Slice thin for salad.

ASIAN VINAIGRETTE:

1 tablespoon sesame oil

1 tablespoon minced fresh ginger

1 tablespoon minced garlic

3 tablespoons pepper jelly

¼ cup light, low-sodium soy sauce

½ cup rice wine vinegar

½ cup vegetable oil

1 pinch cayenne pepper

Heat oil in skillet and sauté ginger and garlic until tender. Add jelly and heat to dissolve. Place mixture into small bowl and blend with remaining ingredients. Serve with sliced yellow-fin tuna and your favorite greens and vegetables. Makes 4 portions.

Main Street Restaurant

· · · · · · · · · · · · · · · · · ·

1102 Main Street
Franklinton, LA 70438
(985) 839-9700

· · · · · · · · · ·

Jeanette Sumrall
Chef/Proprietor

This casual country restaurant features home-cooked meals daily, baby back ribs, steaks, seafood, and sandwiches. Chef Jeanette has been in business for twenty-four years and learned her wonderful cooking skills from her mother.

Peach Cobbler

1½ sticks butter or margarine

2 cups self-rising flour

2 cups sugar

2½ cups milk

2 large cans sliced peaches

Preheat oven to 350°. Melt butter in a 9x13x½-inch pan. Mix together flour, sugar, and milk. Whisk to get any lumps out. Pour over butter; drain peaches, and place over butter. Bake at until golden brown. Crust will rise to the top. Serves 10 people.

Strawberry Pie

3 pints Louisiana strawberries

2 graham cracker pie crusts

2½ cups sugar

3 heaping tablespoons corn-starch

2½ cups water

1 (6-ounce) box strawberry gelatin

1 (12-ounce) container Cool Whip

Wash and drain berries. Slice and place in pie crust; the crust should be full. In a 2-quart saucepan, mix sugar, cornstarch, and water. Boil until thick. Add gelatin. Pour over berries in crust. Cool until set and cover. Top with Cool Whip. Makes 2 pies.

Cream Cheese Cake

1½ cups butter, softened

1 (8-ounce) package cream cheese, softened

3 cups sugar

6 eggs

1 teaspoon vanilla

¼ teaspoon salt

3 cups cake flour

Vegetable spray

Preheat oven to 275°. Cream butter and cream cheese; add sugar and mix well. Add eggs one at a time. Add vanilla and salt, and gradually add flour. Batter will be very thick. Put in a tube cake pan (sprayed with vegetable spray). Bake for 2½ hours. Makes 1 cake.

Cornbread Dressing – Louisiana Style

. . . .

BROTH:

4 to 5 pounds turkey meat

Boil turkey meat in water to cover until tender. Debone and set aside with broth. (Should have 2 to 3 quarts of broth.)

CORNBREAD:

2 cups yellow cornmeal

1 cup self-rising flour

4 heaping tablespoons baking powder

¾ teaspoon baking soda

2 teaspoons salt

2 eggs

4 tablespoons cooking oil

Milk to mix

Preheat oven to 350°. Mix all ingredients well with milk and cook in a greased pan until golden brown.

DRESSING:

2 tablespoons butter

1 celery heart, diced

1 medium bell pepper, diced

1 medium onion, diced

1 bunch green onions, diced

6 hard-cooked eggs, peeled, diced

4 tablespoons mayonnaise

Melt butter in a skillet; sauté celery, bell pepper, onion, and green onions. Crumble cornbread with eggs; add sautéed vegetables, mayonnaise, and deboned turkey. Pour broth over all until well mixed (should be loose and not stiff). Pour in a buttered 9x13x½-inch pan. Drizzle butter on top and bake at 350° until golden brown.

Michabelle Inn and Restaurant

1106 South Holly Street
Hammond, LA 70403
(985) 419-0550
www.michabelle.com

Michel Marcais
Chef/Proprietor

Isabel Marcais
Manager

Chef Michel is a classically trained French chef from Angers, France. He has worked extensively all over Europe, the United States, and the Caribbean. He has prepared banquets for presidents Gerald Ford, Ronald Reagan, and George H. Bush. He participated in the original Great Chefs of New Orleans and was president and one of the founding members of the Chef Association in New Orleans.

Michabelle Inn and Restaurant is located in the historic MacGehee home built in 1908. It is the only home in Hammond on the National Historic Register. Chef Michel and his wife bought the home from the MacGehee family in 1998 and turned it into a French-style country inn. The inn features seven bedrooms, three dining rooms, a library, and a bar. The Greek Revival home is situated on three acres of land that provide room for the extensive gardens and an atrium-style banquet hall, called the Glass Pavilion. Since 1998, Michabelle has been the scene of many of Hammond's cultural and social events. Michabelle has become one of the premier spots for weddings in the North Shore area of Louisiana.

Ile Flottante au Chocolate et au Rhum
· · · · · · · *Floating Island of Chocolate and Rum* ·

6 eggs, separated
1½ cups sugar, divided
3 cups milk
1 cup cream
1 tablespoon cornstarch
1 tablespoon chocolate powder
1 tablespoon rum

Whip egg whites until stiff, then gradually add ¾ cup sugar. Scald the milk in a pan, then scoop egg white on top in 6 large balls. Poach until cooked, then remove and let cool. Mix egg yolks, remaining sugar, chocolate, milk, and cream. Cook until thick. Flavor with rum. Pour cream custard into 6 cups and place egg whites on top. Serves 6.

Rabbit à la Creole
· ·

1 rabbit
1 onion, chopped
2 tablespoons butter
2 tablespoons flour
1 cup tomato purée
1 cup white wine
1 carrot, diced
2 celery stalks, diced
Seasoning

Cut rabbit into pieces, and sauté with onion in butter until brown. Add flour, tomato purée, white wine, carrot, and celery. Cover with water and season to taste. Cook until tender. Serves 6.

Escargot Casserole

36 snails
Butter
1 tablespoon chopped garlic
1 green onion, chopped
2 tablespoons diced bacon
1 teaspoon flour
1 cup white wine
1 tomato, diced
Seasoning

Sauté snails in butter in large skillet. Add garlic, green onion, and bacon; sprinkle with flour. Add white wine. Add diced tomato and season to taste. Serves 6.

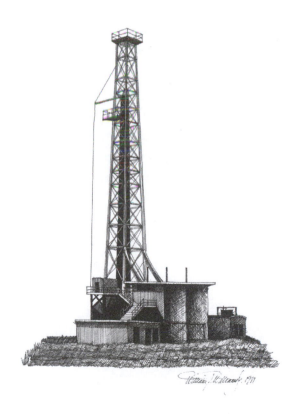

A Taste of Bavaria

Bakery – Restaurant – Deli
14476 Highway 22 West
Ponchatoula, LA 70454
(985) 386-3634

Justine Hedrick and
Lori Reed
Proprietors

A Taste of Bavaria was established in 1985 by Larry and Mary Alice Larrieu who, although not German, both had a passion for Germany. After fifteen years of a hugely successful business, they sold their dream to Justine Hedrick and Lori Reed who intend to carry on the tradition. Justine was born in Bayreuth, located in Bavaria, and lived there twenty-seven years. She brings her true heritage with her, and a knowledge of authentic German cuisine, traditions, and, of course, the language. Lori, originally from Chicago, spent twenty years in the restaurant industry and always dreamed of having her own restaurant. The new owners, friends for sixteen years, are living their dream together along with their families. They are working daily to prepare the freshest baked breads, European pastries, and homemade authentic German cuisine. A trip to Taste of Bavaria is worth remembering!

German Potato Salad

5 pounds sliced red potatoes

1½ pounds bacon, chopped

1 onion, sliced

2 bay leaves

1 large or 2 small cucumbers, peeled and sliced

1 cup balsamic vinegar

½ cup white vinegar

½ cup prepared mustard

¼ cup Worcestershire sauce

Salt and pepper to taste

Boil sliced potatoes until soft, then drain. Sauté bacon, onion, bay leaves, and cucumber until onion is soft. Add balsamic vinegar and simmer. Remove from heat, add remaining ingredients, mix well, and add salt and pepper to taste. Serves 4 to 6.

Bavarian Potato Soup

1 pound bacon, chopped

4 carrots, sliced

8 ribs celery, chopped

1 onion, chopped

2 bay leaves

White wine

1⅔ gallons chicken stock

4 pounds new potatoes, sliced

Salt and pepper to taste

Sauté bacon in heavy-gauge pot until almost crisp; add carrots, celery, onion, and bay leaves. When vegetables begin to soften, add a little white wine to deglaze the bottom of the pot. Add stock and potatoes, bring to a rolling boil, then turn down to a simmer. Cook until potatoes are soft. Salt and pepper to taste. Makes 2 gallons.

Tope Lá!

104 North Cate Street
Hammond, LA 70401
(985) 542-7600
www.topela.com

Tommy Masaracchia
Executive Chef

Nestled in the downtown area of historic Hammond, Tope Lá provides the atmosphere of a friendly small town café combined with fine restaurant professionalism.

Owned by Jim Hebert, Troy Tallo, Tracy Barringer, and Executive Chef Tommy Masaracchia, Tope Lá graces Hammond with the finest food in the area. The name Tope Lá means the joining or clasping of hands, symbolizing the perfect union of French and Louisiana culinary cultures. With excellent service and exquisite food, Tope Lá provides all with an enchanting dining experience.

Crawfish and Andouille Stuffed Pork Loin with Hot Pepper Jelly Demi-Glace

. . . .

1 (4-pound) boneless pork loin

Salt and black pepper to taste

3 ounces butter

1 pound andouille sausage, small dice

1 cup diced onion

1 cup diced green bell pepper

⅓ cup sliced celery

1¼ tablespoons minced garlic

1 Granny Smith apple, peeled, cored, and small dice

4 cups crumbled cornbread

⅓ cup minced fresh parsley

⅓ cup sliced green onion tops

1 cup crawfish tails

¾ to 1 pound smoked Gouda cheese, grated

Cayenne pepper to taste

Chicken stock (optional)

1 pound applewood regular or smoked bacon (optional)

HOT PEPPER DEMI-GLACE:

3 cups demi-glace or beef gravy

1 cup hot pepper jelly (red)

Preheat oven to 350°. Make an incision lengthwise in the top ⅓ of the pork loin so that the loin is butterflied. There will be a thick side and a thin side. Butterfly the thick side so that the loin lays flat and is ready for stuffing. Season with salt and black pepper. Reserve.

Melt butter and sauté andouille sausage until browned. Add onion, bell pepper, celery, garlic, and apple; sauté until vegetables are wilted. Add cornbread, parsley, green onions, and crawfish tails. Mix well and allow to cool. When mixture has cooled, add Gouda and mix. Season with salt, pepper, and cayenne. If mixture is too dry, add chicken stock to achieve desired stuffing consistency.

Fill pork loin with stuffing and roll up to achieve a pinwheel effect. If desired, wrap pork with applewood smoked bacon and secure with butcher's twine. Sear meat on all sides so that bacon is crisp. Place in oven for 45 minutes or until internal temperature is 160°. Allow to cool before slicing.

Heat demi-glace and hot pepper jelly in a saucepot until hot and blended. Serve over stuffed pork loin. Serves 10 to 12 people.

Trey Yuen

Cuisine of China
2100 North Morrison
Hammond, LA 70401
(985) 345-6789

600 N. Causeway
Mandeville, LA 70448
985-626-8293
www.treyyuen.com

An American Dream

James, Frank, John, Tommy, and Joe Wong were all born in Hong Kong after their parents fled the Communist Revolution. The Wong brothers came to America in 1967 with their mother and settled in Amarillo, Texas, where their grandfather had a small Chinese restaurant. After his death, the Wong brothers went their separate ways seeking employment in different states from California to Louisiana.

In 1972, the brothers were reunited in Hammond, where they opened their first restaurant. It was the town's first introduction to Chinese cuisine. The brothers had brought with them new ideas on traditional Chinese cooking. They began creating new and special dishes and offering them to regular customers. The brothers, now world-renowned, operate two beautiful restaurants in Hammond and Mandeville. Authentic Chinese décor, consistently great food, attentive service, generous portions, and the Wong brothers' personal touch all combine to make Trey Yuen "an aesthetic and gastronomic delight."

Pot Stickers

· ·

FILLING:

2 cups ground turkey, or 1 cup ground turkey and 1 cup small bay shrimp

2 cups finely chopped bok choy, blanched and squeezed dry in cheesecloth

1 tablespoon minced ginger

1 tablespoon minced white part of green onion, save green part

1 tablespoon sesame seed oil

2 egg whites

½ teaspoon white pepper

Mix all ingredients in bowl. Cover and place in refrigerator for 1 hour.

WRAPPERS:

1 package pot sticker wrappers or gyoza skins

1 egg white, whipped

Place 1 teaspoon Filling in center of wrapper. Brush egg white around outer edge. Fold in half and tuck. This is a foolproof way to cook pot stickers. Place the desired number of pot stickers on plate and steam 8 to 10 minutes. When done, place flat side in a Teflon-coated skillet with a little polyunsaturated oil (not olive oil—too strong of a taste). Cook over medium-high heat until crispy golden brown. Remove and serve with Soy-Vinegar Sauce for dipping. Garnish with reserved chopped green onions.

SOY-VINEGAR SAUCE:

½ cup low-sodium soy sauce

½ cup vinegar

Crushed chili pepper with oil, to taste

Combine all ingredients.

Hot and Sour Soup

¼ pound pork

1 teaspoon soy sauce

1 teaspoon cornstarch

4 dried Chinese black mushrooms

1 teaspoon dried morel mushrooms

14 tiger lily buds

1 cup hot water

1 square fresh bean curd

1 egg, beaten

5 cups soup stock

1 small green onion, finely chopped

¼ cup bamboo shoots

1½ tablespoons light soy sauce

2½ tablespoons red wine vinegar

½ teaspoon black pepper

Salt to taste

1 teaspoon chili oil, or 1 teaspoon red hot pepper flakes

1 teaspoon sesame seed oil

Cut pork into matchstick-size shreds. Marinate with soy sauce and cornstarch. Soak mushrooms and lily buds in 1 cup hot water for 20 minutes. Rinse, drain, and shred mushrooms. Cut tiger lily buds to 1-inch lengths. Cut bean curds into shreds. Beat egg thoroughly.

Heat soup stock until boiling, add pork, and mix with chopsticks. While soup is boiling, add the dry ingredients and beaten egg. Add soy, vinegar, and seasonings and boil 2 more minutes, stirring a few times.

Szechuan Spicy Alligator

. . . .

¾ pound alligator meat (use fresh alligator for best results)

1 teaspoon cornstarch

1 tablespoon soy sauce

1 tablespoon oil

¼ teaspoon salt

¼ teaspoon white pepper

½ egg white

STIR-FRY:

⅓ cup each: julienne celery, carrot, and onion

⅓ cup chopped red or green bell peppers

2 green onions, cut in 2-inch slices

½ cup plus 3 tablespoons oil, divided

3 dried hot peppers

½ teaspoon finely chopped garlic

1 tablespoon sherry

1 tablespoon vinegar

1 tablespoon soy sauce

½ teaspoon salt

½ teaspoon crushed Szechuan peppercorns (optional)

2 tablespoons sugar

1 teaspoon sesame seed oil

Slice alligator ⅛-inch thick and 2 inches long, removing fat and gristle. Sprinkle with cornstarch, soy sauce, oil, salt, and pepper. Mix thoroughly. Coat with egg white and let marinate for 20 minutes.

Cut all vegetables julienne style, 2 to 2½ inches long. Heat wok or heavy skillet until very hot, adding ½ cup oil for 45 seconds over high heat. Drop alligator into hot oil. Stir gently to separate, and cook until 70% done. Remove meat from pan and drain oil. Reheat pan with remaining oil. Break hot pepper in half, add to oil and cook until brown. Add garlic, then vegetables. Stir-fry for 1 to 2 minutes. Add alligator back into wok. Add sherry, vinegar, soy sauce, salt, peppercorns, sugar, and sesame seed oil. Stir for 30 seconds. Remove from wok to serving platter.

Crawfish with Spicy Lobster Sauce

SEASONINGS:

½ **teaspoon sesame seed oil**

½ **teaspoon dark soy sauce**

¾ **tablespoon cornstarch**

½ **teaspoon peanut oil**

Salt to taste

Mix ingredients together. Set aside.

CRAWFISH STIR-FRY:

1 **tablespoon peanut oil**

4 **ounces finely chopped pork**

½ **teaspoon chopped garlic**

½ **teaspoon chopped ginger**

2 **to 3 chile peppers**

½ **teaspoon sugar**

1 **teaspoon black beans, rinsed and crushed**

2 **white onions, cut in 2-inch strips**

½ **pound crawfish tails**

3 **tablespoons sherry or rice wine**

½ **tablespoon light soy sauce**

½ **cup chicken stock**

1 **egg, beaten**

3 **green onions, white cut in 2-inch slices; green, finely cut for garnish**

Heat wok or heavy skillet until hot. Add peanut oil and pork. Sauté both sides until slightly brown. Add garlic, ginger, chile peppers, sugar, and black beans to oil. Add onions and stir for 10 seconds. Add crawfish; sauté with wine and light soy sauce. Add chicken stock and cover. When mixture comes to a boil, add Seasonings; stir till thickened. Spread beaten egg over mixture. Reduce heat and cover for 10 seconds more. Remove to serving platter and garnish with green onions. Serves 1 to 2.

Plantation Country

History truly comes to life in **PLANTATION COUNTRY**, located in the southeastern region of Louisiana. Come wind your way across the Atchafalaya Basin, through the rolling hills of St. Francisville, and along the Great River Road that begins just west of New Orleans as you travel back to the 1800s. The plantations throughout this region offer tours of the property, gardens, and/or homes. Many of these plantations also offer overnight stays, including The Myrtles, which has been called "the most haunted house in America."

Plantation Country Restaurants

Brec's Magnolia Mound Plantation 139

Cajun Injector, Inc. 142

Joe's Dreyfus Store Restaurant 145

Juban's Restaurant & Catering 148

Maison Lacour 152

Mansur's on the Boulevard 156

Morel's 159

Nottoway Plantation 162

Oak Alley Plantation 167

Primo's 172

Ralph and Kacoo's 175

Saia's Oaks Plantation 178

Magnolia Mound Plantation
Baton Rouge, Louisiana

Brec's Magnolia Mound Plantation

Museum Location:

2161 Nicholson Drive

Baton Rouge, LA 70802

(225) 343-4955

An Accredited Historic House Museum on the National Register of Historic Places

Surrounded by 200-year-old live oaks, Brec's Magnolia Mound has retained its French Creole plan and character for over 200 years. Construction is of cypress beams with bousillage-entre-poteau (mud between posts), and the original cypress flooring runs throughout the house. The original section of the main house, built circa 1791, was expanded to its present size at the beginning of the 19th century.

The plantation, with its garden, pigeonnier, and smoke house, supplied the basic food items that would be supplemented by large amounts of foodstuffs imported through the port of New Orleans. The steamboat, inaugurating upstream travel in 1812, provided easy transportation of imported goods upriver, thus opening the Baton Rouge market to the world.

A French Cake

- -

2½ cups all-purpose flour

1½ cups sugar

1 teaspoon cinnamon, or nutmeg

½ teaspoon salt

5 tablespoons butter, softened

1 cup milk or cream

3 medium eggs

1 teaspoon baking powder

½ teaspoon warm water

Preheat oven to 350°. Mix flour, sugar, cinnamon or nutmeg, and salt together in a bowl. Cream the butter. Add milk or cream to the butter, alternating with the flour mixture. Beat the eggs until very light in a separate bowl and add to the cake batter; beat for 10 minutes. Dissolve the baking powder in warm water and add to batter; stir only long enough to mix well. Butter a deep Bundt or angel food pan, and pour batter in. Bake for 40 to 45 minutes. Good served with hot tea.

Pineapple Sherbet

- -

1½ quarts boiling water

2 ripe pineapples, peeled and sliced

2¼ cups sugar (or 1 cup sugar to each cup of juice)

4 egg whites, lightly beaten

Pour boiling water over pineapple and let it stand 1 to 2 hours. Strain it well and measure the juice. (Be sure to press the pineapple in a strainer to extract all the juice.) Add sugar to the juice; bring to a boil, stirring until the sugar has dissolved. Boil 5 minutes. Cool and then chill. Just before freezing in an ice cream freezer, add the egg whites. Freeze until firm. Makes 2 to 3 quarts.

Oyster Stew

4 tablespoons butter

1 tablespoon flour

1 cup milk or cream

Pinch of cayenne pepper
  (or to taste)

Pinch of nutmeg

1 teaspoon salt

4 (10-ounce) jars oysters

2 egg yolks, beaten

½ cup bread crumbs

In a pan, melt butter and add flour; stir well. Slowly add milk or cream and cook 3 to 4 minutes, stirring all the while. Add cayenne, nutmeg, and salt, then add oysters. Cover and cook until edges of the oysters curl. Turn off heat and gently stir in egg yolks. Place in a serving bowl that can be placed under a broiler; sprinkle with crumbs. Broil to golden brown. Serve at once. Serves 6 to 8.

Shrimp Pie

1½ teaspoons anchovy paste

2 ounces (4 tablespoons) dry
  vermouth

½ teaspoon salt

⅛ teaspoon mace

⅛ teaspoon ground cloves

1 pinch cayenne (optional)

¼ teaspoon thyme (optional)

1 teaspoon dried parsley
  (optional)

4 cups medium shrimp, peeled
  and deveined

1 recipe light pastry dough for
  top crust

Preheat oven to 425°. Measure the anchovy paste in a small bowl and thin with a very small amount of vermouth. Gradually add remaining vermouth; stir in seasonings until salt is dissolved. Pour mixture over shrimp and marinate while you prepare pastry dough. Divide the shrimp equally into 4 au gratin dishes (or put in a pie pan) and cover with crust. Bake for 25 to 30 minutes or until crust is lightly browned. Serves 4.

Cajun Injector, Inc.

Clinton, LA 70722

Note: Call (800) 221-8060 to order Cajun Injector products.

Chef Reese Williams and his mother and late father, Jeanne and Edgar Williams, pioneered the technique of injecting marinades into meats known today as the "Cajun Injector." Cajun Injector, Inc. is now America's leading injectable marinade company with sales topping $20 million. Cajun Injector recipes and techniques have been featured on every major television network from the "Today Show" to "Live with Regis and Kelly." Chef Reece Williams is a regular on the national retail channel, QVC, and the Outdoor Channel's *Louisiana Outdoor Adventures*.

Edgar's Cajun au Jus Beef

This is the technique that made the "Front Porch Prime Rib" famous!

16 fluid ounces Cajun Injector Beef Marinade, Creole Garlic recipe, (2 ounces per pound of meat)

8 pounds boneless beef top round

Pour marinade into separate container and draw into injector. Place roast into 2- to 3-inch deep pan and inject marinade at points every 1 to 2 inches apart. After injecting, pour generous amounts of marinade over roast. Cover with foil and bake at 350° until desired temperature is reached. (You may cook this outside on the pit also.) A whole rib-eye or prime rib prepared this way is wonderful!

Ron's Bar-B-Que Shrimp

If you don't "sop" your bread in the sauce, it's your mistake!

2 dozen jumbo shrimp in shells

½ stick butter

Cajun Injector Creole Garlic Marinade

Black pepper

½ fresh lemon

Wash shrimp thoroughly. Pinch off portion of head from the eyes forward. Melt butter in a large skillet. Place shrimp in a single layer in the butter. Shake marinade well and pour over shrimp until almost covered. Cover the top with black pepper. Cook for 5 minutes, occasionally shaking skillet in a back and forth motion; do not stir. Just before removing shrimp from heat, squeeze ½ fresh lemon on top of shrimp and sauce. Remove from heat; serve immediately in bowls with hot French bread on the side. Serves 2.

Crabmeat au Gratin

• •

¼ cup chopped onion

1 stalk celery, chopped

¼ pound butter or margarine

½ cup all-purpose flour

13 ounces evaporated milk

2 egg yolks, beaten

1 teaspoon salt

½ teaspoon ground red pepper

¼ teaspoon black pepper

1 pound lump crabmeat

½ pound Cheddar cheese

Preheat oven to 375°. Sauté onion and celery in butter or margarine until onions are wilted. Blend flour in well. Pour in the milk gradually, stirring constantly. Add egg yolks, salt, red pepper, and black pepper; cook for 5 minutes. Put crabmeat in a mixing bowl and pour the cooked sauce over the crabmeat. Blend well, folding over and over to keep lump crabmeat from breaking up. Transfer into a lightly greased casserole and sprinkle with grated Cheddar cheese. Bake for 10 to 15 minutes or until light brown. Serves 6.

Joe's Dreyfus Store Restaurant

2731 Highway 77
Livonia, LA 70755

(225) 637-2625

www.joes-dreyfusstore
restaurant.com

Trent and Susan
Lasseigne
Proprietors

This legendary restaurant is located in the heart of Cajun Country. Joe's Dreyfus Store Restaurant features authentic Cajun food sure to tempt the most discriminating diner.

The proprietors, the Lasseigne's, and their friendly staff serve up delicious seafood dishes, gumbo, crawfish étouffée, melt-in-your-mouth filet mignon, and incredible sweet temptations six days a week.

Joe's Dreyfus Store Restaurant is a place where famous faces, tourists and locals alike, come to celebrate and experience the Cajun culture through unique cuisine and a historic location.

Bread Pudding with Rum Sauce

PAN DRESSING:

2 ounces soft unsalted butter

4 ounces powdered sugar

In a small bowl, cream butter and powdered sugar. Generously coat sides and bottom of a 9x13x2-inch cool, dry (preferably glass) cake pan with half the butter-sugar mixture. Reserve the remaining portion. Set cake pan in refrigerator or cool place.

PUDDING:

2 cups sugar

½ teaspoon ground cinnamon

Pinch of nutmeg

1 teaspoon vanilla

4 eggs

2 egg yolks

1 quart whole milk

½ cup raisins

1 cup shredded sweet coconut

1 (1-pound) loaf day-old French bread, ends and bottom crust removed, cut in ½-inch slices

Preheat oven to 325°. In a large bowl, combine sugar, cinnamon, nutmeg, vanilla, eggs, and egg yolks with a whisk. Add milk, raisins, and coconut; stir until thoroughly combined. Add bread slices, gently pushing down into the milk mixture. Do not squeeze! Let soak ½ hour, turning occasionally. Pour into prepared pan. Pat down. Gently push raisins into the mixture so they will not burn. Melt reserved sugar-butter mixture. Pour on top. Bake 45 to 50 minutes in top third of oven. (Best if pan is placed on cookie sheet prior to placing in oven.)

RUM SAUCE:

2 ounces unsalted butter

4 ounces powdered sugar

4 ounces heavy whipping cream

1 tablespoon Myers dark rum

Combine butter, powdered sugar, and cream in a small saucepan. Bring to a boil over medium heat while stirring constantly. Remove from heat. Add rum. Serve over bread pudding.

Rémoulade Sauce

1 cup mayonnaise

½ cup horseradish

½ cup Creole mustard

3 ribs celery, diced

1 large white onion, diced

1 bunch green onions, chopped fine

½ bunch flat leaf parsley, chopped fine

Salt, black pepper, Tabasco sauce, and Lea and Perrin Worcestershire sauce to taste

Lemon juice to taste

Combine all ingredients. Let stand one hour. Mix with any cooked seafood. Serve over shredded lettuce.

Joe's Stuffed Eggplant

2 or 3 young eggplants

2 tablespoons oil

1 large onion, chopped

1 bell pepper, chopped

2 ribs celery, chopped

Butter

¾ pound small shrimp, peeled and deveined

¾ pound crabmeat, white or claw

½ pound ham, diced

Red and black pepper

Salt and sugar to taste

Bread crumbs

Preheat oven to 350°. Split eggplants lengthwise and coat with oil. Place split side down in a shallow pan and bake until tender. Cool. Remove pulp, chop it coarsely, and set aside. Reserve skins. Chop onion, bell pepper, and celery. Cook in a little butter until tender. Add shrimp, crabmeat, ham, and eggplant pulp. Season to taste. Bind mixture with bread crumbs, stuff into skins, and top with bread crumbs. Bake for 20 minutes. Serves 4.

Juban's Restaurant & Catering

3739 Perkins Road
Baton Rouge, LA 70808
(225) 346-8422
www.jubans.com

Miriam Juban
Co-Owner

Carol Juban
Co-Owner

Terry McDonner
Executive Chef

A Creole restaurant with the ambiance of the Vieux Carré

Juban's has received numerous accolades over the years, among them the *Wine Spectator's* Award of Excellence. They offer private dining, a banquet facility, and catering.

Hallelujah Crab

1 ounce backfin crabmeat

1 ounce shrimp

1 ounce crawfish

1 tablespoon butter

1 tablespoon diced onions

1 tablespoon diced green
pepper

1 tablespoon diced celery

Seasoning to taste

Seasoned bread crumbs

1 egg

Water

Milk

Soft-shell crab, cleaned

Self-rising flour

Mix seafood together in a bowl. Melt butter in skillet over medium heat. Add onion, green pepper, and celery. Sweat until tender. Combine seafood and vegetables, folding together gently in skillet. Season to taste. Cook until seafood is done. Add bread crumbs. Cool. Form into 2 soft balls. Lift the points of the crab shell and place seafood ball. Repeat on the other side. Combine egg and milk to make a wash. Place flour in separate container. Dredge stuffed soft-shell crab in flour, egg-milk wash, and again in flour. Drop gently into fryer. (Oil should be 350°.) Cook 6 to 8 minutes. Top with Creolaise sauce (combination of Creole mustard with hollandaise sauce). For presentation, place crab with legs reaching up. Serves 1.

Bayou Pearls

1 pound crabmeat

4 ounces tasso, ground

1 red pepper, diced

1 bunch green onions, sliced
thin

1 tablespoon chopped garlic

2 eggs

3 ounces heavy cream

1 cup Italian bread crumbs

Salt and pepper to taste

1 (8-ounce) package angel hair
pasta, cooked

In a mixing bowl, combine crabmeat, tasso, pepper, green onions, garlic, eggs, and cream. Mix thoroughly. Add bread crumbs to tighten mixture. Season with salt and pepper to taste. Add pasta and mix well. Roll into 1½-inch balls and fry in 350° oil until golden brown, about 2 to 3 minutes.

Stuffed Tomatoes with Crab and Corn Coulis

2 quarts water

½ tablespoon salt

4 medium tomatoes

3 ears fresh corn, shucked

1 red bell pepper, split, seeded, cored

1 sweet yellow pepper, split, seeded, and cored

2 tablespoons olive oil, divided

1 clove garlic, finely chopped

14 ounces fresh lump crabmeat

4 slices bacon, cooked and crumbled

2 tablespoons finely chopped chives

5 basil leaves, julienned

Salt and pepper to taste

½ cup chicken stock

Bring water and salt to a boil in a medium-size pot over high heat. Plunge in tomatoes and boil for 15 to 30 seconds, remove with a mesh skimmer, and cool under cold running water. Peel the tomatoes with a small knife. Cut a ¼-inch cap from the top of the tomatoes. With a small spoon, carefully scoop out and discard the seeds and pulp, leaving the shell intact. Refrigerate the tomato shells with their caps on the side. Return the same water used for the tomatoes to a boil, add the corn, and cook for 3 to 4 minutes. Drain well and transfer to a plate; let cool and set aside.

Preheat broiler. Place red and yellow peppers in a broiler pan skin side up. Broil until the skin turns black, about 8 to 10 minutes. Remove peppers, cool under cold running water, and peel off the burned skin. Dice the peppers into ¼-inch pieces and set aside.

In a sauté pan, heat 1½ tablespoons olive oil over medium heat. Gently fold in garlic. Add peppers, crabmeat, bacon, chives, basil, salt, and pepper to taste. Salt and pepper each tomato shell and fill it with the crab mixture up to just above the rim. Cover with the cap and refrigerate until needed.

(continued)

COULIS:

Reserved corn off cob

Preheat oven to 375°. Cut reserved corn off cob and transfer to a blender or food processor; purée. In a small nonreactive saucepan, heat corn and chicken stock to desired thickness. Just before serving, drizzle remaining olive oil over the tomatoes and warm in the microwave for 2 minutes on high. The tomatoes should not become too soft but the crab mixture should be hot. If you do not have a microwave, cover the tomatoes with foil and warm them in the oven for 10 minutes. Evenly divide the Coulis among 4 warm plates. Place one hot tomato on top of the sauce and decorate each tomato with a sprig of basil. Serves: 4

Orange Chocolate Crème Brûlée

5 ounces sugar

10 egg yolks

10 ounces orange-flavored chocolate

4 vanilla pods

3½ ounces milk

1½ pints heavy cream

Brown sugar

Preheat oven to 250°. Mix the sugar and egg yolks together in a bowl. In a small, dry nonreactive bowl, melt chocolate. Add melted chocolate to egg yolk mixture. Split vanilla pods in half and scrape the seeds out into the milk and cream in a pan; add the pods. Heat gently so that the full flavor of the seeds and pods infuses the liquid. Pour the cream and milk onto the egg yolk mixture, mix well; strain. Divide the mixture between 10 ramekins. Cook in oven in a bain-marie (hot water bath) for 30 to 40 minutes or until just set. Allow to cool and set, then chill. Sprinkle the tops with brown sugar, and glaze under a hot grill. Allow the sugar to set hard, then serve in the dish. Serves 10.

Maison Lacour

11025 North Harrell's Ferry Road

Baton Rouge, LA 70816

(800) 377-7104

www.maisonlacour.com

Michael Jetty
Chef/Proprietor

Eva Jetty
Manager/Proprietor

A cozy place to indulge in French Epicurean delights

Located in a cottage nestled among live oaks and crape myrtles on beautifully landscaped grounds, Maison Lacour is dedicated to the idea of serving the finest food in a memorable setting, and strives to ensure their customers are comfortable and well served. The menu offers classic dishes like the veal chop and venison, as well as culinary creations such as broiled tenderloin medallion with béarnaise, and shrimp with garlic butter and lump crab in puff pastry with hollandaise. Maison Lacour uses the highest quality ingredients offering a wide selection including veal, game, beef, fowl, lamb, and seafood. All are well presented and perfectly cooked.

Stuffed Mushrooms with Crawfish

6 tablespoons butter

½ stalk celery, finely chopped

½ bell pepper, finely chopped

4 tablespoons finely chopped shallots

2 cloves garlic, finely chopped

2 ounces tasso or cured ham

1 pound crawfish tail meat, coarsely chopped

½ teaspoon salt

½ teaspoon cayenne pepper

⅓ cup dry bread crumbs, divided

2 egg yolks

24 medium mushrooms

4 tablespoons olive oil

Preheat oven to 375°. Melt 4 tablespoons butter in a sauté pan. Add the celery, bell pepper, shallots, and garlic. Sauté for 1 minute, being careful not to burn the garlic. Add tasso and crawfish meat. Lower the heat and cook 5 minutes. Add salt, cayenne, and ¼ cup bread crumbs. Remove from heat and allow to cool to room temperature, about 30 minutes. When mixture has cooled, mix in the egg yolks.

Clean mushrooms and discard stems. Brush olive oil on the inside and outside of each mushroom cap. Arrange the caps in a shallow casserole dish. Stuff and mound each mushroom cap with crawfish mixture, sprinkle with remaining bread crumbs, and drizzle with remaining butter. Bake mushrooms 15 minutes, or until brown. Serve immediately. Serves 6.

Soup Jacqueline

2 tablespoons finely chopped shallots

2 tablespoons chopped celery stalk

2 tablespoons vegetable oil

⅓ cup flour

3½ cups clam juice

¼ teaspoon white pepper

1 cup cream

3 ounces Brie, trimmed and cubed

8 asparagus stalks, blanched and diced

8 ounces lump crabmeat

In a medium saucepan, sweat the shallots and celery in oil for about 1 minute. Add the flour and mix well, but do not let it brown. Stir in clam juice, stirring until smooth; season with pepper. After the mixture thickens, add the cream and bring to a boil. Lower heat, simmer for 20 minutes. Add the Brie and stir until the cheese is melted. Add the diced asparagus and crabmeat and cook for 3 minutes. Check seasoning. Ladle into 6 heated soup bowls and serve immediately. Serves 6.

Shrimp Baton Rouge

· ·

2 quarts water

4 tablespoons olive oil, divided

1 pound angel hair pasta

¼ pound butter

⅓ cup salad oil

1 garlic clove, minced

1 shallot, minced

4 tablespoons minced green onions

2 cups heavy cream

Juice of 1 lemon

1 teaspoon ground black pepper

½ teaspoon cayenne

½ teaspoon ground white pepper

1 teaspoon dry mustard

1 teaspoon prepared horseradish

1 teaspoon Worcestershire sauce

1 teaspoon salt

4 tablespoons Dijon mustard

30 shrimp, peeled and deveined

Bring water to a boil. Add 1 tablespoon olive oil. Separate strands of angel hair pasta and drop into boiling water. Cook for 2 minutes. Drain and rinse with hot water. Toss with remaining olive oil and keep warm until ready to serve.

In a large sauté pan, heat butter and salad oil until they foam. Add garlic, shallot, and onions. Cook for 1 minute, being careful not to burn the garlic. Add the heavy cream, lemon juice, spices, horseradish, Worcestershire, and salt. Simmer for 10 minutes. Whisk in Dijon. Add shrimp and cook until plump, about 4 to 5 minutes. Arrange shrimp on angel hair pasta and pour sauce over them. Serves 6.

Sabayon Glacé

This dessert may be made a day ahead, then covered and refrigerated.

1½ cups medium dry white wine

½ cup raspberry liqueur

6 egg yolks

2 tablespoons water

½ cup granulated sugar

1 tablespoon cornstarch

2 cups heavy cream, well chilled

1 teaspoon vanilla

1 pint raspberries, blackberries, strawberries, or blueberries

Mint for garnish

Pour the wine and the raspberry liqueur into a saucepan; bring to a boil and lower heat, letting it simmer for 5 minutes. Meanwhile, combine the egg yolks, water, sugar, and cornstarch in the bowl of a mixer and beat at medium-high speed until the mixture forms a ribbon. Use the low speed of the mixer while pouring in the hot wine and liqueur mixture. Return the mixture to the saucepan and set over low heat, stirring continuously with a whisk until mixture thickens to whipped cream consistency. Remove the pan from the heat. Pour custard into a bowl. Place in the refrigerator to chill for about 3 hours, stirring from time to time to prevent a skin from forming.

Combine the well-chilled cream with vanilla in a chilled mixing bowl and beat at medium speed for 1 to 2 minutes, then increase the speed and beat for another 3 to 4 minutes, until the cream begins to thicken. It should be a little firmer. Do not over-beat or the cream may turn into butter. Still beating, incorporate the cold wine custard and beat for about 3 minutes, until the mixture is homogeneous and very light in texture, like a mousse. Serve in 6 chilled dessert dishes. Garnish with raspberries (or berries of choice) and a sprig of mint. Cover and refrigerate. Serves 6.

Mansur's on the Boulevard

Fine Dining & Catering

5720-A Corporate Boulevard

Baton Rouge, LA 70808

(225) 923-3366

www.mansursonthe boulevard.com

Tim Kringlie
Charles Taucer
Justin McDonald
Brandon McDonald
Owners

Chris Nealy
Executive Chef/Proprietor

In the heart of Baton Rouge lies an experience that one can find in no other restaurant in town. Mansur's, since its 1989 opening and through the determined dedication of its staff, has made a name for itself nationwide for providing award-winning contemporary Creole cuisine and impeccable service to its beloved clientele. Many professional pianists perform nightly.

The restaurant's atmosphere, with its 100-year-old mahogany soda fountain bar, has an intoxicating effect immediately upon arrival. The spirit offerings are endless and Mansur's boasts many honors for its wine list.

Mustard and Cornmeal-Crusted Salmon with Lump Crabmeat and Lemon Butter

1 egg

½ cup cold water

½ cup yellow mustard

½ cup olive oil

2 cups yellow cornmeal

1 tablespoon salt

1 tablespoon pepper

4 (8-ounce) fillets of Pacific salmon, or any fresh fish fillets

1 small shallot, chopped fine

3 ounces white wine

Juice of 1 lemon

3 ounces heavy cream

½ pound fresh jumbo lump crabmeat

2 sticks unsalted butter, room temperature

Whisk together the egg, water, and mustard. Season the cornmeal with salt and pepper. Heat the olive oil in a 12-inch, nonstick sauté pan. Coat the salmon fillets with the mustard-egg wash. Dredge in cornmeal. Carefully place them in the hot sauté pan. Cook for about 4 minutes on medium heat. Flip the fillets over and continue to cook for another 4 minutes. The fillets should be a nice medium rare and the crust should be golden and crispy. Take the fillets out of the pan and drain on paper towels.

Discard the olive oil and return the sauté pan to the heat. Add the shallot and sauté for about 30 seconds. Deglaze the pan with white wine and lemon juice. Add the heavy cream and whisk together until sauce starts to boil and thicken. Add the crabmeat and toss to coat. Start adding the butter, 1 ounce at a time. Allow the butter to melt into the sauce before adding more. Adjust the seasoning with salt and pepper. Put the salmon fillets on 4 separate plates and equally divide the crabmeat and sauce over the top. Serves 4.

Cream of Brie Cheese with Lump Crabmeat Soup

• •

The recipe for this Cream of Brie and Lump Crabmeat Soup, proudly served by Mansur's Restaurant, was awarded a gold medal by Baton Rouge's American Culinary Federation, and was published in Bon Appetit *magazine! Mansur's Corporate Chef Tim Kringlie proudly presents the following recipe for your dining pleasure.*

3 tablespoons cottonseed oil

2 cups finely diced onion, bell pepper, and celery mixture

½ cup unsalted butter for roux

½ cup self-rising flour for roux

6 cups half-and-half

2 tablespoons crab base (may be purchased at specialty food stores)

¼ teaspoon Tabasco sauce

1 tablespoon dry vermouth

⅛ teaspoon lemon juice

1 teaspoon Creole seasoning

1 teaspoon chopped garlic

6 ounces Brie cheese, outer rind removed

6 ounces of fresh crabmeat (not frozen or thawed)

Heat the cottonseed oil in a 5-quart pot and sauté the vegetables until tender. To make the roux, melt the butter, then whisk in flour until smooth and blended. Add remaining ingredients to the onion mixture with the exception of Brie and crabmeat. Bring to a slow boil and thicken with 2 ounces of hot roux. Stir continuously until smooth and silky. Add Brie and crabmeat when ready to serve. Do not bring to a boil after cheese has been added. Makes 8 cups or 4 bowls.

Morel's

210 Morrison Parkway
New Roads, LA 70760
(225) 638-4057
www.morelsrestaurant.com

Buddy and Georgia
Morel
Proprietors

Built over the water along the edge of Morrison Parkway, a wide, paved area along False River, Morel's is located across the parkway to the rear of Morel Inn, a ten-room hotel facing West Main Street.

The restaurant is open seven days a week and offers customers a choice of grilled dishes, plus fried seafood baskets, a variety of salads, a number of freshly made specials each day, and several desserts. Some of the most popular specials are Fried Shrimp on Fried Eggplant Rounds Topped with a Remoulade Sauce, Grilled Red Snapper Topped with Grilled Tomatoes, Onions, and Romano Cheese served on braised spinach, and fried or boiled Shrimp Salad.

The Morels also sell antiques, accessories, and architectural pieces at the restaurant.

Shrimp-Stuffed Bell Peppers

½ cup butter
⅔ cup minced onions
½ cup minced celery
½ cup minced bell pepper
1 clove garlic, minced
1 pound shrimp, or crawfish
¼ teaspoon pepper
1 teaspoon salt
¼ teaspoon cayenne pepper
Dash of Tabasco sauce
1 teaspoon Worcestershire
⅓ cup chopped green onions
½ cup chopped fresh parsley
½ cup Italian bread crumbs
2 cups plain bread crumbs
Chicken broth
10 bell pepper halves, blanched*

Melt butter. Add onion, celery, and bell pepper. Sauté until translucent. Add next 9 ingredients. Cook 10 minutes. Remove from heat. Add bread crumbs. Add small amount of chicken broth if mixture appears dry. Stuff into blanched bell pepper halves. Warm in microwave before serving. Stuffs 10 bell pepper halves.

* Blanched bell peppers are those that have been halved, seeds removed, and placed in boiling water for 5 minutes.

Kitty Kimball's Broccoli Soup

3 tablespoons butter

5 ounces chopped onions

4 tablespoons flour

1 (10-ounce) package frozen, chopped broccoli

1 teaspoon pepper

1 tablespoon salt

2 cloves garlic, minced

1/8 teaspoon celery salt

1/2 cup beef broth

1 cup chicken broth

1 3/4 cups half-and-half

Melt butter. Sauté onions in butter until translucent. Slowly add flour until blended. Add next 7 ingredients. Cook 15 minutes. Process mixture in food processor. Add half-and-half. Heat through and serve immediately. Makes 6 cups.

Nottoway Plantation

Restaurant and Inn
30970 Highway 405
White Castle, LA 70788
(866) 4-A-VISIT
www.nottoway.com

Johnny "Jambalaya"
Percle
Executive Chef

The Largest Plantation Home in the South

Nottoway was completed in 1859 for Mr. and Mrs. John Hampden Randolph and their eleven children. The Greek Revival and Italianate mansion boasts 53,000 square feet! Randolph acquired over 7,000 acres of land, making his fortune in sugarcane.

Savor the excitement, beauty, and drama of the Old South. Stay in one of Nottoway's thirteen guest rooms, each with its own private bath. Overnight guests receive a tour of the mansion, a welcoming beverage upon arrival, an early morning wake-up call of sweet potato muffins, coffee, juice, and a full plantation breakfast. The restaurant is also open daily for lunch and dinner. "One of the top twenty-five American inns with super chefs," says *Condé Nast Traveler.*

Johnny Jambalaya's Beat the "Summertime Blues" Pasta Salad

- 1 cup low-fat mayonnaise
- 1 cup Johnny Jambalaya's Herb Dressing
- 12 ounces elbow macaroni, cooked and cooled
- 2 cucumbers, peeled and sliced
- 2 large Creole tomatoes, quartered and sliced
- 3 ribs celery, chopped
- 1 Vidalia onion, chopped
- Lemon pepper to taste
- 2 tablespoons parsley flakes

Mix mayonnaise and Herb Dressing in a large bowl. Add macaroni and mix. Add cucumbers, tomatoes, celery, and onion. Mix all ingredients well. Sprinkle with lemon pepper and mix. Refrigerate at least 1 hour. Serve in chilled, lettuce-lined bowl and sprinkle with parsley flakes. Serves 8.

Bacon, Lettuce, and Tomato Soup

- 1 pound bacon, cut into 1-inch pieces
- ½ pound butter
- 6 large tomatoes, cut into wedges
- 2 tablespoons Pickapeppa Sauce
- 2 tablespoons Worcestershire
- 2 tablespoons Tony's Seasoning
- 1 quart half-and-half
- 1 (10¾-ounce) can cream of asparagus soup
- 1 head lettuce, cut into 1-inch pieces

Cook bacon in large saucepan. Remove bacon before crisp and set aside. Add butter to bacon drippings and add tomato wedges. Add Pickapeppa, Worcestershire, and Tony's Seasoning. Add half-and-half and asparagus soup, and heat thoroughly, but do not allow to boil. Add bacon back to soup. Serve over lettuce.

Mandy's Cheese-Stuffed Mushrooms

- -

14 large mushrooms

2 tablespoons olive oil

⅓ cup Italian bread crumbs

4 tablespoons Johnny Jambalaya's Herb Dressing and Marinade, divided

1 cup chopped onion

1 tablespoon garlic, minced

½ teaspoon Italian seasoning

1 teaspoon lemon pepper

½ teaspoon parsley flakes

2 tablespoons salsa

2 tablespoons butter

½ cup Italian bread crumbs

2 tablespoons Parmesan cheese, grated

½ cup white wine

Pull stems out of mushroom caps, set aside caps, and mince stems. Place nonstick skillet over medium-low heat until hot. Combine olive oil and ⅓ cup Italian bread crumbs. Add olive oil mixture and 2 tablespoons Herb Dressing; swirl in bottom of pan. Once oil is hot, add onions and sauté 5 minutes until onions start to brown. Add garlic, chopped mushroom stems, Italian seasoning, lemon pepper, parsley, and salsa. Stir and sauté 5 minutes. Melt butter into mixture and stir in ½ cup Italian bread crumbs. Add cheese and stir. Remove from heat and allow to cool.

Preheat oven to 350°. Spray large glass baking dish with cooking spray. Stuff mushrooms with mixture and place in pan. Mix together wine and remaining Herb Dressing and Marinade, and pour into bottom of pan. Cover with foil and bake for 30 minutes. Uncover and bake 15 minutes more until browned.

JJ's Meaux Jeaux Pork Medallions

6 boneless pork chops, approximately 1½ pounds total

¼ cup plus 2 tablespoons JJ's Herb Dressing and Marinade, divided

2 tablespoons olive oil

1 cup sliced onion

2 tablespoons dry sherry

1 tablespoon minced garlic

¼ cup chopped yellow bell pepper

1 teaspoon dried parsley

1 teaspoon lemon pepper

2 teaspoons cornstarch, dissolved in ¼ cup water

¼ cup sliced green onions

SAUCE:

Juice of I lemon

Juice of I lime

½ cup orange juice

½ cup chicken broth

4 tablespoons salsa

4 tablespoons sweet orange marmalade

2 tablespoons JJ's Herb Dressing and Marinade

1 tablespoon Worcestershire

1 tablespoon dark brown sugar

Rinse pork and place in shallow glass pan. Coat with ¼ cup JJ's Herb Dressing. Chill 30 minutes while preparing Sauce and remaining ingredients.

Place a nonstick skillet over medium-high heat until hot. Add olive oil and remaining JJ's Herb Dressing, swirling to coat bottom of pan. Add pork and brown for 2 minutes on each side; remove from pan. Add onion and reduce heat to medium. Sauté until onions are brown on edges. Add sherry and swirl to deglaze pan. Sauté 1 to 2 minutes. Add garlic, bell pepper, parsley, and lemon pepper to pan and stir well. Sauté 3 minutes over medium heat. Return pork to pan; reduce heat to low. Pour Sauce over pork; cover and simmer 20 minutes, turning pork once. Uncover skillet and stir in cornstarch and green onions. Simmer, uncovered 5 to 6 minutes, turning medallions once. Remove pork from skillet and place on 6 plates. Spoon Sauce over and serve. Serves 6.

Combine the Sauce ingredients in a small glass bowl; set aside.

Serving Suggestions: Serve over a bed of cooked wild rice and top with Sauce. Garnish with orange slices.

Bread Pudding

- -

1 cup water, warmed

¼ pound margarine, melted

1 loaf sliced white bread, broken in pieces

1 cup milk

½ teaspoon vanilla

3 eggs, beaten

1 cup sugar

RUM SAUCE:

1 stick butter

½ cup sugar

2 (16-ounce) cans whipped topping

6 ounces white rum, or to taste

Preheat oven to 350°. Mix water and margarine in large bowl. Put broken bread into the mixture and stir. Add milk and stir. Add vanilla, eggs, and sugar, and stir well. Pour into a 12x16-inch baking pan and bake for one hour. Serve warm topped with rum sauce. Makes 20 (6-ounce) servings.

Melt the butter; add sugar and mix together in a bowl till the sugar is dissolved. Add the whipped topping and whip with a wire whip. Drizzle the rum into the mixture a little at a time. Cover and keep mixture in the freezer until ready for use. Makes 20 (2-ounce) servings.

Nottoway Plantation
The largest plantation home in the South ~ White Castle

Oak Alley Plantation

Restaurant and Inn
3645 Highway 18
Vacherie, LA 70090
(225) 265-2151
**www.oakalleyplantation
    .com**

Tracie Chiquet
Executive Chef

Oak Alley Plantation begins with its spectacular trees. A quarter-mile alley of twenty-eight sheltering oaks nearly 300 years old, still greets you today. The present-day plantation, a National Historic Landmark, was built between 1837–39 by Jacques Telesphore Roman, a wealthy French Creole sugar planter. It was built along the Great River Road when southern aristocracy ruled the land. Oak Alley offers daily guided tours of the antebellum mansion. Luscious grounds, a charming restaurant, gift shop, and overnight cottages, plus a calendar of delightful seasonal special events complete the Oak Alley experience. The restaurant serves authentic Creole/Cajun specialties and is located on the grounds of the plantation.

Bananas Foster French Toast

BANANAS FOSTER SYRUP:

1½ cups good quality maple syrup

2 tablespoons butter

4 bananas, peeled, halved, and sliced lengthwise

1 teaspoon rum-flavored extract, or 1 tablespoon dark rum

In a small saucepan, heat syrup over medium heat; add butter and stir until melted and syrup is bubbling. Add bananas and heat thoroughly. Remove from heat and add rum or extract. Return to slow heat and keep warm.

FRENCH TOAST:

6 large eggs

2 teaspoons vanilla

½ cup heavy cream

6 tablespoon butter

8 slices French bread, preferably a few days old

Whisk eggs. Add vanilla. Pour in cream and whisk until well blended. Melt 1 to 2 tablespoons butter over medium-high heat. Dip slices of bread into batter and soak thoroughly. Place 2 slices at a time in melted butter and cook each side until golden brown. Repeat with remaining slices, using remaining butter. Serve slices with warm syrup and bananas.

Oak Alley Plantation
Vacherie, Louisiana

Chicken and Andouille Gumbo

3 quarts chicken broth or stock

¼ cup picante sauce

2 bay leaves

1 pound andouille sausage, divided

1⅓ cups vegetable oil

1⅓ cups flour

1½ cups diced onions

½ cup diced bell pepper

¼ cup diced celery

½ tablespoon dry Italian seasoning

1 tablespoon parsley flakes

Creole seasoning to taste

1 teaspoon sugar

3 pounds smoked sausage

1½ pounds chicken

In an 8-quart stockpot, bring chicken broth to a boil with picante sauce, bay leaves, and half the andouille. Heat oil in a large Dutch oven. Add flour and make a dark roux. Add onions, bell pepper, celery, Italian seasoning, parsley, Creole seasoning, and sugar. Cook until vegetables are tender. Carefully add roux mixture to boiling chicken broth, stirring constantly until roux dissolves. Add smoked sausage, chicken, and remaining andouille and bring to a boil; simmer for 2 hours. Makes 8 to 12 servings.

The Shrimp and Andouille Pasta

2 pounds penne pasta

2 quarts heavy cream

½ cup Creole mustard

Salt and pepper to taste

2 cups julienned onions

1 cup julienned red bell peppers

1 cup julienned yellow bell peppers

½ cup olive oil

2 pounds 50/60-count shrimp

2 pounds andouille, diced

Boil pasta and set aside. Bring heavy cream to a boil in a large saucepan. Simmer for 20 minutes or until reduced by ¼. Add Creole mustard and salt and pepper to taste. Sauté onions and peppers in olive oil until tender. Add shrimp and andouille sausage and cook until shrimp are almost cooked. Add heavy cream mixture and simmer for 30 minutes. Toss with pasta and cook until pasta is heated through. Serves 8 to 12.

Fried Eggplant with Crawfish Monica Sauce

CRAWFISH MONICA SAUCE:

4 tablespoons butter

⅔ cup minced onions

1 cup Ro-Tel tomatoes

2 tablespoons minced garlic

1 pound crawfish

1 quart heavy cream

4 ounces freshly grated Parmesan cheese

1 cup green onions, divided

Creole seasoning to taste

Melt butter in medium saucepan. Add onions, tomatoes, and garlic. Cook until onions are tender. Add crawfish and cook until heated through. Add heavy cream and bring to a boil. Add Parmesan cheese and half of the green onions. Season to taste. Bring back to a boil and simmer until sauce thickens.

FRIED EGGPLANT:

¼ cup vegetable oil

2 cups flour, divided

1 cup water

Creole seasoning to taste

2 eggplants, cut in ½-inch thick slices

2 cups Italian bread crumbs

Creole seasoning to taste

Heat oil in a frying pan. Mix 1 cup flour with water and season. Mix well until lumps are dissolved. Season eggplant. Toss eggplant in remaining flour, then into flour/water mixture, then into bread crumbs. Pan-fry until golden brown. Place on paper towels to drain.

Layer eggplants with Crawfish Monica Sauce and garnish with remaining green onions. Makes 8 appetizer portions.

Praline Bread Pudding

2 tablespoons butter, softened

1 cup light brown sugar

3 large eggs, well beaten

¼ teaspoon cinnamon

1 pinch freshly grated nutmeg

2 tablespoons pure vanilla extract

4 cups heavy cream

1 large loaf stale French bread, torn in 1-inch cubes (about 6 cups)

½ cup finely chopped and lightly toasted pecans

PRALINE SAUCE:

½ cup light brown sugar

½ cup white sugar

¼ cup butter (no substitutes)

1 cup heavy cream

½ cup pecan halves, lightly toasted

1 teaspoon pure vanilla extract

Preheat oven to 325°. Generously butter a 11x3½x3-inch baking dish. In a large mixing bowl, combine sugar, beaten eggs, cinnamon, nutmeg, vanilla, and heavy cream. Mix with electric mixer for 3 to 4 minutes. Place torn bread pieces in buttered baking dish, then cover with egg and cream mixture. Push down with the back of a spoon to insure there are no dry pieces. Sprinkle with pecans. Cover with plastic wrap and refrigerate for 2 hours. Place bread pudding pan in a larger pan filled with water. Bake for 55 to 60 minutes until set in center (until it slightly jiggles). Remove bread pudding pan and set on a wire rack to cool for about 45 minutes. Serve with warmed Praline Sauce.

Place sugars in a heavy saucepan over medium-low heat. When sugar starts to turn color, carefully shake and swirl the pan to uniformly brown. Add butter and mix well. Remove from heat and add cream carefully, as this will steam. Stir until thoroughly incorporated. Add pecans and vanilla.

Primo's

Steak and Louisiana Cuisine

**5454 Bluebonnet
   Boulevard, Suite A**

Baton Rouge, LA 70809

(225) 291-9600

www.primosrestaurant.com

Matt Merchant
General Manager

Michelle Cassano
Executive Chef

Primo's Steak and Louisiana Cuisine is located in Baton Rouge, the capital and heart of Louisiana. It is casual fine dining at its best with superb service in a warm, relaxed atmosphere. Diners are presented with a dazzling array of Black Angus steaks, Louisiana specialties, and the freshest seafood available. In addition to the unique dining experience, Primo's offers the Mahogany Room, an exquisite lounge with a distinctive assortment of fine wines and liquors, hand-rolled cigars, and exceptional appetizers.

Veal Primo

- -

3 veal medallions per serving

3 ounces butter, divided

3 to 4 ounces crabmeat, divided

Lemon juice

Salt and pepper to taste

4 thin slices Gruyère cheese, divided

Preheat oven to 450°. In a skillet, quickly brown veal medallions in 2 ounces of butter and set on paper towels to drain. Sauté crabmeat in remaining butter with lemon juice and seasoning to taste. In a separate skillet or pan, layer a veal medallion, ½ the crabmeat, and ½ the cheese, repeating the process with veal medallion, remaining crab, and remaining cheese, finishing with the last veal medallion. Place pan in oven for 3 minutes (just long enough to melt the cheese).

SAUCE:

1 tablespoons crushed black peppercorns

⅓ cup brandy

2 cups demi-glace

2 ounces foie gras paté

In a skillet, roast peppercorns for approximately 1 minute. Take skillet off heat and carefully add brandy (it will flame). When brandy has finished flaming, add demi-glace and reduce to proper consistency. Finish by swirling in foie gras paté. Top with Meunière and Hollandaise Sauces.

MEUNIÈRE SAUCE:

2 quarts demi-glace

⅓ cup lemon juice

1½ pounds butter, softened

2 teaspoons seasoning salt

Heat demi-glace to a simmer. Add lemon juice, and cook to reduce, 2 to 3 minutes. Quickly whisk in butter. Remove from heat. Add seasoning salt.

HOLLANDAISE SAUCE:

½ cup white wine

4 egg yolks

2 whole eggs

Juice of 1 lemon

½ pound butter, melted

Salt, pepper, and Tabasco to taste

Bring wine to a simmer in a small saucepan. Whisk eggs with lemon juice; whisk in warm wine. Whisk while cooling in a bain-marie until mixture is a smooth custard consistency. Remove from heat. Whisk in melted butter. Season to taste.

Stuffed Portobello Mushrooms

. . . .

4 medium yellow onions, chopped

8 shallots, chopped

12 cloves garlic, chopped

8 ribs celery, chopped

Butter

2 pounds claw crabmeat

2 cups white wine

6 cups béchamel

2 tablespoons Herbsaint

2 eggs

Italian bread crumbs

15 large portabello mushroom caps, or 30 small ones

Preheat oven to 375°. Sauté all veggies in butter; make sure they don't brown. Sauté in 2 pounds crabmeat, then deglaze with 2 cups white wine. Cook until there is no liquid at all. Add béchamel, Herbsaint, eggs, and bread crumbs until desired thickness is achieved. Cook down on low heat for about 20 minutes. Season to taste. Place a scoop of stuffing on each mushroom cap (where the stem was). Bake 20 minutes for large or 15 minutes for small.

Old State Capitol – Baton Rouge

Ralph and Kacoo's

The Seafood Restaurant
6110 Bluebonnet Boulevard
Baton Rouge, LA 70809
(225) 766-2113
www.ralphandkacoos.com

Ralph and Kacoo's offers fresh, affordable seafood, and is celebrating nearly forty years of providing quality seafood and courteous service. Bring the family 'cause they are open for lunch and dinner. Private dining rooms are available.

Ralph and Kacoo's Seafood Gumbo

4½ cups all-purpose flour

3 cups vegetable oil

8 cups chopped onions

2 cups chopped bell peppers

3 cups chopped celery

3 tablespoons chopped garlic

3 (14-ounce) cans whole tomatoes with juice, hand squeeze

1 (8-ounce) can tomato sauce

3 tablespoons salt

3 tablespoons black pepper

2 teaspoons red pepper

1 gallon water

3 pounds fresh shrimp

¾ cup chopped parsley

1 cup green chopped onions

2 pints oysters

2 pounds lump crabmeat

Make a roux by stirring flour and vegetable oil until a well-browned, peanut butter color develops. Do not burn! When roux is made, add onions, bell peppers, celery, and garlic. Cook, stirring, until vegetables are limp, being careful not to burn. Add hand-squeezed tomatoes, tomato sauce, salt, and peppers. Cook and stir until well blended. Add water and cook 50 minutes. Turn fire off. Let sit until ready to serve. Just before serving, bring to a light bubble. If too thick, add more water. Add shrimp. Cook 10 minutes. Add parsley, green onions, oysters, and crabmeat. Cook 5 minutes more. It is important not to overcook the seafood. Serve immediately.

Ralph and Kacoo's Stuffed Crabs

½ cup margarine

2¼ cups chopped onions

2 tablespoons garlic

3 pounds crabmeat, fresh and drained

½ cup chopped green pepper

⅔ cup chopped parsley

5 cups stale bread crumbs

2 teaspoons black pepper

½ teaspoon red pepper

2 teaspoons salt

2 eggs

10 to 12 crab shells

Preheat oven to 450°. In a saucepan, melt margarine. Add onions and garlic. Simmer until onions are wilted. Remove from heat and add all other ingredients, reserving some crumbs. Mix well. Stuff crab shells and top with remaining crumbs. Dot with butter. Place stuffed crabs into oven until thoroughly heated throughout and crumbs are brown.

Note: This is also great for crab balls. Roll in a light batter and deep-fry.

Shrimp Butter

2 cups cooked shrimp

1 stick butter, softened

1 (8-ounce) package cream cheese, softened

3 tablespoons mayonnaise

1 tablespoon lemon juice

3 tablespoons grated onion

½ teaspoon garlic powder

¼ cup chopped parsley

2 teaspoons Tabasco sauce

½ teaspoon red pepper

1 teaspoon Worcestershire sauce

Mince shrimp or run through food processor. Blend butter and cream cheese together until fluffy. Add shrimp, mayonnaise, lemon juice, onion, garlic powder, parsley, Tabasco, red pepper, and Worcestershire. Mix well. Shape into ball. Refrigerate until firm. Serve with crackers.

Saia's Oak Plantation

20 Avenue of Oaks
Destrehan, LA 70047
(985) 764-6410

At Saia's Oak Plantation, you can enjoy the perfect atmosphere, delicious food, quality drinks and a professional staff. They also serve a variety of entrées from Cajun trout specials, to veal dishes, to sizzling steaks. The elegance and charm of the plantation, located off historic River Road, offers a romantic view of the 160-year-old oak trees. A friendly face is always waiting to cater to all your needs at Saia's.

Crawfish, Corn, and Potato Chowder

• •

ROUX:

3 ounces vegetable oil

3 ounces flour

Heat oil in pan over medium heat. Add flour and stir constantly until roux is a light blonde color, about 4 to 5 minutes; remove from heat.

CHOWDER:

2 large yellow onions, chopped

2 green onions, chopped

½ stalk celery, chopped

4 garlic cloves, minced

2 green bell peppers, chopped

¾ teaspoon celery seed

¾ tablespoon dill weed

¾ tablespoon thyme

¾ teaspoon basil

1½ ounces extra virgin olive oil

½ gallon seafood stock

½ gallon chicken stock

1 teaspoon liquid crab boil

1½ pounds diced red potatoes, skin on

1 tablespoon Crystal cayenne seasoning with garlic

3 ounces sugar

1 (16-ounce) package frozen whole-kernel corn

¾ cup half-and-half

2 pounds crawfish tail meat

In a braiser, sauté vegetables in the olive oil over medium heat until soft. Whisk in the blonde roux. Add warm seafood and chicken stock, crab boil, potatoes, cayenne seasoning, and sugar. Let simmer for 15 minutes and reduce heat. Add the corn, half-and-half, and crawfish tails with the fat. Cook over low flame for 10 more minutes. Makes 1½ gallons.

Veal Delmonico

. . . .

1 ounce butter

1 ounce white wine

1 ounce lemon juice

6 shrimp

4 artichoke quarters

1 ounce whipping cream

½ teaspoon blue cheese dressing

Green onions, chopped

Mushrooms, sliced

Veal, panéed

Cook all ingredients (except veal) until shrimp are done. Serve on top of panéed veal. Serves 1.

Flaming Almonds Amaretto for Two

. . . .

¾ stick butter

1 cup brown sugar

3 ounces amaretto

1 cup toasted almonds

½ lemon, juiced

¼ shot 151 rum

Cinnamon

4 scoops vanilla ice cream

Melt butter in copper saucepan. Mix in brown sugar; dissolve. Stir in amaretto, almonds, and fresh lemon juice; add rum and flame. Throw cinnamon for sparkles. Serve immediately over 2 scoops of vanilla ice cream per person. Serves 2.

Cajun Country

Stretching across the Gulf of Mexico and up into south-central Louisiana, the region known as CAJUN COUNTRY offers breathtaking views of bayous. The first French Canadians settled here and forever changed the landscape and culture of Louisiana. Resourceful, stoic, and inventive, these were the people who turned soup into gumbo, washboards into musical instruments, and made the swamp a mystical paradise.

In Cajun Country you'll discover crawfish étouffée, dance to Zydeco music, and learn a whole lot of new and interesting words.

Cajun Country Restaurants

Blue Dog Café. 183

Café Des Amis. 185

Catahoula's 189

Chef Roy's Frog City Café 191

Clementine Dining and Spirits 193

Cristiano's Ristorante. 196

D.I.'s Cajun Food & Music 200

Don's Seafood and Steakhouse. 202

Dupuy's Oyster Shop 204

Fezzo's. 207

Flanagan's 209

Fremin's 213

The Grapevine Café and Gallery 218

Hanson House 222

Harbor Seafood Restaurant 226

Lafayette's 228

Landry's Restaurant 230

Maison Daboval. 232

Mr. Lester's Steakhouse 234

Nash's Restaurant 237

The Palace Café 242

Pat's of Henderson 246

Prejean's Restaurant 248

Pujo St. Café 251

SNO'S Seafood and Steakhouse 253

Thai Cuisine. 257

Walker's Cajun Dining 260

Yellow Bowl Restaurant 262

Blue Dog Café

1211 West Pinhook Road
Lafayette, LA 70503
(337) 237-0005

Steve Santillo
Owner

Blue Dog Café is a favorite of locals and visitors alike. Offering award-winning food, friendly and knowledgeable service, and the world's largest private collection of Blue Dog artwork by world-famous artist, George Rodrigue. Blue Dog boasts that it "has it all." Many of the dishes on the menu have earned their chefs prestigious culinary awards. In addition to Cajun favorites such as crawfish étouffée, seafood gumbo, and a delicious seafood platter, Blue Dog Café offers fusion cuisine such as Crawfish Enchiladas with Cumin Mornay Sauce and their signature appetizer of Seafood Wontons with a Plum-Ginger Sauce. They offer an impressive wine list and homemade desserts such as their popular Bread Pudding with Pecan Praline Sauce.

Pan-Grilled Grouper with a Crabmeat and Curry Coconut Cream Sauce

ROASTED GARLIC SEASONED RUB:

4 ounces roasted garlic

1¼ tablespoons salt

1 tablespoon black pepper

2 teaspoons onion powder

2 teaspoons ginger

1 tablespoon white pepper

1 teaspoon tandoori paste

1 grouper fillet

1 tablespoon butter

Preheat oven to 350°. Place all ingredients except fish and butter into a food processor and purée until pasty. Brush grouper thoroughly with paste. Heat pan over medium heat. Add butter. Cook both sides approximately 2 minutes and finish in oven until done, about 6 minutes.

CURRY CREAM:

1 cup diced onions

¼ pound butter

4 ounces Chardonnay wine

6 ounces yellow curry powder

1 teaspoon salt

2 teaspoon rosemary

1 quart heavy cream

13½ ounces coconut milk

Blonde roux as needed

1 pound white lump crabmeat

Sauté onions in butter until clear, then deglaze with Chardonnay. Add all dry seasonings then cream and coconut milk. Bring to a gentle boil and thicken with blonde roux. Add crabmeat to sauce and keep warm for plate assembly.

Café Des Amis

140 East Bridge Street
Breaux Bridge, LA 70517
(337) 332-5273
www.cafedesamis.com

Dickie Breaux
Owner

Josh Robin
Executive Chef

When Dickie Breaux originally purchased the building where Café Des Amis is now housed, the downstairs was used as an art studio and the upstairs became a living area. As time passed, the decision was made to include a coffee shop along with the studio, and Café Des Amis was born in 1992. Before long food was served too, depending on how much catfish they could buy for $200 that week. As demand from the customers grew, so did the menu and the Café Des Amis family.

Vinaigrette Dressing

4 cups extra virgin olive oil

2 cups olive oil, lesser grade

1 cup apple cider vinegar

1½ cups red wine vinegar

1 cup Romano cheese

1 cup minced garlic

1 cup sugar

4 tablespoons granulated garlic

1 cup lemon juice

1 teaspoon black pepper

1 teaspoon cracked black
pepper

1 teaspoon cayenne pepper

2 tablespoons Italian seasoning

1 tablespoon celery seeds

1 tablespoon basil

1 tablespoon rosemary

5 tablespoons salt

Mix all of the above ingredients in a bowl and stir well. Best if refrigerated overnight. Great to mix this with blue cheese dressing as a nice dressing combination.

Gateau Sirop

Syrup Cake

Delicious served with vanilla or chocolate ice cream.

1 cup canola or peanut oil

1 cup raw sugar

1¼ cups cane syrup

⅓ cup dark molasses

2 teaspoons baking soda

1 cup boiling water

4 eggs

2 teaspoons ground cinnamon

2 teaspoons ground cloves

2 teaspoons ground ginger

2 tablespoons vanilla extract

2 cups sifted flour

¾ cup chopped pecans

Preheat oven to 350°. Mix oil, sugar, cane syrup, and molasses in a bowl. In separate container stir baking soda into boiling water. Add to above mixture. Add all other remaining ingredients. Beat well at medium to high speed with an electric hand mixer. Pour into a large baking pan that has been sprayed with a nonstick spray. Bake about 30 minutes. Test to see if middle is still wet. Turn pan around in oven to insure even baking. When the middle of the cake begins to firm up, add ¾ cup chopped pecans on top and continue baking until the cake is done throughout. Cake is sliced by cutting cake down the middle and then making 4 cuts horizontally for a total of 8 pieces. Cake is served warm on a plate and garnished with cane syrup drizzles.

Note: Great to also garnish with fresh mint leaves, when available.

Spinach and Andouille Stuffing

Try this spicy tasty stuffing with chicken breasts, fish, or mushrooms.

5 cups chopped andouille

2½ cups Creole mix (chopped onions and bell peppers)

¼ pound (1 stick) butter

2½ tablespoons minced garlic

1 tablespoon lemon juice

1 (10-ounce) package frozen chopped spinach

1 teaspoon chicken bouillon granules

½ cup Romano cheese

¾ cup bread crumbs

Chop andouille in food processor. Sauté down all ingredients through lemon juice in an iron skillet until onions are tender. Remove from fire and blend in spinach, chicken base, cheese, and bread crumbs. Blend thoroughly by stirring.

Catahoula's

234 King Drive
Grand Coteau, LA 70541
(888) 547-2275
www.catahoulasrest.com

Jude Tauzin
Owner/Chef

In the heart of Cajun country and in the center of a rare rural historic district sits Catahoula's, a superbly renovated country store turned fine dining restaurant. Catahoula's has been featured in such publications as *Gourmet*, *Southern Living*, *Reader's Digest*, and *USA Today*. The cuisine, however, can be described as south Louisiana with sophisticated influences. The seasonings and tastes are more interesting than traditional Louisiana "hot and spicy" flavors. Catahoula's is located eleven miles north of Lafayette just off I-40, Exit 11 at Grand Coteau.

Shrimp Saint Charles

- -

2 to 3 tablespoons butter and oil blend

5 jumbo shrimp

2 tablespoons diced roasted red pepper

2 tablespoons chopped green onions

2 tablespoons sun-dried tomatoes

⅓ cup quartered artichoke hearts

1 teaspoon Creole seasoning

1 cup shiitake mushrooms, slivered

2 tablespoons white wine

½ cup chicken stock

1 tablespoon lemon juice

⅓ cup béchamel sauce

¾ to 1 cup cooked angel hair pasta

1 tablespoon pesto for garnish

2 tablespoons freshly grated Parmesan cheese for garnish

In skillet heat 2 to 3 ounces butter-infused oil over medium-high heat. Add 5 large peeled and deveined shrimp and sauté 1 minute each side. Add next 6 ingredients and sauté about 3 minutes. Deglaze pan with white wine for about 30 seconds, then add chicken stock and lemon juice. Sauté 1 minute more. Stir in béchamel and cook 3 minutes more. Serve over angel hair pasta. Garnish with a tablespoon of pesto and sprinkle with freshly grated Parmesan cheese. Serves 1.

Chef Roy's Frog City Café

1131 Church Point Highway
Rayne, LA 70578
(337) 334-7913

- - - - - - - - -

Roy Lyons, CEC
Chef/Proprietor

Chef Roy is an active member of a number of prestigious professional organizations, among them the National Association of Chefs Federation, to which he has belonged for seventeen years and which has recognized him as a "Certified Executive Chef." He has also been recognized in Louisiana for his culinary achievements by being named "Chef of the Year."

Chef Roy became an Honorary Member of the Avignon Chef's Association in Avignon, France. He was also invited to join and became a member of the Confrerie du Vin de Suresnes, a prestigious wine society based in Suresnes, France, a suburb of Paris. More recently, Chef Roy became an honorary member of the distinguished "White Chef Hats" organization of the Vaucluse Region in France.

Chef Roy's Frog Wellington

- -

5 frog legs (2- to 4-count)

1 teaspoon Chef Roy's seafood seasoning, divided

5 hickory-smoked bacon slices

1 tablespoon butter

1 tablespoon olive oil

1 tablespoon minced onion

½ teaspoon minced garlic

1 teaspoon minced parsley

2 tablespoons dry vermouth wine

⅓ cup chicken stock

¾ cup cooked pasta

1 tablespoon diced seedless tomato (¼-inch-dice)

½ teaspoon minced chives

Parmesan to taste (optional)

Season the frog legs with ½ teaspoon seasoning, wrap with partially cooked bacon, and secure with toothpick. In a saucepan, add the butter and olive oil; heat. Add the frog legs and cook for 2 minutes on both sides. Add remaining seasoning, onion, garlic, and parsley. Cook for 2 minutes. Deglaze with wine and add stock. Reduce the liquid by half. Dish the frog legs over the pasta and top with the sauce. Top the frog legs with diced tomato and sprinkle with the minced chives. Sprinkle with a little grated Parmesan if you wish.

Clementine Dining and Spirits

113 E. Main Street
New Iberia, LA 70560
(337) 560-1007
www.clementinedown town.com

Clementine, located in New Iberia's Downtown Historic District, invites you in to soak up the artistic ambience, relax and enjoy cocktails at one of the most beautiful antique bars in Acadiana, or indulge in fine dining service and cuisine by candlelight.

Clementine, named for owner Wayne Peltier's favorite artist, Clementine Hunter, features local artwork, and showcases local bands on Friday and Saturday nights.

Clementine has been featured in *Southern Living*, *Gourmet* and most recently, *1,000 Places to See in the USA and Canada Before You Die.*

Roasted Red Pepper and Wild Mushroom Bisque with Crabmeat

1 large yellow onion, diced small

1 tablespoon minced garlic

4 tablespoons clarified butter

20 shiitake mushrooms, sliced

5 portobello mushrooms, chopped

10 dried morels, rehydrated and sliced

8 red peppers, roasted and puréed

2 cups water reserved from morels

2 quarts heavy cream

2 quarts half-and-half

2 teaspoons dried thyme

2 teaspoons granulated garlic

2 bay leaves

2 tablespoons crab base

1 tablespoon chicken base

Sweat onion and garlic in butter. Add shiitake and portobello mushrooms and sauté for 5 minutes. Next add morels and pepper purée. When purée comes to a boil, add the reserved water, heavy cream, half-and-half, thyme, garlic, and bay leaves. Simmer for 10 minutes, then add bases. Stir well and simmer for 10 more minutes. Thicken with blonde roux, if desired. Serves 10 to 12.

Tuna au Poivre

Olive oil

1 (8-ounce) tuna steak, sashimi grade

Kosher salt to taste

Cracked black pepper to taste

½ cup brandy

¼ cup chopped green onions

1 cup heavy cream

Chopped parsley for garnish

Coat the bottom of a heated skillet with olive oil. Season tuna with salt and pepper and sear in skillet for 1 minute on each side. Remove from skillet and keep warm. Deglaze hot skillet with brandy; add green onions. When brandy is reduced almost completely, add heavy cream and reduce to desired consistency. Ladle sauce over tuna. Garnish with chopped parsley. Serves 1.

Houmas House
Burnside, Louisiana

Cristiano's Ristorante

Lounge and Wine Boutique
724 High Street
Houma, LA 70360
(985) 223-1130

. . . .

Cristiano Raffignone
Chef/Proprietor

Starting at the age of eighteen, restaurant owner and businessman Cristiano Raffignone has worked in dozens of international locations, including Italy, London, Australia, and New York City. Eventually, he settled in Houma and opened Cristiano's. While Cristiano's specializes in Italian cuisine, Raffignone admits that he loves to involve Cajun as well as Asian touches into his traditional Italian dishes. Some of his most famous experiments have produced savory dishes like Ravioli di Campagna (truffle ravioli with melted fontina cheese), Spaghetti Fruitte di Mare (crawfish, shrimp, and scallops sautéed in extra virgin olive oil, garlic, red pepper flakes, white wine, and tomato sauce), or Crespelle al Granchio (crabmeat dressing rolled in crêpes, served with a light tomato and béchamel sauce). Cristiano's restaurant is stocked with comfortable sofas, beautiful works of art, and antiques, giving it a very homey atmosphere. Customers can also enjoy soft, live music every Thursday night in the Cristiano lounge, and a daily happy hour featuring free delicious hors d'oeuvres prepared by his staff.

Fried Green Tomatoes with Crabmeat Rémoulade

Antipasto

2 cups all-purpose flour, seasoned to individual's taste

Iced club soda or water

1 cup cornstarch

2 (½-inch-thick) slices fresh green tomato per person

2 cups processed Italian bread crumbs

¾ cup processed Japanese bread crumbs (panko)

Mix flour with club soda or water; add cornstarch. Mix well. Place slices in seasoned flour and cornstarch mix, completely covered on each side. Place slices into a mixture of Italian and Japanese bread crumbs, covering slices evenly on both sides. Fry in medium-hot oil until golden brown, or crisp.

RÉMOULADE:

6 tablespoons mayonnaise

½ tablespoon ketchup

¼ teaspoon Tabasco sauce

¼ teaspoon Worcestershire sauce

Pinch of salt

Pinch of cayenne pepper

Mix all ingredients together. Set aside.

CRABMEAT:

1 pound white crabmeat

1 pound crab claw meat, cleaned of shells and strained

Grape tomatoes for garnish

Fresh parsley, finely diced for garnish

Fresh chives, finely diced for garnish

Fold white crabmeat and claw meat into Rémoulade mixture. Place about 1 teaspoon Rémoulade in the center of plate. Put a slice of fried tomato on top. Place a teaspoon of Rémoulade on each side of the bottom slice. Cut other tomato in half and angle on top of the Rémoulade. Place another teaspoon in the center of the angled slice. Garnish top of dish with a small amount of spring medley, then place 3 slices of grape tomatoes in symmetry at the bottom of the dish and top with finely diced parsley and chives placed in center of the top of the Rémoulade.

Francese

• • • • • Salad •

1 tablespoon clarified butter

1 tablespoon chopped pancetta bacon

2 tablespoons blue cheese

¼ to ⅓ cup chicken stock

2 heads frisée (Belgium endive, radicchio, or other assorted greens)

4 seasoned croutons

Heat skillet with butter. Toss in pancetta until crisp, then throw in blue cheese and stir with tongs until cheese breaks down just a little. Add chicken stock. Let reduce to a creamy consistency. Pour mixture over frisée and seasoned croutons.

Spaghetti Fruitte di Mare

• •

½ cup clarified butter

1 cup shrimp

1 cup scallops

1 cup crawfish

½ teaspoon kosher salt

Minced garlic to taste

Crushed red pepper to taste

⅔ cup white wine

2 cups pomodoro tomato sauce

6 cups cooked spaghettini or pasta of choice

Parsley, diced fine, for garnish

Basil, diced fine, for garnish

Heat butter in skillet. After butter turns clear, toss in shrimp, scallops, crawfish, kosher salt, minced garlic, and crushed red pepper. Let seafood simmer until almost done. Deglaze with white wine and tomato sauce. Let reduce to a sauce consistency, then add pasta. Place on dish and garnish with parsley and basil.

Crespelle

Italian Pancake

CRÊPES:

1½ eggs

1 cup milk

⅔ cup all-purpose flour

½ teaspoon salt

1 tablespoon butter, divided

In a bowl, beat the eggs until foamy. Gradually beat in milk until blended. In a large bowl, stir together the flour and salt. Gradually whisk in the egg mixture. The batter should be as thin as heavy (double) cream. If it is too thick, add a little water. Cover and let rest for 30 minutes.

Lightly brush a 6- to 8- inch crêpe or omelet pan with a little of the butter. Heat the pan over medium heat. To test if hot enough, sprinkle in 1 or 2 drops of batter. If it sets quickly, the pan is ready. Stir the batter. Holding the pan in one hand, use a small ladle to pour in about 2 tablespoons of the batter. Immediately tilt the pan so that the batter spreads out evenly. There should be just enough to cover the bottom with a thin layer. Cook until just set and lightly browned around the edges, about 1 minute. With a spatula, flip the crêpe over and cook the other side until speckled brown, about 30 seconds. Transfer the crêpe to a plate. Repeat with the remaining batter, brushing the pan with remaining butter as needed. As the crêpes are cooked, stack them, placing a strip of wax paper between each layer. Let cool completely before filling.

D.I.'s Cajun Food & Music

6561 Evangeline Highway
Basile, LA 70515
(337) 432-5141
www.discajunrestaurant
.com

Daniel and Sherry
Fruge
Owners

This restaurant has won several first places in the "Crawfish Étouffée Cook-Off" in Eunice, Louisiana. The restaurant has also been featured in *Southern Living* magazine. D.I.'s restaurant presently seats 275. This Cajun family restaurant has had two major expansions. The second expansion included a bandstand and dance floor. The restaurant features live Cajun music nightly on Tuesday, Thursday, Friday, and Saturday and a Cajun jam session on Wednesday. Families enjoy dancing with young children to Cajun music while dining.

Angels on Horseback

Appetizer

8 fresh-shucked oysters

Italian dressing

½ teaspoon hot sauce

8 slices bacon

1 package Louisiana Fish Fry, or fish flour

Marinate oysters for ½ hour in Italian dressing and hot sauce. Drain, wrap oyster in bacon, and roll in Louisiana Fish Fry or fish flour. Deep-fry at 325° in oil until golden brown.

Crawfish Bisque

Entrée

1 medium onion, chopped

1 medium bell pepper, chopped

1 (10-ounce) can Ro-Tel tomatoes

1 stick margarine

2 tablespoons tomato paste

2 teaspoons flour

Salt and pepper to taste

5 cups water

½ cup roux

2 cups clean crawfish tails

Sauté onion, bell pepper, and tomatoes in margarine until transparent. Add tomato paste and stir in flour. Add salt and pepper. Add water and simmer. Add roux while simmering. Add crawfish tails and simmer until thick. Serve over rice, like a gumbo or soup.

Don's Seafood and Steakhouse

The Original
301 East Vermilion
Lafayette, LA 70501
(337) 235-3552
www.donsdowntown.com

Ashby D. Landry, Jr.
Owner

Take one look at the menu at Don's Seafood and Steakhouse and you will get a broad introduction to this region's most delicious dishes and their tantalizing names. Try one of the wonderful gumbos, or crawfish étouffée, bisque, or jambalaya, or tempt yourself with the stuffed tilapia, and surely you'll find yourself asking, "What is Don's secret?" The secret . . . that's what everyone wants to know. Just what is the secret behind the great food at Don's Seafood and Steakhouse? Well, there are many. First, all of the ingredients are the absolute freshest available, and our seafood is locally caught and bought so each dish is as fresh as it could possibly be. Then there's our creativity in the kitchen—we're not afraid to improve on a good idea. And finally, there's the Landry family's 194 years of combined cooking experience.

Crawfish Fettuccini

3 sticks margarine

2 large onions, chopped

1 large bell pepper, chopped

3 ribs celery, chopped

3 pounds crawfish

2 (6-ounce) rolls jalapeño cheese

1 (6-ounce) roll garlic cheese

2 pints sour cream

1 (12-ounce) package fettuccini noodles, cooked and drained

4 ounces Kraft shredded Swiss cheese

Sauté onions, bell pepper, and celery. Add crawfish, jalapeño and garlic cheeses, and sour cream. Mix in noodles. Pour into a prepared 9x13-inch casserole. Top with shredded cheese. Bake until cheese is melted. Serves 6 to 8.

Crabmeat à la Landry

1 cup finely chopped onions

1/3 cup finely chopped celery

1 stick margarine or butter

Pinch of sage

Pinch of thyme

Pinch of nutmeg

Pinch of oregano

Pinch of marjoram

1 teaspoon salt

1/2 teaspoon cayenne pepper

1 tablespoon flour

1 (12-ounce) can evaporated milk

1 cup cornflakes

1 pound white crabmeat

1 cup crushed Ritz Crackers

Preheat oven to 375°. Sauté onions and celery in margarine or butter until onions are wilted. Add sage, thyme, nutmeg, oregano, marjoram, salt, cayenne, and flour. Add milk, stirring constantly. Toast the cornflakes, then crumble and mix well with the crabmeat. Combine crabmeat with the milk mixture and put into ramekins or casseroles. Sprinkle with crumbled Ritz Crackers. Add a pat of butter and bake for 20 to 25 minutes. Serves 6.

Dupuy's Oyster Shop

108 South Main
Abbeville, LA 70510
(337) 893-2336

Jody and Tonya Hebert
Chefs/Proprietors

Dupuy's Oyster Shop was established by Joseph Dupuy in 1869. Mr. Dupuy harvested his own oysters and sold them for five cents a dozen! Joseph started a tradition, which continued through the next three generations—more than 130 years of success in its original location! This restaurant is world-famous for its oysters on the half shell and outstanding seafood. This success continues today with the present owners, Jody and Tonya Hebert.

Eggplant Dupuy

* *

Fried eggplant topped with a shrimp and tasso herb cream sauce.

2 whole eggplants

1 quart buttermilk

5 cups bread crumbs

2 quarts heavy cream

3 cups diced tasso

2 tablespoons dry basil

¼ cup chopped green onions

1 tablespoon minced garlic

2 tablespoons chopped parsley

½ cup margarine, melted

1 cup all-purpose flour

1 pound baby shrimp, peeled

1 tablespoon salt, or to taste

1 tablespoon black pepper, or to taste

2 quarts vegetable oil

Peel eggplant, slice in ¼-inch thick, round medallions. Dip eggplant medallions in buttermilk, then in bread crumbs; repeat twice. Set eggplant aside until later. In a medium-size pot, pour heavy cream, tasso, dry basil, green onions, minced garlic, and chopped parsley on medium heat and let cook for 15 minutes, stirring occasionally. In a small bowl, mix melted margarine and flour to make a white roux until thick paste forms. With a small spoon, add small amounts of white roux to cream mixture until slightly thick. Add shrimp, salt, and pepper. Cook until shrimp are done. Fry eggplant in vegetable oil until golden brown. Place eggplant on plate, add shrimp, tasso, and herb cream sauce on top of eggplant. Excellent appetizer for 8 or entrée for 4 (recommend serving with pasta).

White Chocolate Bread Pudding with Frangelico Cream Sauce

. . . .

1 cup Frangelico liqueur, divided

1 (12-ounce) can evaporated milk, divided

4 cups sugar, divided

1 loaf white bread

2 cups white chocolate chunks

¼ cup vanilla extract

5 eggs, beaten

Preheat oven to 350°. In small pot, mix ½ cup Frangelico, ½ cup evaporated milk, and 2 cups sugar. Let cook on low until it thickens a little. Set aside. In large bowl, tear bread into pieces. Pour remaining evaporated milk on bread, and add remaining sugar, chocolate chunks, vanilla, and eggs; mix well. Soak for about 20 minutes and pour into greased baking pan. Bake for 1 hour; let cool, then cut in squares. Top with remaining ½ cup Frangelico liqueur before serving. Serves 10 to 12.

Fezzo's

Seafood, Steakhouse and Oyster Bar
2111 N. Cherokee Drive
Crowley, LA 70526
(337) 783-5515
www.fezzos.com

Fezzo's II
720 South Frontage Road
Scott, LA 70583
(337) 261-2464

Fezzo's III
Reception & Banquet Hall
109 Lions Club Drive
Scott, LA 70583
(337) 261-2464

Phil Faul and
Pat Bordes
Proprietors

Joshua Spell
Executive Chef

The Story Behind the Name:

A long time ago when Phil's father was a young boy in Church Point, Louisiana, he was very creative with his toys. His favorite toys were things he made with his mother's empty wooden spools. In Cajun French, the word for these wooden spools is *fezzo*. Everywhere he went he always had these spool toys with him. One day, the local postmaster began calling him Fezzo, a name he would carry with him the rest of his life.

In July 1979, Phil's family opened a grocery store in Rayne, Louisiana, and called it Fezzo's Supermarket. Phil and Pat worked in the store for a long time. In July 1999, twenty years to the month later, Phil and Pat opened their first restaurant in Crowley. When it came time to decide on the name it was clear. In honor of Phil's dad, they named it Fezzo's.

Creamy Cajun Crawfish and Tasso Sauce

1 cup diced onions

½ cup diced bell peppers

¼ pound butter or margarine

¼ pound smoked pork tasso, diced

1 (10¾-ounce) can cream of mushroom soup

1 quart heavy whipping cream

2 pounds crawfish tails, seasoned with ¼ cup Fezzo's Cajun Seasoning

2 tablespoons cornstarch

½ cup water

2 cups shredded American cheese

Sauté onion and bell pepper in butter until translucent; add tasso and simmer for 5 minutes; stir regularly. Add cream of mushroom soup. Add heavy whipping cream and cook for 10 minutes. Add seasoned crawfish, cook for 10 minutes. Stir in cornstarch and water. Turn off heat and add shredded cheese. Serve over angel hair pasta. Serves 6 to 8.

Flanagan's

1111 Audubon Avenue
Thibodaux, LA 70301
(985) 447-7771
www.fremins.net

Scarlet Rutter
General Manager

Kevin Templet
Executive Chef

Located between Nichols State University and Regional Medical Center sits Thibodaux's premier dining experience, Flanagan's Creative Food and Drink. Established in 1983, Flanagan's has built a reputation for outstanding food in a casual yet refined atmosphere. A team of culinary experts are eager to create an excellent meal featuring Black Angus beef, only the freshest seafood available, pasta favorites, and Cajun specialties headed by Executive Chef Kevin Templet. Under the leadership of General Manager Scarlet Rutter, the restaurant also features an extensive wine menu and specialty bar drinks, such as Flanagan's own "Long Island Ice Tea." Recently awarded 4½ Crawfish by *Gumbo Magazine*, Flanagan's constantly strives for 100% customer satisfaction.

Bar-B-Que Shrimp

· ·

2 tablespoons olive oil

20 large shrimp, 10/12 count, peelings and heads on

Salt, pepper, and Season-All to taste

1½ tablespoons minced garlic

1 (12-ounce) can beer

1 tablespoon dry basil

2 tablespoons chopped fresh rosemary

3 tablespoons chopped green onions

¼ cup barbeque sauce, smoky

½ stick butter

Heat olive oil in pan. Season shrimp with salt, pepper, and Season-all. Place in skillet and cook on each side 2 to 3 minutes until pink almost all the way through. Add garlic. Let it cook for 1 minute. Deglaze with beer. Add basil, rosemary, and green onions. Add barbeque sauce and reduce by ⅓. Turn off fire and melt butter in sauce. Serve over toasted French bread slices.

Southern Pecan Chicken Champignon

PECAN BUTTER:

- 2 sticks sweet butter
- 3 basil leaves, diced, or 3 tablespoons dry basil
- 2 tablespoons brown sugar
- 1 pinch cayenne
- 1 pinch blackening seasoning
- ½ cup pecans

Mix all ingredients together in a food processor. Roll in log shape in wax paper and refrigerate or freeze for future use.

CHICKEN:

- 4 boneless skinless chicken breasts
- ½ cup Southern Comfort whiskey, divided
- 4 tablespoons diced onion
- 2 cloves garlic, minced
- Juice of ½ orange, seeds removed
- 1 cup all-purpose flour, seasoned to taste
- 3 tablespoons olive oil
- 3 tablespoons butter
- 4 ounces sliced mushrooms
- 4 tablespoons roasted pecan pieces
- 8 tablespoons Pecan Butter
- 12 ounces whipping cream
- Salt and pepper to taste
- 4 tablespoons chopped parsley

Marinate the chicken breasts in half the Southern Comfort, diced onion, garlic, and orange juice for 1 hour.

Dredge in seasoned flour and pan-fry in olive oil and butter mixture. After golden brown, remove from skillet, and finish cooking in 350° oven, then hold warm.

Discard most of oil from skillet and deglaze with marinade. Reduce for 2 to 3 minutes. Add mushrooms, roasted pecan pieces, and Pecan Butter. Sauté mushrooms for 3 to 4 minutes; add remaining Southern Comfort and flame off. Add whipping cream and reduce to coat a spoon. Salt and pepper to taste. Fold in fresh parsley and spoon over panned chicken. Serves 4.

Note: This dish is excellent with your favorite stuffing or wild rice dish. For a more formal presentation, serve this sauce with game hens, quail, or duck.

Seafood au Gratin

. . . .

½ stick butter

½ large onion, diced

2 pounds shrimp, 90/110 count, peeled

1 pound crawfish meat

1 pound claw crabmeat

1 pint half-and-half

1 bunch green onions, chopped

4 dashes hot sauce

2 tablespoons parsley

1½ tablespoons onion powder

1½ tablespoons garlic powder

½ to 1 teaspoon cayenne pepper

1 teaspoon white pepper

Salt and pepper to taste

2 sticks butter for roux

1¾ cups flour for roux

1 cup shredded Cheddar cheese

Melt butter and sauté onion. Add shrimp and sauté until almost done (4 to 5 minutes). Add crawfish and crabmeat and sauté 2 minutes. Add half-and-half. Add green onions, hot sauce, and all dry seasonings. In a separate pan, melt butter and stir in flour to make roux. Stir constantly for 2 minutes; turn off fire. Bring seafood and half-and-half mixture to a simmer; slowly add small amounts of roux while stirring until desired consistency is reached. Spoon in serving dishes and sprinkle cheese over au gratin. Melt cheese in broiler. Serve with toasted French bread slices.

Fremin's

402 West 3rd Street
Thibodaux, LA 70301
(985) 449-0333
www.fremins.net

Randy Barrios
Corporate Chef

Kevin Templet
Executive Chef

Nestled in the narrow streets of downtown Thibodaux, across from the historic Lafourche Parish Courthouse, sits Fremin's Restaurant, Thibodaux's newest Epicurean delight. The building, decorated in magnificent millwork, with mahogany bars, original longleaf pine floors, wrought-iron balcony, beveled glass, pressed tin ceiling, Italian ceramic tile floors, and solid brass throughout the building, defines the character and cornerstone of Fremin's philosophy. With a long history of personality, quality, and tradition in the restaurant industry, this newest restaurant endeavor boasts "the new taste of Thibodaux" with a menu created by Corporate Chef Randy Barrios, Executive Chef Kevin Templet, and Sous Chef Erin Michot. The marriage of Creole-style and Italian cooking come together in perfect harmony.

Artichoke and Oyster Soup

3 tablespoons butter

3 tablespoons olive oil

1 medium onion, diced

1 medium bell pepper, diced

2 ribs celery, diced

5 cloves garlic, minced

1 teaspoon salt

½ teaspoon black pepper

¼ teaspoon cayenne

2 bay leaves

8 level tablespoons flour

8 cups (64 ounces) water

3 level tablespoons fish bouillon

1 teaspoon dried thyme

3 ounces oyster liquor

10 artichoke hearts, quartered, chopped medium

5 ounces dry sherry

18 oysters, chopped medium fine

3 tablespoons finely chopped parsley

½ cup heavy cream

¼ level teaspoon white pepper

Slurry of 1 ounce water and 3 teaspoons cornstarch

Place first 10 items in heavy bottom saucepot and sauté until translucent, approximately 8 to 10 minutes. Add flour and cook for 3 minutes. Add water and bring to a boil. Add fish bouillon, thyme, and oyster liquor; simmer for 12 minutes. Add artichokes and dry sherry. Simmer for 15 minutes. Add oysters and parsley and simmer for 6 more minutes. Add heavy cream and white pepper. Simmer with slurry for 2 minutes, then remove from heat. Makes ½ gallon.

Cajun Hot Bites

Eat the chicken and chew the cane!

60 (1-ounce) chicken tenderloins

4 large eggs

4 tablespoons water

4 tablespoons Tabasco

8 cups flour

6 tablespoons salt

6 tablespoons black pepper

2 tablespoons cayenne pepper

1 gallon oil

60 (5-inch) sugarcane skewers

GLAZE:

6 tablespoons butter

3 ounces cane syrup

16 ounces Tabasco pepper jelly

6 tablespoons chipotle pepper sauce

8 tablespoons water

Marinate the chicken tenderloins in the egg, water, and Tabasco mixture for 30 minutes. Cut skewers from the meat of the sugarcane stick. Skewer the tenderloins on the cane sticks in an in-and-out crochet fashion. Mix together the flour, salt, pepper, and cayenne. Bread the chicken kabobs in the seasoned flour mixture and deep-fry at 360° until golden brown and crispy. Drain on paper towels.

Combine all ingredients in a skillet and simmer for 3 to 4 minutes until of glaze consistency. Toss the sugarcane skewered fried tenderloins in the hot Glaze and serve by crossing the cane skewers in the center of service dish with cane leaves as garnish. Serves 12.

Abbeville Pork

· ·

2 (6-ounce) cornbread mixes

1 onion

1 green bell pepper

2 tablespoons butter

1 pound crawfish, chopped

2 bunches green onions

1 boneless pork loin, cut into 8-ounce portions

Salt and pepper to taste

Bake cornbread according to the package directions and break into small pieces. Chop the onion and bell pepper. Sauté in butter until lightly browned. Add chopped crawfish and sauté lightly. Add crumbled cornbread and finish with green onions. Season with salt and pepper and mix well. Set aside to cool.

Form a pocket in the pork "chop" and stuff with the cooled stuffing, using a pastry bag. Grill the pork to desired doneness and when almost cooked, glaze with the Cane Syrup Glaze. Serves 6 to 8.

CANE SYRUP GLAZE:

2 cups cane syrup

1 cup white wine

1 pound butter

Salt and pepper to taste

Combine cane syrup and wine and start to reduce. Add the butter slowly to combine and cook down to sauce consistency. Season to taste.

Smoked Pork Fettuccini

6 ounces fettuccini pasta

2 tablespoons olive oil

4 mushrooms, sliced

¼ green bell pepper, diced

¼ yellow bell pepper, diced

¼ red bell pepper, diced

4 ounces pork loin, smoked, julienned

4 sun-dried tomatoes, julienned

1 tablespoon brandy

½ cup heavy cream

Salt and pepper to taste

1 tablespoon grated Parmesan cheese

1 teaspoon truffle oil

Cook pasta until al dente, shock, and oil. Heat olive oil. Add mushrooms and peppers. Let sauté for 1 to 2 minutes. Add pork loin and tomatoes. Cook for an additional 2 to 3 minutes. Deglaze with brandy. Add heavy cream, salt and pepper. Let reduce until of sauce consistency. Add heated pasta and cook until pasta is coated with sauce. Twist pasta into bowl. Sprinkle with Parmesan cheese and drizzle with truffle oil. Top with cracked black pepper. Serves 1.

The Grapevine Café and Gallery

211 Railroad Avenue
Donaldsonville, LA 70536
(225) 473-8463
www.grapevinecafeand
gallery.com

Steve and Cynthia Schneider
Owners

The Grapevine Café and Gallery opened its doors in February 2001 in a 1920's two-story, commercial building in historic downtown Donaldsonville. The concept of the Grapevine Café and Gallery, as defined by owners Cynthia and Steve Schneider, is to provide authentic Louisiana Creole and Cajun cooking in a comfortable art gallery atmosphere. Their award-winning cuisine has been written up in numerous national and international publications.

Crawfish Cornbread

4 eggs

4 cups yellow cornmeal

6 teaspoons baking powder

2 teaspoons salt

4 cups cream-style corn

2 cups milk

1 stick butter, melted

4 teaspoons sugar

2½ cups shredded Cheddar cheese

1 (1-pound) package crawfish tails

Mix all ingredients in a large bowl. Pour into a stainless steel full-size baking pan that has been sprayed with pan spray. Bake at 375° for about 1 hour. Serve as an appetizer plain or topped with crawfish étouffée. Also great served as an entrée topped with fresh grilled fish. Makes 16 slices.

Praline Yams

10 to 12 yams (9 cups mashed)

5 eggs

¾ cup milk

2½ cups sugar

1½ cups butter

2½ teaspoons vanilla extract

1 teaspoon cinnamon

Bake yams until tender. Cool and peel. Mash potatoes in a large bowl. Add all remaining ingredients and put into a stainless steel pan. Sprinkle mixture with Topping.

TOPPING:

1 cup butter, melted

1½ cups flour

3 cups light brown sugar

2½ cups chopped pecans

Preheat oven to 350°. Mix all of the above ingredients and sprinkle on top of potato mixture. Bake 30 minutes (or until hot and bubbly).

Peach or Kumquat Sauce

• •

1 cup sugar

5 peaches, sliced, or kumquats, halved

4 cups orange juice

¼ cup Peach Schnapps

¼ cup Grand Marnier

Cornstarch and water blend for thickening

Caramelize sugar in pot, then add remaining ingredients. Thicken with cornstarch mixture to a thin, smooth texture (put through a blender to make it smooth, if desired). Serve with roasted quail, or as a glaze over pork tenderloin.

Chocolate Pecan Pie

• •

⅔ cup raw sugar

1 cup dark Karo syrup

4 eggs

2 tablespoons melted butter

1 tablespoon flour

1 tablespoon vanilla extract

1 cup mini semisweet chocolate chips

1 pie crust, unbaked

1½ cups broken pecan pieces

Preheat oven to 325°. Beat sugar, syrup, eggs, butter, flour, and vanilla in bowl until well blended. Pour semisweet chocolate chips in bottom of pie shell. Pour pecans on top of chocolate chips. Pour liquid mixture over pecans, making sure all of the pecans are coated. Bake for 45 minutes to 1 hour until done. Makes 8 slices.

Cheesecake

. . . .

CRUST:

15 sugar cookies

6 tablespoons butter, melted

Grind cookies in food processor until fine. Mix with the melted butter. Press mixture in bottom and sides of 8½-inch springform pan that has been greased with a pan spray.

FILLING:

3 pounds cream cheese, softened

2 cups sugar

6 eggs, beaten

1 cup sour cream

2 tablespoons pure vanilla extract

Preheat oven to 350°. In a bowl, mix cream cheese, sugar, eggs, sour cream, and vanilla. Beat with electric mixer until creamy. Pour over Crust. Wrap bottom of pan with aluminum foil, enough to cover the sides so that water from the water bath does not get into the pan. Bake in a water bath for 45 minutes to 1 hour until firm. Refrigerate, preferably overnight, before serving. Makes 12 slices.

Hanson House

114 East Main Street
Franklin, LA 70538-6164
(337) 828-3271
www.hansonhouse.bigdogz
.com

Colonel Clarence B.
and Bettye Kemper
Proprietors

Hanson House is a five-bedroom antebellum home set on four acres in Franklin's historic district between Bayou Teche (of Evangeline fame) and the Old Spanish Trail, one of the first coast-to-coast, east-west routes in American history. Hanson House has been in the family since 1852. The current owner, Colonel Clarence B. Kemper, Jr., is the great-great-grandson of Albert Hanson, the man who made Hanson House the home that it is today. The home is decorated in a style appropriate to its use and growth over the 150-plus years that it has been in the family.

Date Nut Bread

2 cups brown sugar

¼ cup butter or margarine

2 eggs, beaten

1¾ cups hot coffee

2 cups chopped dates

3 cups all-purpose flour

2 teaspoons baking powder

1 teaspoon salt

1 teaspoon vanilla

1 cup finely chopped nuts, toasted

Preheat oven to 350°. Mix the above ingredients thoroughly and bake for 1 hour in a greased loaf pan.

Apple Loaf

4 cups peeled, finely diced Granny Smith apples

2 cups sugar

¼ cup lemon juice

Zest of 1 large lemon

1 cup butter, melted and cooled

3 cups all-purpose flour

2 teaspoons baking soda

2 teaspoons nutmeg

1 cup finely chopped pecans, toasted

2 large eggs

1 teaspoon vanilla

1 teaspoon salt

Mix apples, sugar, lemon juice, and zest in a large bowl. Marinate approximately 2 hours.

Preheat oven to 325°. Mix dry ingredients and stir into apples; add remaining ingredients. Mix well. Bake 1 to 1¼ hours in large greased pan, or 45 minutes for miniatures. Cool. Refrigerate until serving time.

Peach Marmalade

. . . .

12 to 15 peaches, peeled

3 large ripe oranges

1 (16-ounce) can crushed pineapple

1 cup sugar for each cup fruit

Mix ingredients in food processor (do not over-mix). In large pot, cook slowly and stir often until thick. Process in sterile jars.

Greek Spread

. . . .

1 stick butter, softened

1 (8-ounce) package cream cheese, softened

⅓ cup chopped chives

1 (4-ounce) can chopped olives

⅓ cup chopped scallions

½ teaspoon garlic powder

½ teaspoon Tabasco sauce

1 teaspoon Worcestershire sauce

1 cup finely chopped toasted walnuts

Mix together and chill. Serve on toast points or Melba toast with fruit plate.

English Apple Pie

8 apples, pared and sliced
½ cup water
1 cup sugar
Juice of 1 lemon
Zest of 1 lemon

Preheat oven to 325°. Place apples in pie dish. Mix water, sugar, lemon juice, and zest and pour over apples.

CRUMBLE:

1 cup brown sugar
1 cup all-purpose flour
½ cup butter

Combine and sprinkle over apples. Bake for 45 minutes to 1 hour. Serve warm. Serves 8.

Harbor Seafood Restaurant

Restaurant and Catering
500 Universe Street
Bayou Vista, LA 70380
(985) 395-3474

Virginia Bailey
Owner

Harbor Seafood is a casual-dining, family restaurant featuring seafood, steaks, sandwiches, salads, and Italian dishes.

Crawfish Casserole

1 small block Velveeta cheese

1 (10¾-ounce) can cream of mushroom soup

1 cup chopped onion

1 cup chopped bell pepper

1 floret broccoli, cut-up

1 stick unsalted butter

1 (1-pound) package crawfish tails with juice

Creole seasoning to taste

Jalapeño peppers

1 cup mushrooms

3 cups cooked rice

Preheat oven to 350°. Melt cheese and soup together in microwave. Sauté onion, pepper, and broccoli in unsalted butter. Add crawfish and juice to sautéed mixture. Season as desired. Sauté until crawfish are cooked. Add jalapeño peppers and mushrooms. Cook until soft. Add cooked rice and cheese mixture and mix together in a 9x13-inch pan. Bake for 25 minutes covered and 25 minutes uncovered. Serves 4 to 6 people.

Bread Pudding

1½ loaves French bread

3 (12-ounce) cans evaporated milk

4 eggs

1 cup sugar

3 tablespoons vanilla extract

MERINGUE:

6 egg whites

¼ cup sugar

Preheat oven to 350°. Tear French bread into pieces into a buttered 9x13-inch pan. Add evaporated milk, eggs, sugar, and vanilla extract. Stir well into a thick, soupy mixture. Bread should soak up majority of liquid. (Add additional sugar and vanilla to taste, if needed.) Bake 30 to 45 minutes, until firm (be sure not to dry out.)

Beat egg whites until stiff. Add sugar slowly. Continue to beat until fluffy. Spread on bread pudding and bake until lightly brown. Serves 10 to 12 people.

Lafayette's

1025 Kaliste Saloom Road
Lafayette, LA 70508
(337) 216-9024
www.lafayettes.com

Jude Tauzin
Executive Chef

Celebrating the Food and History of Acadiana

Lafayette's offers a full menu of Cajun favorites such as their world-championship seafood gumbo—loaded with shrimp, crab, and crawfish, corn and crab bisque, Lafayette's Caesar Salad, premiere seafood platters, Angus certified filets and ribeyes, Mississippi pond-raised catfish, and fabulous desserts!

Lafayette's Crawfish and Artichoke Bisque

2 cups chopped onions

1 cup chopped bell pepper

¼ cup chopped garlic

½ cup chopped celery

4 ounces butter

4 cups artichoke hearts, quartered

2 cups chopped fresh basil

½ cup chopped fresh oregano

1 tablespoon fresh thyme

1 pound fresh peeled Louisiana crawfish

4 tablespoons Cajun seasoning

2 pints rich chicken stock

1 quart heavy cream

2 ounces blonde roux

1 (8-ounce) packages sliced American cheese

In a large saucepot, cook onions, bell pepper, garlic, and celery in butter until onions are clear. Add artichoke hearts and herbs; simmer for 5 minutes. Add crawfish and seasoning; mix well. Add stock and simmer for 5 minutes. Add cream and simmer for 10 minutes. Fold in roux and simmer for 10 more minutes. Add cheese, allow to melt, and serve. Serves 8 to 10.

Shrimp and Tasso Pasta

8 ounces diced tasso

8 ounces butter, divided

1 pound (26/30 count) shrimp, peeled

1 cup diced onion

½ cup diced bell pepper

¼ cup diced celery

3 tablespoons minced garlic

1½ cups white wine

2 tablespoons Cajun seasoning

In a medium saucepot, sauté tasso in 2 ounces of butter for 3 minutes. Add shrimp and cook for 3 minutes. Add onion, bell pepper, celery, and garlic. Cook for 7 minutes. Add white wine and seasoning. Simmer for 2 minutes. Fold in remaining butter on low heat until dissolved. Serve with angel hair pasta. Serves 6.

Landry's Restaurant

2318 Hwy 90 West
New Iberia, LA 70560
(337) 369-3772

David and Grace Landry
Owners

Landry's Restaurant of New Iberia was founded in 1969 by E.G. Landry. David Landry and his wife Grace purchased the business upon the death of his father and were the first to offer a seafood buffet in the New Iberia area. The restaurant offers a luncheon buffet serving home cooking Tuesday, Wednesday, and Thursday and a seafood luncheon buffet on Friday. The Seafood Grand Buffet on Friday and Saturday evenings and Sunday at noon boasts a wide variety of fried seafood, étouffée, gumbo, pasta, and boiled seafood when available. Landry's steaks are fresh and delicious. On Friday and Saturday evenings, guests can enjoy live Cajun music and dancing. The restaurant also offers banquet facilities for seating up to 175 people.

Crawfish Étouffée

2 large onions, diced

2 medium bell peppers, diced

2 stalks celery, diced

2 cloves garlic, diced

Salt and pepper to taste

Cayenne pepper to taste

½ cup (1 stick) butter or margarine

2 pounds crawfish tails, cooked

2 tablespoons flour

1 cup water

¼ cup chopped onion tops

Cook vegetables and seasonings in butter over low heat until tender, stirring often. Add crawfish tails; mix well. Add flour, mix until smooth. Add water; stir well. Add onion tops and remove from heat. Serve hot over rice.

Blackened Catfish

4 catfish fillets

Salt and black pepper

Cayenne pepper

Paprika

Garlic powder

½ cup (1 stick) butter

Sprinkle catfish fillets with seasonings (heavy on the paprika). Melt butter in black iron skillet. Place catfish fillets in butter. Let cook about 5 minutes on each side, turning once. Serves 4.

CAJUN FISH:
Place Blackened Catfish on a dish and top with Crawfish Étouffée for a delicious entrée.

Maison Daboval

305 East Louisiana Avenue
Rayne, LA 70578
(337) 334-3489
www.dabovalbb.com

Gene and Martha Royer
Proprietors

A French Bed and Breakfast

Martha and Gene Royer's home was featured on HGTV's *If Walls Could Talk* (episode number "WCT-601"). HGTV was inspired by the rich history of the home and the extensive renovation work done by Martha and Gene. Maison Daboval has five bedrooms decorated with antiques. Each has a private bath and all have claw-foot bathtubs. Every morning a Cajun breakfast is served. Both French and English are spoken.

Once you have enjoyed Martha's Cajun breakfast, you will quickly start making plans to come back for another visit.

Egg Soufflé

18 slices bread, buttered on one side

2 pounds spicy breakfast sausage

1 onion, chopped

½ chopped bell pepper

1 bunch green onions, chopped

1 pound mozzarella, grated

20 eggs

½ pint milk or whipping cream

1 stick butter, melted

Preheat oven to 350°. Cut crusts off bread; butter one side; put buttered side down in large 9x13-inch pan. Sauté sausage with vegetables until sausage is brown and vegetables are tender. Drain off excess fat. Layer meat and vegetable mixture with cheese. Repeat the process until all is used, approximately 3 layers. Pour beaten eggs, milk, and melted butter over top. Refrigerate overnight. Bake for 1 hour until done. Serves 8 to 10

Sweet Potato Muffins

1¾ cups all-purpose flour

1 teaspoon baking soda

½ teaspoon ground cinnamon

¼ teaspoon salt

2 eggs

1 cup sugar

½ cup packed brown sugar

½ cup vegetable oil

1 (17-ounce) can sweet potatoes, drained and mashed

½ cup chopped pecans

1 cup chopped dates

¼ cup all-purpose flour

Preheat oven to 350°. Sift first 4 ingredients in a bowl. Combine eggs and next 4 ingredients in another bowl and mix well. Mix sweet potato mixture and dry ingredients together. Dust pecans and dates with flour; add to muffin mixture. Grease muffin pans and bake for 27 to 30 minutes. Makes 1½ dozen.

Mr. Lester's Steakhouse

**832 Martin Luther King
Road
Charenton, LA 70523
(800) 284-4386**

Scott McCue
Executive Chef

Mr. Lester's Steakhouse, established in 1995 and located within Cypress Bayou Casino, is known throughout the state and beyond for it's prime beef, bold portions, extensive wine and cigar selection, exceptional service, friendly staff, and unique and enticing décor and environment. With the amazing talents of Chef Scott McCue, Mr. Lester's continues to build customer loyalty and exceed guests' expectations. Chef Scott, born and raised in Tucson, Arizona, has not only adapted to the Cajun culture and its cuisine, but also has cultivated his talents to enhance traditional Cajun dishes as well as solely create unique and delicious recipes. He is an active and founding member of the Atchafalaya Basin Chapter of the American Culinary Federation and has attained many medals for his skills in the many facets of his profession.

Filet Mignon au Poive

12 (6-ounce) prime beef tenderloin filets

Kosher salt and ground
   peppercorn melange to taste

AU POIVE SAUCE:

3 cups fine cognac

4 cups heavy cream

4 cups demi-glace

2 tablespoons coarse-ground
   peppercorn melange

Kosher salt to taste

Preheat oven to 500°. Season all sides of the filet with salt and pepper; sear on a hot broiler. Place into oven and cook to desired temperature.

Heat a small saucepot and add cognac; let alcohol burn off. Add the cream and demi-glace; let reduce to 4 cups. Add pepper, melange, and salt to taste; reserve warm. When filet is cooked, top with the sauce and serve. Serves 12.

White Chocolate Bread Pudding Soufflé

1 quart heavy whipping cream

1 pound white chocolate,
   chopped

8 whole eggs

2 cups milk

2 cups granulated sugar

2 tablespoons vanilla extract

2 teaspoons cinnamon

½ cup white rum

3 to 4 loaves day-old French
   bread

Bring heavy cream to a boil; stir in white chocolate until smooth. Mix remaining ingredients together, except bread, and stir into cream mixture until fully incorporated. Grind up or slice bread thin; soak bread in the custard for a couple of hours.

Preheat oven to 350°. Butter a large baking pan and fill the pan with the bread pudding. Bake about 40 minutes, until the bread pudding is firm to the touch and golden brown on top.

After pudding cools, crumble some by hand into a bowl (about 6 cups). Make a basic meringue with 2 egg whites and ½ cup sugar; whip the meringue to stiff peaks, and fold into crumbled bread pudding. Fill 4 (16-ounce) soufflé dishes full. Bake at 350° for about 40 minutes. Serves 15.

Acadiana Creamy Crab Cakes

. . . .

2 tablespoons whole butter
⅔ cup diced yellow onions
⅓ cup diced sweet red pepper
⅓ cup chopped green onions
1 pound cream cheese, softened
**1 pound jumbo lump blue crab-
    meat**
½ tablespoon chopped parsley
Salt to taste
Pinch of cayenne
Pinch of granulated garlic
Pinch of ground black pepper
Dash of Tabasco sauce

Heat butter in sauté pan and sauté onions, pepper, and green onions until soft. Let cool. Mix cream cheese and sautéed onion mixture until mixed well. Fold in crabmeat, parsley, and dry ingredients. Add dash of Tabasco. Portion into 12 (4-ounce) cakes. Let firm up in refrigerator for 1 hour.

BREADING:

3 cups bread crumbs
1 tablespoon chopped parsley
Pinch of salt
Pinch of cayenne pepper
12 crab cakes
2 cups all-purpose flour
2 cups egg wash

Combine bread crumbs, parsley, salt, and pepper. Remove crab cakes from cooler and dust with flour, then dip into egg wash, and last into breadcrumb mixture. Pan-fry or deep-fry the cakes to a golden brown, let drain, and serve. Serves 12.

Nash's Restaurant

101 East Second Street
Broussard, LA 70518
(337) 839-9333

Nash Barreca, Jr.
Chef/Proprietor

Chef Nash Barreca is a third-generation restaurateur following in the footsteps of his grandfather, Frank, and his father Nash, Sr., who owned the famous Frank's Steak House in New Orleans for forty-five years. He continued his profession as an executive chef with his brother David, who owns and operates Barreca's Restaurant in Metairie, Louisiana—still the favorite place in Metairie where the locals go to dine. Chef Nash came to Lafayette in 1999 with his wife Jenny to establish Nash's Restaurant in an old historical home built in 1908 in Broussard, approximately five miles south of Lafayette off Highway 90. He brings with him traditional recipes brought down from the Creole chefs that taught him, from age fifteen, at his grandfather and father's restaurant.

Chicken Braciuolini

. . . .

¼ cup Italian-seasoned bread crumbs

¼ freshly squeezed lemon, deseeded

1 tablespoon grated Parmigiana cheese

½ teaspoon granulated garlic

1 tablespoon extra virgin olive oil

Pinch of ground rosemary

Pinch of ground sage

Pinch of black ground pepper

4 (6-ounce) boneless skinless chicken breasts

1 artichoke, chopped

1 hard-cooked egg, shredded

2 slices prosciutto, julienned

Mozzarella cheese

Marinara sauce (red gravy)

In a mixing bowl, add bread crumbs, lemon juice, Parmigiana, garlic, olive oil, rosemary, sage, and black pepper. Mix well by hand rubbing together until the mix is moist. Set aside.

Preheat oven to 350°. Flatten raw chicken breasts to ¼-inch thickness. Layer the mixed bread crumbs over the top of the chicken. Add chopped artichoke, boiled egg, and prosciutto in layers on top of the bread crumb mix. Top with mozzarella cheese and hand roll chicken, stretching the sides and folding so that the ingredients inside will not fall out. Use 1 or 2 toothpicks to hold together. Place the chicken in a casserole dish and smother with marinara. Cover with foil and bake 40 minutes. Take out and serve with angel hair pasta. Serves 4.

Note: You may use baby veal or round steak instead of chicken. If using round steak, cook for 1 hour until meat is tender.

Shrimp and White Beans

BEANS:

½ pound ham or seasoning meat

1 medium onion, finely chopped

½ medium bell pepper, chopped

4 ribs celery, chopped

Salt and pepper to taste

2 teaspoons minced garlic

1 tablespoon margarine

1 cup chicken broth

1 pound Great Northern beans

8 to 10 cups water

1 tablespoon fresh parsley chopped

In a stockpot, sauté meat, onion, pepper, celery, salt, pepper, and garlic in margarine. Add chicken broth and beans. Add 8 to 10 cups water. Let cook for 2 hours until beans are tender. If necessary, add water while cooking. Add parsley, and more salt and pepper, if needed.

SHRIMP:

1 tablespoon unsalted butter

½ teaspoon chopped fresh garlic

½ pound shrimp, peeled

¼ cup shrimp stock

¼ cup chopped green onions

Sauté unsalted butter, garlic, and shrimp. Add shrimp stock and green onions. Let simmer until the shrimp are cooked. Add 8 ounces cooked white beans to shrimp mixture. Let simmer until heated, stirring occasionally. Pour over steamed rice. Approximately 4 servings per sauté pan.

Grilled Eggplant, Tomato, Fresh Mozzarella, Portobello Mushrooms, and Fresh Basil Salad

Extra virgin olive oil

Salt and pepper to taste

3 (¼-inch) slices eggplant, skin on

3 (¼-inch) slices vine ripe or Creole tomatoes

3 (¼-inch) slices portobello mushroom

3 (¼-inch) slices fresh mozzarella cheese

2 tablespoons finely chopped fresh basil leaves

2 cups freshly grown spring salad mix

Balsamic or raspberry vinaigrette

Coat a sauté pan with a thin layer of extra virgin olive oil. Salt and pepper eggplant, tomatoes, and mushroom. Grill all 3 vegetables in the same sauté pan on both sides. Remove from sauté pan and place on paper towel to dry. On a platter, lay spring mix on top. Layer each vegetable and slices of fresh mozzarella cheese, rotating each vegetable. Sprinkle fresh sweet basil on top.

Note: You may add grilled chicken, duck breast, or fish to this salad, also. A vinaigrette dressing such as balsamic or raspberry will complement this dish.

Shrimp and Corn Bisque

- -

3 pounds medium-size shrimp, peeled and deveined (save shells for stock)

1¼ gallons water

½ pound (2 sticks) unsalted butter

1 cup bleached all-purpose flour

1 gallon shrimp stock

2 cups heavy cream

2 (17-ounce cans) whole-kernel or creamed corn

2 cups finely chopped onions

1 cup finely chopped celery

½ red pepper, diced

1 tablespoon chopped fresh thyme

1 teaspoon granulated white pepper

2 tablespoons granulated garlic

3 bay leaves

1 tablespoon chopped fresh tarragon

1 tablespoon chopped parsley

Boil shrimp in plain water; drain and set aside. Boil shrimp peelings in 1¼ gallons of water so that you have enough stock for your bisque. Strain and set aside. In a stockpot, melt butter and add flour. Stir to make a white roux (10 minutes). Add shrimp stock. Let come to a boil. Add heavy cream, corn, onion, celery, pepper, thyme, white pepper, garlic, and bay leaves. Let come to a boil. Add cooked shrimp. Let come to a boil, then reduce het and simmer for 30 minutes. Add tarragon and parsley. Makes 8 servings.

The Palace Café

135 West Landry
Opelousas, LA 70570
(337) 942-2142

Tina D. Elder and
  Bill Walker
Owners

The Palace Cafe in Opelousas is a family restaurant serving local flavor, primarily Cajun cuisine. The fried chicken salad is a favorite among visitors.

Tina's Vegetable Soup

3 quarts water

1½ pounds diced beef or soup bone

2 large onions, chopped

1 large bell pepper, chopped

3 ribs celery, chopped

1 (15-ounce) can crushed tomatoes

2 potatoes, cut in small pieces

3 carrots, chopped

1 (16-ounce) bag mixed frozen vegetables

1 (17-ounce) can whole-kernel corn

½ cup shredded cabbage

In a 6-quart covered pot, add water, meat, onions, bell pepper, celery, and tomatoes; bring to a boil, then simmer for 2½ hours. Take soup meat from pot and remove from bone. Chop into bite-size pieces, discarding bone and fat. Return meat to broth, add potatoes and cabbage, and cook ½ hour more. Add frozen vegetables and corn during last 15 minutes of cooking. Serves 8 to 10 people.

Joseph Jefferson House
Rip Van Winkle Gardens
New Iberia, Louisiana

Baklava – Steve Doucas' Original

SYRUP:

3 cups sugar

4 cups water, boiling

1 pound honey

2 lemons, clear juice only

Make a simple syrup by dissolving sugar in boiling water. Simmer over medium-low heat for 1 hour and 14 minutes (this is simple syrup). Add honey, and bring to a slow boil. Mixture will foam; skim off foam until foam stops forming, then add lemon juice. Allow Syrup to cool to at least room temperature. (May be made well ahead of time.)

PECAN FILLING:

3 pounds ground pecans

2½ cups white sugar

3 tablespoons cinnamon

1¼ pounds sweet butter, melted

1½ (16-ounce) packages phyllo dough leaves

Combine ground pecans, sugar, and ground cinnamon until uniform. In a separate pan, melt butter. Thaw phyllo leaves; lay out ready to separate and use. Butter bottom and sides of a 18x13-inch pan. Lay 8 phyllo leaves, one at a time, on pan bottom, buttering each leaf completely before adding another leaf. Add ⅓ of pecan mixture to pan, smooth, and pat down evenly. Add 4 more phyllo leaves, using same procedure. Add second ⅓ of pecan mixture, smooth, and pat down evenly. Add 4 more phyllo leaves, same procedure as before. Add last ⅓ of pecan mixture, smooth, and pat evenly. Add 8 more phyllo leaves, using same procedure. Be generous in adding butter to top layer. Place pan in refrigerator for about 45 minutes, or until butter throughout surface hardens, evenly. (This step can be eliminated, if desired.)

(continued)

With a sharp, thin knife, cut 10 uniform-width rows lengthwise. Make an angled cut cat-a-corner across pan; cut uniform rows cat-a-corner on either side of center cut. All pieces should be diamond shaped. Trim excess phyllo from sides of pan to give smooth appearance.

Preheat oven to 375°. Place pan in oven for 20 minutes. Lower heat to 350°, cook for an additional 20 minutes. Lower heat to 325°; cook an additional 20 minutes. Turn off heat; leave pan in oven an additional 20 minutes (top surface should be golden brown). Remove pan from oven, pour cool Syrup onto hot Baklava evenly. Do not separate or serve Baklava until next day!

Note: Cuts do not go to bottom of crust. After baking, firmly re-cut in original grooves to bottom of pastry.

Pat's of Henderson

1500 Siebarth Drive
Lake Charles, LA 70615
(337) 439-6618
www.patsofhenderson.com

Richard and Nancy Perioux
Owners

Note: Pat's products may be ordered by calling (866) 711-7287 or visiting our website at www.patsofhenderson.com.

This restaurant has won numerous awards: Best Restaurant in Southwest Louisiana, Best Cajun Restaurant, Best Place for a Business Lunch, Best Gumbo, Best Seafood, and Best Cajun Dish!

Seafood Gumbo

2 quarts water

½ cup Pat's Roux

¼ cup chopped onions

¼ cup chopped bell pepper

¼ clove garlic

Season to taste with Pat's Spicy
　Seasoning

1 cup shrimp, peeled

1 cup crawfish tails

1 cup raw oysters, pasteurized

Heat water until it starts to boil. Dissolve roux in water by stirring on medium heat. Add onions, bell peppers, garlic, and ¼ cup seasoning to roux mixture. Add shrimp, crawfish tails, and raw oysters to mixture. Cook on low heat for 45 minutes. If more seasoning is needed, add to desired taste. Serve over rice.

Chicken and Sausage Gumbo

1 large hen

Pat's All-Purpose Seasoning to
　taste

1 cup Pat's Roux

3½ quarts water

1 medium onion, chopped

1 medium bell pepper, chopped

2 cloves garlic, minced

1 pound sausage, sliced

Cut up hen and season to taste. Fry hen until light brown and set aside. In a separate pot, dissolve roux in water over medium heat. Add seasoning to taste. Add onion, bell pepper, and garlic to the water and boil for 20 minutes. Add hen and sausage to the water mixture. Cook on medium for 1½ to 2 hours or until meat is tender. If more seasoning is needed, add to desired taste. Makes 6 to 8 servings.

Prejean's Restaurant

3480 I-49 North
Lafayette, LA 70507
(337) 896-3247
www.prejeans.com

Bob Guilbeau
Owner

Donovan Solis
Executive Chef

For a genuine Cajun experience go to Prejean's Restaurant. It is a large place with 350 seats, a fourteen-foot stuffed alligator called "Big Al," and a live Cajun band. Owner Bob Guilbeau can trace his Cajun heritage back to the founding of this region. Prejean's culinary team has won more culinary competitions, and more medals and trophies than any restaurant in the South. The restaurant offers guests a wide array of seafood specialties, steaks, and wild game dishes.

Bread Pudding with Jack Daniel's Sauce

PUDDING:

3 loaves stale bread

4 cups milk

8 eggs

1 (12-ounce) can evaporated milk

⅓ can water

¾ cup butter

2 cups sugar

2 tablespoons vanilla

1 teaspoon cinnamon

½ pound (2 sticks) butter, cut into pieces

JACK DANIEL'S SAUCE:

½ cup sugar

½ cup water

1 stick butter

2 tablespoons vanilla

2 ounces Jack Daniel's Black Label whiskey

All ingredients should be at room temperature.

Preheat oven to 325°. Cut bread into cubes. Combine all ingredients except bread and ½ pound butter pieces. Mix well and pour over bread into a buttered, 9x13-inch pan. Let bread soak in milk mixture for 15 minutes. Top bread mixture with butter pieces. Bake for 1 to 1½ hours, or until pudding mixture has risen about 1 inch.

Mix sugar and water together until dissolved. Add butter and vanilla and simmer until melted. Cook over high heat for 2 minutes. Add Jack Daniel's and simmer 3 to 5 minutes. Serve warm on top of bread pudding. Makes 25 servings.

Crawfish Étouffée

- **2 tablespoons plus 1 cup butter, divided**
- **2 tablespoons flour**
- **¾ cup chopped onion**
- **½ cup chopped celery**
- **⅓ cup chopped green onion tops**
- **⅓ cup chopped green onion bulbs**
- **¼ cup plus 2 tablespoons chopped parsley, divided**
- **1 tablespoon paprika**
- **1 teaspoon cayenne pepper**
- **½ teaspoon garlic powder**
- **½ teaspoon black pepper**
- **3 tablespoons chicken bouillon**
- **4 cups water**
- **3 pounds crawfish tails**
- **Chopped green onion tops for garnish**

Melt 2 tablespoons butter in a small skillet. Stir in flour. Cook over medium heat until brown to form a roux, stirring constantly; set aside. Sauté the onion, celery, green pepper, and onion bulbs in remaining butter in a large saucepan until tender. Add ¼ cup parsley, paprika, cayenne, garlic powder, pepper, and bouillon and mix well. Cook for 2 minutes. Add the water and bring to a boil. Stir in the roux. Cook until thickened, stirring occasionally. Add the crawfish. Cook just until the crawfish are tender. Stir in remaining parsley and green onion tops. Serve over steamed rice. Serves 12.

Pujo St. Café

901 Ryan Street
Lake Charles, LA 70601
(337) 439-2054
www.pujostreet.com

This casual, yet elegant restaurant is conveniently located just six blocks off I-10 in the heart of historical downtown Lake Charles. Housed in what once was the old Gordan's Drug Store, it comes highly recommended by the locals. As featured in *Southern Living* magazine, Pujo St. Café offers courtyard dining, steaks, seafood, salads, and pastas—complemented by a full bar and an excellent wine list.

Oysters Pujo
Appetizer

STUFFING:

½ tablespoon minced garlic

½ tablespoon minced shallot

¾ cup minced tasso

½ teaspoon olive oil

¾ cup minced, smoked Gouda cheese

4 cups fresh spinach

¼ cup Southern Comfort bourbon

½ cup heavy whipping cream

Sauté garlic, shallot, and tasso in olive oil over high heat. After 3 minutes, add Gouda and cook another 3 minutes; add spinach and wilt down 1 minute. Deglaze with Southern Comfort. Add cream. Reduce by half; set aside.

OYSTERS:

Oysters

Flour

Buttermilk

Pecans, finely chopped

Vegetable oil

Preheat oven to 400°. Dust oysters with flour and dip in buttermilk; roll in pecans and fry for 1 to 2 minutes in vegetable oil. Place each oyster in a half shell and top with stuffing mixture; bake for 5 to 7 minutes. Serve on a bed of greens garnished with a lemon twist. Serves 6 to 8.

SNO'S Seafood and Steakhouse

13131 Airline Highway
Gonzales, LA 70797
(225) 647-2632
www.snos.com

Todd and Candy Sheets
Owners

David W. Tiner
Executive Chef

Chef Tiner is a Louisiana native. He attended the Culinary Art Institute of Louisiana in 1995. Previous restaurant stints included Dajonel's as sous chef and chef at Tezcuco Plantation Bed and Breakfast. Chef Tiner began working at Sno's Seafood in September 1999, where he really developed his style of cooking, creating a combination of Cajun, Creole, and French dishes. Chef Tiner claims that most of his best and creative dishes are made up on the spot!

Crawfish Étouffée

. . . .

¾ cup butter, divided
1 medium onion, diced
1 medium bell pepper, diced
2 ribs celery, diced
2 pounds crawfish tails, whole
¼ teaspoon thyme
¼ teaspoon finely chopped
    fresh parsley
¼ cup sliced green onions
¼ teaspoon cayenne pepper
1 teaspoon salt
1 teaspoon black pepper
1 tablespoon granulated garlic
1 cup water
½ cup all-purpose flour

In a large pot or Dutch oven, melt ¼ cup butter, and sauté the vegetables until tender. Add the crawfish tails and seasonings; cook until tender. Add the water and remaining butter; stir until the mixture comes to a boil. Sprinkle the flour over the top of boiling mixture and whisk in, cooking until thick (just a few minutes). Adjust the seasoning for salt and pepper to desired taste. Serve over hot rice with fresh French bread. Makes 8 servings.

Shrimp Diablo

Oil for frying

2 cups milk

2 whole eggs

2 cups all-purpose flour

½ teaspoon habanero chili powder

1 teaspoon chili powder

1 teaspoon granulated garlic

1 teaspoon salt

24 (26/30-count) shrimp, peeled and deveined

SAUCE:

1 pint ketchup

½ teaspoon habanero chili powder

1 teaspoon chili powder

1 teaspoon granulated garlic

2 sticks butter, melted

Chopped green onions for garnish

Preheat enough oil for frying to 350°. In a bowl combine milk and eggs; mix well. In another bowl, combine flour and ½ teaspoon of habanero chili powder, and first set of seasonings; blend well. Dredge shrimp in flour mixture, then dip into the egg wash and back into the flour mixture; fry until golden brown. Makes 4 servings.

In a food processor or blender, combine the ketchup and seasonings; turn on high and slowly pour in butter. After blending, taste and adjust seasonings. Gently coat each shrimp in the blended mixture, place 6 to a plate, garnish with green onions, serve with a side of blue cheese dressing for dipping.

Note: Habanero peppers are extremely hot, so use sparingly. The habanero seasoning can be found at your local supermarket with the dried spices or specialty spices. You can substitute the habanero for a less hot pepper such as cayenne, or use none at all if you are not heat tolerant.

Chocolate Bread Pudding

. . . .

2⅔ cups sugar

3 whole eggs

½ cup melted butter

1 (12-ounce) can evaporated milk

½ cup half-and-half

1 pound semisweet chocolate chips

1 tablespoon vanilla

1 loaf French bread, cut in 1-inch pieces

1 teaspoon cinnamon

½ teaspoon nutmeg

Preheat oven to 350°. In a bowl, combine sugar and eggs; mix well. In a small pot, combine butter, milk, half-and-half, and chocolate. Heat on medium until chocolate is melted and mixture is smooth, then add vanilla and remove from heat. Slowly pour the chocolate mixture into the sugar mixture, whisking the sugar constantly to prevent curdling eggs. Once combined, place bread into a large bowl, then pour chocolate mixture over bread, gently tossing to coat evenly. Allow to set up for 5 minutes. Pour bread mixture into a greased 9x13-inch pan, and sprinkle top with cinnamon and nutmeg. Bake 20 minutes or until done. Serve warm or cold topped with chocolate syrup.

Note: Fresh bread works best; makes a more moist pudding. Makes 8 servings.

Thai Cuisine

607 B Kaliste Saloom Road
Lafayette, LA 70508
(337) 261-0000
www.thaicuisinellc.com

Yai O'Neal
Chef/Proprietor

This authentic Thai restaurant offers an excellent alternative to the great Cajun cuisine in the area. Like Cajuns, Thai people enjoy a little spice in their life, and the uniqueness and versatility of their cooking style will afford you an opportunity to enjoy an important part of their culture. Chefs On, Yai, and Toi incorporate fresh herbs and spices into recipes from southern, central, and northeastern Thailand that have been passed down for generations.

Pad Thai

• •

4 tablespoons cooking oil

2 garlic cloves, finely chopped

½ pound meat, cut into small slivers (shrimp, pork, or chicken)

1 cup thinly sliced tofu

3 tablespoons chopped pickled radish

2 eggs, beaten (optional)

12 ounces fresh flat rice noodles

3 tablespoons fish sauce

2 tablespoons sugar

4 tablespoons tamarind juice or vinegar

1 cup bean sprouts

1 tablespoon chopped green onions

½ cup ground roasted peanuts

Heat cooking oil in wok and sauté garlic. Add meat and cook until shrimp turns bright orange and chicken turns white. Add tofu and radish; fry until tofu is nearly cooked. If desired, continue to stir and slowly drizzle in the eggs to form a fine ribbon of cooked egg. Add remaining ingredients except for bean sprouts, shallots, and nuts, and cook until noodles are done. Add half the bean sprouts and shallots; fry for about 30 seconds. Transfer to platter, sprinkle with peanuts, and serve topped with bean sprouts.

Note: It is possible to use less oil than indicated by adding small amounts from time to time to keep the noodles from drying.

Red Curry

Gaeng Daeng

1 tablespoon cooking oil

1 tablespoon red curry paste

12 ounces chopped meat (beef, chicken, pork, or shrimp)

1½ cups coconut milk

½ cup water or chicken stock

2 tablespoons fish sauce

½ teaspoon sugar

3 to 4 fresh kaffir lime leaves

1 medium-size red or green bell pepper, sliced

2 to 3 sweet basil leaves

Heat wok; add oil and curry paste, stirring for 30 seconds. Add meat and cook until almost done. Add coconut milk and remaining ingredients; cook 2 to 3 minutes until meat is done. Add basil; remove from heat.

Lemon Grass Soup

Tom Yum Goong

3 cups chicken stock

1 lemon grass stem, cut into short lengths

4 slices fresh galangal

2 to 3 kaffir lime leaves, torn

5 large shrimp, shelled and deveined

¾ cup mushrooms, halved

5 tablespoons lime juice

3 tablespoons fish sauce

5 to 6 Thai chiles, just broken with pestle

1 dash Ac'cent (optional)

2 coriander (cilantro) plants, chopped coarsely

1 shallot, chopped

Heat the stock to boiling. Add the lemon grass, galangal, and lime leaves. Return to a boil, add shrimp and mushrooms, and cook until shrimp are done. Season to taste with lime juice, fish sauce, chiles, and Ac'cent. Add coriander and shallot. Remove from heat. Serve hot.

Walker's Cajun Dining

Located in the Holiday Inn
603 Holiday Drive
Jennings, LA 70546
(337) 616-0766

- - - - - - - - -

Mike Walker
Chef/Proprietor

Adjacent to exit 64 on I-10 in Jennings, Walker's Cajun Dining specializes in seafood, steaks, gumbo, salads, pasta, and po-boys. The restaurant has seating for 200 people, a banquet room for 100, and accepts all major credit cards. Walker's is a member of the Louisiana Restaurant Association.

Baked Stuffed Red Snapper

4 pounds Red Snapper Fillets

Salt, red pepper, and lemon pepper to taste

1 stick butter, melted

Season fillets with salt, red pepper, and lemon pepper. Cut pocket in snapper for Stuffing. Rub butter on both sides of fillets. Lay in greased baking pan, covered.

STUFFING:

3 cups chopped onions

1 cup chopped bell pepper

½ cup chopped celery

3 sticks butter

1 pound small shrimp, cleaned

1 pound white crabmeat

4 cloves garlic, finely chopped

alt, black pepper, and red pepper to taste

2 tablespoons paprika

2 eggs, beaten

5 slices bread, broken, mixed with beaten eggs

S3 cups bread crumbs

¼ cup chopped parsley

½ cup chopped green onions

Sauté all vegetables in butter until clear. Add shrimp. Cook for 10 minutes. Add crabmeat, seasoning, and bread mixed with eggs. Cook for additional 15 minutes on medium heat. Add bread crumbs, parsley, and green onions. Stuff fillets. Bake at 375° for 20 minutes.

Yellow Bowl Restaurant

Highway 182
Jeanerette, LA 70544
(337) 276-5512

T. K. and Colleen Roberts Hulin
Proprietors

In 1953, Tony and Margaret Roberts bought the Yellow Bowl, moving their family from Breaux Bridge to Jeanerette. Tony Roberts was a pioneer in moving the lowly crawfish onto the restaurant tables of Louisiana. He originated the ever famous fried crawfish, which remains one of our most sought-after recipes. Margaret Roberts was a wonder in the kitchen, every meal reflecting the traditions and pride of the Bayou Teche area.

From 1988 to 2000, Neal and Kay Roberts, second generation owners, operated the Yellow Bowl, carrying on the prideful traditions started by Tony and Margaret Roberts. The new millennium brings a new look and a new Roberts as owner of the Yellow Bowl! T. K. Roberts and Colleen Roberts Hulin welcome you and promise continued superior service, with the guidance of Tony and Margaret Roberts, and the Yellow Bowl tradition of "good food with good friends." The Yellow Bowl has been featured in *Southern Living, Coastal Living,* and *Ford Times.*

Chef Floyd Clavelle's Snapper and Garlic Cream Sauce

. . . .

SAUCE:

½ quart half-and-half

½ cup mozzarella

½ cup Romano

½ cup Cheddar

½ cup Parmesan cheese

1 teaspoon garlic powder

1 teaspoon thyme

1 teaspoon basil

1 teaspoon Ac'cent seasoning

3 tablespoons chicken base

1 cup shrimp stock

Flour to thicken

Add all ingredients except flour and simmer for approximately 20 minutes or until cheeses are melted. Dissolve flour in small amount of water and add to thicken sauce.

SNAPPER:

2 tablespoons butter per person

¼ cup water per person

1 teaspoon lemon juice per person

1 snapper fillet per person

Parlsey for garnish

In a skillet, heat butter, water, and lemon juice. Add skinless snapper fillet and cook on each side until fish flakes. Remove fish from skillet and pour ¼ cup Sauce over the fish. Garnish with parsley and serve.

Holiday Pumpkin Cheesecake

CRUST:

1½ cups graham cracker crumbs

2 tablespoons sugar

¼ cup margarine, melted

1 teaspoon grated lemon rind

Preheat oven to 350°. Mix ingredients and press mixture firmly on the bottom of a 9-inch spring-form pan. Bake 5 minutes, then set aside.

FILLING:

3 (8-ounce) packages cream cheese, softened

1 cup sugar

3 eggs

1 (15-ounce) can 100% pure pumpkin

¾ teaspoon vanilla extract

Beat cream cheese at high speed until fluffy. Gradually add sugar, eggs, pumpkin, and vanilla. Pour mixture into Crust and bake at 375° for 30 to 35 minutes.

SOUR CREAM TOPPING:

1 (16-ounce) carton sour cream

3 tablespoons sugar

½ teaspoon vanilla

Mix sour cream, sugar, and vanilla on medium speed of mixer for 2 minutes. Spread Sour Cream Topping on top of cheesecake and bake at 500° until topping melts. Remove cheesecake from oven and let cool. Chill 8 hours before cutting. Makes 1 cheesecake.

Crossroads

Located right in the center of the state, the CROSSROADS region gives visitors a taste of all things Louisiana. For a sampling of southern hospitality, you'll want to visit Natchitoches, the inspiration for the movie and play *Steel Magnolias*, where the women had big hair and even bigger hearts. The Crossroads region is home to some of the South's most charming bed and breakfast inns and antique shops.

Crossroads Restaurants

Cajun Landing 267

Cypress Bend 270

The Landing Restaurant 273

Lasyone's Meat Pie Kitchen 276

Lea's Lunch Room 279

The Magnolia Room 282

Mariner's 288

Tunk's Cypress Inn 290

Cajun Landing

2728 MacArthur Drive
Alexandria, LA 71303
(318) 487-4913
www.cajunlanding.com

Lonnie and Sandy Lee
McDonald
Owners

Voted #1 for Seafood Dining in Alexandria by the national publication *Where America Eats*, Cajun Landing serves seafood, as well as USDA Choice steaks, chicken, catfish, and burgers, plus some of the best desserts in town. Cajun Landing is open Monday through Saturday for lunch and dinner.

Cajun Rice Mix

· ·

½ large onion, chopped

1 pound hamburger meat

1 pound ground pork

1 tablespoon granulated garlic

¾ tablespoon black pepper

1 tablespoon beef base

2½ ounces Worcestershire sauce

1 ounce Tabasco sauce

1 teaspoon Prudhomme's blackening seasoning

Cooked rice

Chopped green onions for garnish

Sauté onion; add hamburger meat and pork to brown (thoroughly cook). Add garlic, black pepper, beef base, Worcestershire, Tabasco, and blackening seasoning. Mix thoroughly with cooked rice. Garnish with green onions. Serve warm. Serves 4 to 6.

Potato, Leek, and Onion Soup

5 tablespoons olive oil

3 large leeks, white and pale green parts only, sliced

1½ pounds potatoes, peeled and diced

1 large white onion, chopped

4 (14½-ounce) cans vegetable broth

3 large garlic cloves, chopped

½ cup chopped green onions

Salt and pepper to taste

Heat olive oil in heavy, large pot over medium-low heat. Add leeks, potatoes, and onion. Sauté until onion is tender, stirring occasionally, about 12 minutes. Add broth, garlic, and green onions; bring soup to a boil. Reduce heat to medium-low. Simmer until all vegetables are tender, about 20 minutes. Working in batches, purée 5 cups soup in a blender. Return purée to soup in the pot. Season with salt and pepper. Serves 6 to 8.

Garlic Beurre Blanc Sauce

1½ cups chopped white ends green onions, split

2 tablespoons chopped garlic

1½ cups white wine

1 cup white vinegar

Pinch of pepper

1 cup heavy cream

2 pounds unsalted butter

Mix the onions, garlic, wine, and vinegar; heat. Reduce but do not let onions and garlic brown. Add pepper. Add heavy cream. Add butter gradually, bring almost to a boil, then turn off. Pour through strainer.

Cypress Bend

Golf Resort and Conference Center
2000 Cypress Bend Parkway
Many, LA 71449
(877) 519-1500
www.cypressbend.com

J. D. Duggan
Executive Chef

Mike Barnhill
Sous Chef

Cypress Bend Golf Resort and Conference Center is located on Toledo Bend Lake, which rests along the borders of Louisiana and Texas. The lake is the fifth largest man-made reservoir in the United States with 186,000 acres of water and 1,200 miles of shoreline. Nestled in a forest of oak and pine trees, this resort will prove to be a tranquil refuge. You can sit and admire azaleas, camellias, and daylilies, all artfully designed into a breathtaking showcase of acres and acres of greenery and color—some of the most beautiful landscaping you will ever see. Add into this an eighteen-hole championship golf course that is a charter member of the Louisiana Audubon Golf Trail and you've found the perfect spot for a meeting to convene. If golfing is not your game, enjoy fishing in Toledo Bend Lake.

From bountiful American breakfast and theme luncheons buffets, to gourmet Chef's Choice specials and fine dining in the evening, the Cypress Bend dining room will satisfy your every culinary craving.

Redfish Pontchartrain

1 redfish (other fish may be substituted)

6 tablespoons Prudhomme's Redfish Blackening Spice

2 tablespoons crabmeat

3 tablespoons fresh crawfish tails

4 large sliced mushrooms

½ teaspoon garlic

2 dashes Louisiana hot sauce

½ tablespoon butter

HOLLANDAISE:

2 large egg yolks

1 teaspoon fresh lemon juice

1 dash Louisiana hot sauce

2 teaspoons water

Salt and fresh-cracked pepper to taste

¼ pound unsalted butter, melted

In hot cast-iron skillet, blacken fish with blackening spice. Sauté crabmeat, crawfish, mushrooms, garlic, and hot sauce together in butter and let simmer.

In a stainless steel bowl set over pot of simmering water (do not let bowl touch the water), whisk yolks with lemon juice, hot sauce, and water until slightly yellow in color. Season with salt and pepper. Remove bowl from pot, and while whisking, add melted butter, 1 tablespoon at a time, until it is full incorporated. Add sautéed ingredients with the Hollandaise and simmer for about 30 seconds, giving time for the different flavors to melt together. Serve over the cooked fish. It can be garnished with sliced lemon and or fried leeks. Serves 1.

Roasted Corn and Poblano Chowder

- -

5 cups whole-kernel corn

4 poblano peppers

1 diced onion

3 cups diced celery

2 cups diced russet potatoes, cooked

1 tablespoon garlic

3 dashes Louisiana hot sauce

½ cup chicken stock

2 quarts heavy cream

2½ cups milk

Tony Chachere's seasoning to taste

½ tablespoon black pepper

Place corn on well-sprayed baking sheet. Cook at 350° for 20 minutes; rotate and stir every 10 minutes. Set aside. Place poblanos on the hottest part of the grill. Leave peppers on grill until all sides are relatively charred. Place peppers in a container and tightly seal. Let peppers sit for about 10 minutes; peel off the charred skin, seed, and de-stem. Set aside.

Simmer peppers and remaining vegetables with garlic, hot sauce, and chicken stock. Once vegetables are soft, add cream and milk. Bring to a boil then simmer until chowder thickens. Add Tony's to taste with black pepper.

The Landing Restaurant

530 Front Street
Natchitoches, LA 71457
(318) 352-1579

. . . .

Kent Gresham
Proprietor

Established in 1988, The Landing Restaurant uses only the freshest ingredients, vegetables, and seafood. The steaks are aged USDA Choice Black Angus cut fresh in house. All of the spice mixtures are made in their own kitchen. The restaurant is open for lunch and dinner Tuesday through Saturday, and for the Sunday champagne brunch buffet. Closed Monday. Banquet facilities are available for receptions, weddings, parties, or any special occasion.

Easy Beef Brisket

1 (5-pound) brisket of beef
Celery salt
Garlic salt
Onion powder
1 (3-ounce) bottle liquid smoke
Salt and pepper to taste
Worcestershire sauce

Sprinkle brisket generously with celery salt, garlic salt, and onion powder. Pour bottle of liquid smoke over brisket, cover with foil, and refrigerate overnight.

When ready to cook, preheat oven to 275°. Sprinkle brisket lightly with salt, pepper, and lots of Worcestershire. Cover and bake for 6 hours. Serves 4 to 6.

Beef Stew Crockpot

2 tablespoons vegetable oil
2 pounds beef stew meat, cut into 1-inch cubes
¼ cup flour
Salt to taste
½ teaspoon black pepper
1 teaspoon Worcestershire sauce
1 bay leaf
3 potatoes, diced and uncooked
1 stalk celery, chopped
1 teaspoon paprika
2 onions, chopped
2 teaspoons Kitchen Bouquet

In a crockpot, place vegetable oil, meat, flour, salt, and pepper; stir to coat meat. Cook on low until meat and flour brown. Add all remaining ingredients and stir until well mixed. Cover and cook on LOW for about 10 hours or on HIGH for 4 to 6 hours. Serves 4 to 6.

Baked Chicken and Rice

3 cups water

6 cups chicken broth

1 tablespoon butter

1 cup uncooked rice

1 small onion, chopped

½ green bell pepper, chopped

½ cup chopped celery

8 to 10 pieces chicken

Salt and pepper to taste

Preheat oven to 350°. In a Dutch oven, bring water to a boil. Add chicken broth. Add other ingredients, except chicken, to water. Season chicken with salt and pepper; place on top of rice/water mixture. Cook for about 1½ hours. Serves 4 to 6.

Pork Chops and Potato Bake

6 pork chops, nice-size

Salt and pepper to taste

1 (10¾-ounce) can cream of mushroom soup

1 soup can whole milk

¼ teaspoon Tabasco sauce

¼ teaspoon Worcestershire sauce

6 to 12 red potatoes, halved

Preheat oven to 400°. Season the pork chops with salt and pepper; brown on both sides using a Dutch oven. Combine the soup, milk, Tabasco, and Worcestershire; set aside. Cut the potatoes and place on top of the pork chops. Pour the soup mixture on top of everything. Bake for 1 hour and serve. Serves 4 to 6.

Lasyone's Meat Pie Kitchen

622 Second Street
Natchitoches, LA 71457
(318) 352-3353
www.lasyones.com

James, Joann, Angela,
and Tina Lasyone
Proprietors

Lasyone's Meat Pie Kitchen is the place to go for an authentic Creole/Cajun cuisine experience. A favorite with the locals and travelers alike, this family-owned and operated restaurant, famous for their meat pies, lets you feel like a real Louisiana native the moment you walk through the door and take in the aroma of good, down-home cooking! Lasyone's Meat Pie has been recognized and raved about by a score of magazines including *Southern Living*, *The New Yorker*, *Glamour* magazine, and *Gourmet* magazine. It has also made its way on the national airwaves being featured by *On the Road* with Charles Kuralt and *Good Morning America* with Bryant Gumble.

Crawfish Étouffée

2 heaping tablespoons plain flour, to make roux

Vegetable oil, enough to make roux

3 cans chicken broth

1 medium bell pepper, chopped

2 medium onions, chopped

3 ribs celery, chopped

1 (10¾-ounce) can cream of mushroom soup

1 (15-ounce) can tomato sauce

½ can water

1 tablespoon parsley flakes

1 teaspoon Ac'cent

3 pods garlic, chopped

Salt and pepper to taste

¼ teaspoon sweet basil

¼ teaspoon poultry seasoning

1 teaspoon Worcestershire sauce

1 teaspoon lemon juice

1 pound crawfish tails, thawed

½ cup chopped green onion tops

Mix flour and oil together to make roux. Put over medium heat and stir constantly until roux is brown. Do not burn. In a heavy Dutch oven, add all ingredients except crawfish and green onions. Let this cook until vegetables are tender. Add roux and let cook for 30 minutes over medium heat. Add crawfish and green onions and cook for 10 minutes longer. Do not overcook after adding crawfish. Serve over bed of hot rice. Serves 4.

Lasyone's Red Beans and Sausage

1 pound dry red kidney beans, picked and washed

½ cup vegetable oil, or bacon drippings

½ cup dry parsley flakes

10 cups water

1 teaspoon Ac'cent

2 teaspoons salt

1 medium bell pepper, chopped

2 ribs celery, chopped

2 tablespoons sugar

¼ teaspoon red pepper

1 teaspoon granulated garlic

1 cup chopped smoked sausage

In a 4-quart pot, combine all of the ingredients except the smoked sausage. Add sausage the last 30 minutes of cooking time. Cook approximately 2 hours or until beans are tender, uncovered on medium fire. More water may be added as needed. Serve over fluffy, white rice. For additional sausage, cut smoked sausage in links and pan-fry. Place on top of red beans and rice to serve. Serves 6.

Lea's Lunch Room

1810 Highway 71 South
Lecompte, LA 71346
(318) 776-5178

Ann Johnson
Owner

Established in 1928, Lea's has been a traditional place to stop not only for Louisiana residents, but for visitors from all over the world. Lea's restaurant is famous for its pies and southern country cooking. Over 65,000 pies are baked annually! The pies are so famous that the Louisiana Legislature named the town of Lecompte the "Pie Capital of Louisiana" because of Lea's. Lecompte has a pie festival every October with thousands of people attending. Lea Johnson was on the *Johnny Carson Show* when he was ninety-five years old because of a customer writing an article about his restaurant in the New Orleans paper. Lea's is in the Louisiana Restaurant Hall of Fame.

Sweet Potato Pie

- -

2 tablespoons softened butter

¾ cup light brown sugar

3 large eggs

½ teaspoon salt

½ teaspoon nutmeg

¼ teaspoon cloves

¼ teaspoon cinnamon

1 cup evaporated milk

1½ cups cooked mashed sweet potatoes

1 (9-inch) pie shell, unbaked

Preheat oven to 425°. Cream butter and sugar together. Add eggs. Add salt and spices. Add evaporated milk and mashed sweet potatoes. Bake in pie shell until firm. This pie is good with toasted, chopped pecans on top, or with whipped cream.

Corn Salad

1 large red bell pepper, diced

2 ribs celery, diced

1 medium yellow onion, diced

2 whole peeled tomatoes, diced

¼ cup sugar

1 cup sweet pickle relish

4 cups corn (frozen or canned)

Salt and pepper to taste

Miracle Whip

Mix all ingredients together and toss with Miracle Whip. Refrigerate for 3 hours or overnight. Serve cold.

New Potatoes with Cream Sauce

3 or 4 pounds new red potatoes, quartered, not peeled

Pot of lightly salted water

1 stick butter

1 cup evaporated milk

3 tablespoons cornstarch

Salt and pepper to taste

Put potatoes in a large pot, and cover with lightly salted water. Cook until tender (about 5 minutes). Do not overcook. Drain off half the water. Cut up butter over hot potatoes. When melted, add evaporated milk. Make a paste with the cornstarch and a small amount of hot water. Add to potatoes to make a thick sauce. Add more salt if needed and black pepper to taste.

The Magnolia Room

The Bailey Hotel
200 West Magnolia
Bunkie, LA 71322
(866) 346-7111
www.baileyhotel.com

Mr. and Mrs. Thomas T. McNabb, Jr.
Proprietors

Linda Chambers
Executive Chef

From the onset of the 2001 renovation of the Bailey Hotel, closed for nearly a half century, the Magnolia Room Restaurant was the vanguard of the group spearheading the return to prominence of the hotel. Chef Linda Chambers was hired as lead chef to run the restaurant operation because of her vast culinary reputation with other restaurant/hotel groups. She has won numerous awards both nationally and internationally throughout the years and has demonstrated her expertise in catering large functions including weddings, receptions, and special events.

Green Shrimp Salad

1 pound small shrimp

3 cups mayonnaise

2 tablespoons lemon juice

2 ripe avocados

1 bunch celery, chopped

2 bunches green onions, chopped

Sauté shrimp in saucepan with your desired seasonings. Cool down shrimp with ice. Mix mayonnaise, lemon juice, and avocados in a blender until the consistency is creamy. Finally, mix in the shrimp, celery, and green onions.

Corn Fest Bailey Bisque

4 tablespoons butter

3 tablespoons flour

1 large onion, chopped

1 quart half-and-half

1 pound lump crabmeat

1 (16-ounce) can cream-style corn

1 (10¾-ounce) can cream of potato soup

2 tablespoons chopped green onions

2 tablespoons dry sherry

1½ cups shredded Swiss cheese

⅓ cup Bailey's Irish Cream

1 teaspoon mace

Tony's Seasoning to taste

2 tablespoons parsley

In a pot, melt butter; add flour to make a light roux. Sauté onions until tender; add half-and-half, crabmeat, corn, and potato soup. Bring to a boil and reduce heat. Add green onions, sherry, cheese, and Bailey's. Finally add seasoning to taste. Sprinkle with parsley.

The Very Best Seafood Gumbo

- -

This recipe requires two days preparation time, but is well worth the extra effort.

DAY 1: PREPARE STOCK AND OBTAIN FAT FOR ROUX.

1 Long Island duckling, washed

Salt and pepper to taste

Granulated garlic to taste

2 cups water

1 large onion

4 to 5 stalks celery

Several bay leaves

4 to 5 whole carrots

Preheat oven to 350°. Season duckling with salt, pepper, and granulated garlic. Place in roasting pan. Place cut-up onion and other vegetables along with bay leaves inside duck cavity and around duck in pan. Roast for 2 hours or until skin is golden brown and crispy. Cool completely. Debone duck (reserving meat for other uses). Place skin, bones, and pan drippings in a large stockpot, adding enough water to measure approximately 4 quarts. Simmer for 1 hour. Strain stock and discard bones and skin. Refrigerate liquid overnight.

DAY 2:

Oil

4 onions, diced

1 stalk celery, chopped

1½ cups chopped okra, may use frozen

3 cloves garlic, chopped

¼ cup butter or vegetable oil

2 cups plain flour

Salt to taste

¼ teaspoon ground red pepper

¼ teaspoon ground white pepper

½ teaspoon ground black pepper

1 tablespoon granulated garlic

1 teaspoon dried oregano

1 teaspoon dried basil

1 teaspoon dried thyme

1 (10-ounce) can of Ro-Tel tomatoes

2 pounds shrimp, peeled and deveined

2 pounds crawfish tails

1 pound crab claw fingers

2 quarts oysters with juice

Heat oil in large Dutch oven over medium heat; add vegetables and sauté until okra no longer ropes and color darkens. (Frozen okra will not be as prone to roping as fresh.) Set aside.

Skim fat from duck stock. Add enough butter to duck fat to measure 2 cups. Heat fat in a large Dutch oven or heavy stockpot until it no longer sizzles (very hot). Rapidly whisk in flour. You will need to work this flour in small amounts, but work very quickly. (This is very hot and adheres to skin if splattered, so use extreme caution). Stirring constantly, over medium heat, cook until roux is the color of chocolate. DO NOT BURN the roux, or you will have to start over from scratch. Add vegetable mixture to roux. You will need a large pot to complete the cooking of the gumbo as the total quantity will be approximately 2 gallons of gumbo. Again, exercise extreme caution when handling the roux. Add reserved duck stock and add the seasonings and tomatoes. Simmer for 30 minutes on low heat. Stir in shrimp, crawfish, and crab claw fingers. Simmer until seafood is done (shrimp should be pink and opaque.) Stir in oysters with juice; simmer until oysters are plump, 5 to 10 minutes. Serve generous portions over rice as a main course. Serves 10 to 12.

Bailey's Crawfish Cake with Jack Daniel's Corn Sauce

· ·

2 pounds crawfish tails, divided

1 onion, chopped

2 tablespoons chopped garlic

¼ cup chopped green onions

1 tablespoon cayenne pepper

⅓ teaspoon ground thyme

Salt and black pepper to taste

10 cups bread crumbs, divided

Grind 1 pound of crawfish tails. Chop 1 pound of crawfish tails. Combine all of the ingredients except the bread crumbs. Mix well. Add 2 cups bread crumbs to form a patty that will not fall apart. Coat the patties with the remaining bread crumbs. Deep-fry until golden brown.

JACK DANIEL'S CORN SAUCE:

½ pound butter

2 minced green onions

4 cups fresh or canned corn (fresh is preferred)

1 cup Jack Daniel's whiskey

1 quart whipping cream

White pepper and salt to taste

Cornstarch (optional)

Combine ingredients and cook to thicken. Use a tablespoon of cornstarch, if necessary.

Cheese Salad with Basil Olive Vinaigrette

2 bags mixed gourmet salad greens

8 ripe tomatoes, preferably Roma

16 ounces goat cheese, fresh if available

1 red onion, sliced

BASIL-KALAMATA OLIVE VINAIGRETTE DRESSING:

4 ounces fresh basil

4 to 5 cloves fresh garlic

¾ cup Kalamata olives, pitted

1 cup extra virgin olive oil

½ cup red wine vinegar

1 teaspoon salt

½ teaspoon black pepper

Place lettuce mix on chilled salad plates. Layer sliced tomato, goat cheese, and red onion slices. Repeat layers if desired. Top with dressing. Serves 4.

Combine all ingredients in a food processor or blender until smooth.

Mrs. Carmen's Lemon Meringue Pie

2 egg yolks

1 (14-ounce) can sweetened condensed milk

½ cup freshly squeezed lemon juice

1 teaspoon vanilla extract

1 graham cracker pie crust

2 egg whites

4½ teaspoons white sugar

Preheat oven to 350°. Beat egg yolks and combine with milk; mix very well. While beating egg mixture, pour in lemon juice and vanilla extract and mix well. Pour lemon mixture into graham cracker crust. In another bowl, beat egg whites until soft peaks form. Gradually beat in sugar and continue beating egg whites until stiff peaks form. Spoon on pie. Bake until golden brown. Cool. Makes 1 pie.

Mariner's

Seafood and Steak House

**On Beautiful Sibley Lake,
Highway One Bypass**

Natchitoches, LA 71458

(318) 357-1220

**www.marinersrestaurant
.com**

*Don and Jennifer
Nichols*

Proprietors

When you visit Natchitoches, the flavor of Louisiana is only moments away at Mariner's Restaurant. This family-owned restaurant specializes in Cajun/ Creole, fresh seafood, and heavy aged beef. This restaurant is only minutes from downtown Natchitoches.

Seafood Gumbo

1 cup flour

7 ounces vegetable oil

1 bell pepper, chopped

1 large onion, chopped

1 celery rib, chopped

2 quarts seafood stock

1 tablespoon salt, or to taste

1 teaspoon black pepper, or to taste

1 teaspoon cayenne pepper, or to taste

½ cup chopped fresh parsley

½ cup chopped green onions (tops and bottoms)

1 pound lump crabmeat

1 pound shrimp, already cooked, peeled and deveined

1 pound crawfish tails, cooked

Cook flour and oil to a dark roux, but do not burn. Add chopped pepper, onion, and celery, (this stops the browning process). Cook 10 minutes, stirring constantly. Add stock and seasonings. Bring to rolling boil, then reduce heat. Simmer for 1 hour.

Add parsley and green onions; continue to cook for 4 more minutes. Add cooked crabmeat, shrimp, and crawfish tails. Bring almost to a boil, remove from heat, and serve with steamed rice. This recipe will yield approximately 1 gallon of gumbo and you will need approximately 2 quarts of steamed, white rice to accompany the gumbo. Should be enough for 8 to 10 people. Enjoy!

Tunk's Cypress Inn

9507 Highway 28 West
Boyce, LA 71409
(Alexandria area)
(318) 487-4014
www.tunkscypressinn.com

Jimbo and Sandy
Thiels
Proprietors

This rustic, casual dining establishment was opened in 1978. Nestled on the edge of Kisatchie National Forest, customers dine overlooking beautiful Kincaid Lake. Tunk's features "Louisiana cuisine" specializing in fresh Gulf seafood and USDA Choice steaks. Gumbo, alligator, crawfish, and catfish are specialties of the house. This unique family eatery is home-owned and operated by the family of its founder, Tunk Andries.

Miss Mayme's Seafood Gumbo

10 quarts water

1 (3½-pound) fryer chicken

2 teaspoons salt

1 teaspoon black pepper

3 cups vegetable oils

4½ cups all-purpose flour

3 cups chopped onion

2 cups chopped celery

1½ cups chopped bell pepper

1 tablespoon chopped garlic

½ teaspoon red pepper

1 teaspoon ground thyme

5 bay leaves

1 tablespoon garlic powder

¼ cup Worcestershire sauce

3 (8-ounce) cans whole tomatoes, chopped

1 pound crabmeat

1½ pounds catfish fillets

2 tablespoons seafood base, divided

5 pounds medium shrimp, peeled and deveined

Salt and pepper to taste

Cooked rice

Pour 10 quarts water into large stockpot. Place chicken, salt, and pepper into pot. Boil until chicken is tender. Remove chicken from stock; cool. In black iron pot, heat oil just under the smoking point (about 350°). Gradually add flour with a wire whip until all is incorporated. Stir roux constantly over medium heat until it turns a dark brown color. Be careful not to burn! Add chopped vegetables to the roux and stir about 3 to 4 minutes. When vegetables soften, add contents of pot to chicken stock. Stir well. Add seasoning ingredients and Worcestershire. Add tomatoes and juice. Bring gumbo to a boil. Skim fat as it comes to top. Reduce heat to simmer. Cook about 1½ hours, stirring often to avoid sticking.

In 2 separate pots, cook crabs and catfish (each covered with water and each with 1 tablespoon seafood base) until tender. Pour the stock from each of these pots into the gumbo pot. Pick crabmeat out and break fish into small pieces. Set aside. Debone chicken and chop. Set aside. Continue cooking and skimming the grease that rises to top. Add shrimp, fish, crabmeat, and chicken. Cook about 15 to 20 minutes. Add salt and pepper to taste. Serve over hot steamed rice. Makes 3 gallons.

Tunk's Crawfish Étouffée

. . . .

1 cup finely chopped onion

½ cup finely chopped celery

½ cup finely chopped bell pepper

2 sticks margarine

1 (10-ounce) can Ro-Tel tomatoes and green chiles, drained

2 (10¾-ounce) cans cream of mushroom soup

1½ teaspoons paprika

½ teaspoon minced garlic

1 tablespoon Creole seasoning

¾ cup crawfish juice (add ¾ cup water to bag of crawfish tails to make juice)

¼ teaspoon Tabasco sauce

1 pound crawfish tails, peeled

Sauté onion, celery, and bell pepper in margarine about 10 minutes until just tender. Blend tomatoes and soup in food processor. Add to onion mixture. Add remaining ingredients. Cook over medium heat about 20 minutes. Serve over steamed rice. Makes 6 servings.

Snapper Pontchartrain

· ·

4 (8-ounce) red snapper fillets

4 tablespoons melted butter

2 teaspoons Creole seasoning

Preheat oven to 350°. On a buttered baking pan, place fish fillets skin side down. Brush with melted butter and sprinkle lightly with Creole seasoning. Bake about 20 minutes until just done. While fish is baking, make Cheese Sauce.

CHEESE SAUCE:

¼ pound (1 stick) butter

¼ cup flour

2 cups half-and-half

8 ounces Velveeta pasteurized cheese, cubed

¼ pound cooked, peeled shrimp

¼ pound cooked lump crabmeat

¼ pound cooked, peeled crawfish tails

4 tablespoons chopped green onion tops

Melt butter in heavy saucepan over medium heat. Add flour, whisking until smooth. Cook about 4 minutes, stirring constantly. Do not brown; remove from heat. Add half-and-half, whisking until smooth. Return saucepan to fire; cook until sauce thickens. Slowly add cheese. Blend until smooth and remove from heat. Add shrimp, crabmeat, and crawfish tails to sauce. Stir to mix. When fish is done, place on serving plates. Cover with warm Cheese Sauce. Garnish with green onions. Serve immediately. Makes 4 servings.

Fresh Berry Pie

. . . .

1 (8-ounce) package cream cheese, softened

1 (14-ounce) can sweetened condensed milk

⅓ cup lemon juice

1 (8-ounce) tub Cool Whip topping

2 pounds fresh strawberries, hulled, or 2 pints blueberries or blackberries

1 (9-inch) deep-dish pie shell, baked

Cream cheese in mixer until smooth. In separate bowl, mix condensed milk and lemon juice. Add to cream cheese. Beat until smooth. Add Cool Whip. In large bowl, fold in berries. Spoon into pie crust. Refrigerate. Makes 1 pie.

Sportsman's Paradise

SPORTSMAN'S PARADISE is thick, piney woods that flourish with wildlife and clear, sparkling lakes abundant with bass and trout. It is also mysterious bayous and lush, rolling hills. And it is heaven for birdwatchers, photographers, campers, and anyone who loves nature. For those who love history, this is where Native Americans trapped deer and traded pottery at Poverty Point. This is where brave Confederate soldiers fought and fell at the Battle of Mansfield. And right outside of Arcadia is where the notorious Bonnie and Clyde took their last ride in 1933.

Sportsman's Paradise Restaurants

Bella Fresca Restaurant 297
Bountiful Foods Catering 300
The Brandy House Restaurant 303
Chef Hans' Gourmet Foods 306
Chianti Restaurant 311
Country Place Restaurant 313
Dominic's Italian Restaurant 316
Enoch's Café and Pub 319
Fertitta's 6301 Restaurant 321
Follette Pottery 326
Gerald Savoie's 329
The Glenwood Village Tearoom 331
Jesse's Steak and Seafood 334
Ms. Lucy's Classic Cajun 336
Olive Street Bistro 339
Slayden's Bar-B-Q 342
Superior Grill 344
Uncle Earl's Pea Patch Café 348
The Village Restaurant 350
Waterfront Grill 353

Bella Fresca Restaurant

6307 Line Avenue
Shreveport, LA 71106
(318) 865-6307

David Bridges
Chef/Proprietor

Chef Bridges was raised in New Orleans and graduated from the New England Culinary Institute in 1994. He has honed his culinary skills in Florida, St. Croix, U.S. Virgin Islands, and New Orleans.

"Festive Fare, Swanky Setting, Great Service"— *Southern Living* magazine

Bella Fresca Restaurant is a favorite among locals and visitors alike. They serve a unique variety of dishes, and the service is impeccable. For great food, an excellent wine list, and a friendly professional staff, Bella Fresca is the place to dine.

Korean BBQ Oysters

Appetizer

3 tablespoons tomato paste

4 garlic cloves

3 shallots

¼ cup chopped cilantro

1 teaspoon ground pepper

½ cup rice vinegar

4 tablespoons white vinegar

½ cup brown sugar

½ cup sesame oil

½ cup olive oil

2 tablespoons fresh-grated
ginger

1 teaspoon cayenne pepper

¼ cup white sugar

2 lemons, juiced

¾ cup teriyaki

½ cup soy sauce

6 dashes Tabasco sauce

24 oysters in the shell

Combine ingredients except oysters in a food processor to make barbeque sauce. Shuck oysters, leaving them in the shell. Place 1 tablespoon of sauce on top of each oyster. Place oysters on top of the grill. When the oysters start to bubble, cook for 30 seconds then serve. Serves 8 (3 per person).

White Chocolate/Macadamia Crème Brûlée

8 ounces white chocolate

1 quart heavy cream

8 egg yolks, beaten

4 ounces chopped macadamia nuts, divided

8 tablespoons unrefined sugar, or sugar in the raw, divided

Preheat oven to 325°. Place white chocolate into a stainless steel bowl. Place cream into a pot and bring to a simmer. Pour cream over chocolate and stir until mixture is smooth. Temper in egg yolks. Divide mixture into 8 (6-ounce) soufflé cups. Place 1 tablespoon macadamia nuts into each cup. Bake in a pan with a water bath for 40 minutes or until the custard looks firm. Take out of the oven and let the custard cool for 15 minutes. Sprinkle 1 tablespoon sugar on top of each custard. Caramelize the sugar using a blowtorch or a salamander and serve. Serves 8.

Bountiful Foods Catering

1807 Pine Street
Monroe, LA 71201
(318) 325-0062

Phyllis O'Toole
Catering Chef

Bountiful Foods Catering is a full-service, off-prim-ise catering and event-planning company specializ-ing in contemporary American and Cajun cuisine. Only the freshest of ingredients are prepared and served by our expert culinary and service team.

Crawfish Chowder

2 tablespoons butter

1 small diced onion

½ cup diced bell pepper

¼ cup chopped celery

2 tablespoons chopped garlic

1½ cups shrimp stock

2 cups diced raw potatoes

1 cup diced tasso ham

1 pound crawfish tail meat, cooked

2 cups half-and-half

1 tablespoon Old Bay seasoning

Fresh parsley

Over medium heat, melt butter in pot and add onion, bell pepper, celery, and garlic. Sauté until wilted. Add stock, potatoes, and tasso. Cook until potatoes are tender. Add crawfish. About 10 minutes before serving, add half-and-half and seasoning. Cook over low heat until flavors combine. Just before serving, add fresh parsley. Serves 4 to 6.

Cheesy Chicken and Spaghetti

1 quart water

1 pound cooked chicken meat, large dice

2 cups combined roasted onions and bell peppers

½ cup diced celery

¼ cup chopped garlic

2 (4-ounce) cans mushroom stems and pieces

1½ pounds Pepper Jack cheese

2 quarts half-and-half

1 tablespoon chicken base

¼ cup Italian seasoning

Roux

Bring water to a boil, then turn down to medium heat. Add chicken, vegetables, mushrooms, and cheese. Cook until cheese has completely melted. Add half-and-half, chicken base, and seasoning. Slowly add roux to desired consistency. Serve over spaghetti or angel hair pasta. Serves 6 to 8.

Mocha Brownies

• •

¼ cup butter

8 ounces semisweet chocolate

3 eggs

½ cup sugar

1 tablespoon instant coffee

1 tablespoon hot water

½ cup self-rising flour

½ cup chopped pecans

FROSTING:

2 ounces semisweet chocolate

½ cup butter

1 cup powdered sugar

2 tablespoons Kahlúa

Jimmies (chocolate sprinkles)

Preheat oven to 350°. Grease and flour a 9-inch square pan. In a double boiler, combine butter and chocolate; melt. Remove from heat and cool slightly. Beat eggs and sugar with electric mixer until light and lemon colored. Dissolve coffee in water and add to egg mixture. Blend on low. Fold in flour; mix well at low speed. Add pecans and stir by hand. Pour batter into prepared pan. Bake 20 to 25 minutes. Frost when cool.

Melt chocolate in a double boiler. Cream butter and powdered sugar together. Stir in chocolate and Kahlúa. Spread on cooled brownies and sprinkle jimmies over top. Let sit at least 30 minutes before serving.

The Brandy House Restaurant

The Atrium Hotel
2001 Louisville Avenue
Monroe, LA 71201
(318) 325-0641
www.theatrium.biz

John E. Peters
Executive Chef

A graduate of Northeast Louisiana University and a member of the American Culinary Federation, Chef Peters had his formal training at Commanders Palace.

Jack McPhail
Sous Chef

Jack McPhail led a varied career before turning to his first love...cooking. He learned at his mother's knee and still loves the Low Country cooking he grew up with.

The Brandy House has live entertainment at both lunch and dinner. If you are just in the mood for an appetizer and a cocktail, feel free to enjoy it at The Brandy House's ice bar. It's the "coolest" thing in town. Guests can choose from ten different beers, all on tap at the same time, at twenty-four degrees, and served through a tap that is encased in ice. The "ice bar" runs the length of the bar and changes colors with a lighting program that works through the ice. Unusual? To say the least...it is one of only a couple in the country.

As for the menu, our chefs have hand-selected only the finest ingredients for your palate. Guests may choose from a variety of regional seafood selections, just the perfect amount of exotic items to dazzle the diner who chooses from the "wild side," hand-cut black Angus steaks, fresh gulf fish, homemade breads, and desserts. The Atrium Hotel has long been famous for its Sunday champagne brunch with live entertainment and mimosas. Stop by and treat yourself to one of our specialties.

Bayou Stir-Fry

3 tablespoons pecan oil

½ cup cubed chicken breast

½ cup cubed alligator meat

½ cup julienned onion

¼ cup julienned celery

½ cup julienned mirliton

1 teaspoon minced garlic

½ cup chiffonade turnip greens

½ cup chicken stock

½ cup hoisin sauce

¼ cup Norris cane syrup

Cornstarch slurry

Salt to taste

2 cups pecan rice

½ cup spiced pecans

In a wok, heat pecan oil until almost smoking; add chicken and alligator meat. When meat is almost cooked, add vegetables. Cook slightly and deglaze with chicken stock. Add hoisin sauce and cane syrup. Thicken with slurry. Salt to taste. Serve over pecan rice. Top with Spiced Pecans.

SPICED PECANS:

½ cup butter

½ cup brown sugar

1 teaspoon salt

¼ to ½ teaspoon cayenne pepper

1 pound pecan halves

Preheat oven to 250°. Melt butter, add brown sugar, salt, and cayenne. Pour over pecans, toss quickly, then spread on sheet pan. Place in oven for just a few minutes. Let cool.

J.E.'s Salmon Confit

This recipe takes two days to prepare.

1 (4- to 5-pound) salmon fillet, fresh as possible, should smell sweet, not fishy at all

1 cup dry vermouth

Wash and dry-pat salmon fillet. Soak salmon in vermouth for 1 hour, turning fillet at midpoint.

DRY RUB:

26 tablespoons kosher salt

1 teaspoon ground cinnamon

1 teaspoon ground allspice

1 teaspoon dried dill

¼ teaspoon white pepper

¼ teaspoon cayenne pepper

¼ teaspoon black pepper

¼ cup light brown sugar, packed

Mix ingredients. Rub into salmon on both sides and pack on fillet. Place in a 2x12x18-inch pan with drip pan inserts and wrap pan with plastic wrap. Refrigerate overnight.

CONFIT OIL:

10 bay leaves, broken

6 sprigs fresh thyme, bruised

1 tablespoon freshly-cracked black peppercorns

2 stars dried anise

6 dried juniper berries

½ teaspoon grated nutmeg

½ gallon extra virgin olive oil

The next day, add herbs and seasoning to olive oil and heat to 180° for 45 minutes. Scrape salmon fillet and place in a clean 2x12x18-inch pan. Pour hot oil over fillet making sure oil reaches all surfaces of fish. When oil has cooled, strain fillet and serve with crackers or salads, or mix with dips, etc.

Chef Hans' Gourmet Foods

310 Walnut Street
Monroe, LA 71210-3252
(318) 322-2334
www.chefhansgourmet-foods.com

Hans Korrodi
Chef/Proprietor

Note: If unavailable at your local grocery, Chef Han's products may be purchased by contacting:
Chef Hans' Gourmet Foods
310 Walnut Street
Monroe, LA 71201
Phone (318) 322-2334
or Fax (318) 322-2340
www.chefhansgourmetfoods.com

Born in the German-speaking region of northern Switzerland, Hans Korrodi came to the United States in 1969, after a tour in the Swiss Merchant Marine, and having developed his cooking skills in prestigious establishments in Switzerland, Norway, and England. After completing a sailor's apprenticeship on the Rhine River, he obtained a visa under the sponsorship of restaurateur and fellow Swiss, Andres Meyer, who ran the famous Waterville Valley resort on White Mountain in Hew Hampshire. Korrodi served as assistant chef there and head chef in Vermont, and discovered Louisiana cuisine while on a vacation in New Orleans. It was here that "Chef" found his true calling, training at the posh Commander's Palace while simultaneously holding the executive chef spot at Brennan's in Houston. It was at the Palace where Chef learned from two other of Louisiana's great culinary artists, Paul Prudhomme and Ella Brennan, whom he credits as two of his greatest influences. In 1990, he started another business, Chef Hans Gourmet Foods, Inc., where he is fulfilling his dream of sharing Louisiana's cuisine with the rest of the world.

Chef Hans' Crawfish in Heaven

2 tablespoons butter

1 cup finely chopped onion

2 tablespoons flour

2 cups milk

1 pound cooked crawfish tails

¼ cup half-and-half

½ cup finely chopped green onions

1 tablespoon finely chopped parsley

1 tablespoon Chef Hans' Creole Seasoning

1 tablespoon Chef Hans' Blackened Fish Seasoning

2 ounces dry white wine

1 ounce sherry

Chef Hans' Hot Sauce to taste

8 ounces angel hair pasta, cooked

Melt butter in saucepan over medium heat. Add onion. Cook until tender. Add flour and stir continuously with wooden spoon for 2 minutes. Using wire whisk, add milk slowly. Simmer for 5 to 10 minutes on low heat. Add crawfish tails and half-and-half; fold crawfish into sauce. Add green onions, parsley, seasonings, wine, and sherry. Add hot sauce to taste. Serve over angel hair pasta. Serves 4 to 6.

Note: Shrimp may be substituted for crawfish.

Chef Hans' Shrimp Rémoulade

. . . .

½ cup ketchup

½ cup mayonnaise

½ cup finely chopped celery

2 tablespoons finely chopped
   parsley

2 tablespoons horseradish

2 tablespoons red wine vinegar

2 tablespoons salad oil

1 tablespoon Creole or Dijon
   mustard

1 tablespoon finely chopped
   onion

2 cloves garlic, finely chopped

½ medium dill pickle, finely
   chopped

1 teaspoon Chef Hans' Hot
   Sauce

2 pounds shrimp, cooked,
   peeled, and deveined

Combine all ingredients except shrimp and blend well with a wire whisk. (A food processor or blender may be used.) The flavors will be more intense if the sauce mixture is left standing for a while before serving. Shrimp Rémoulade is traditionally served on a bed of lettuce. Place shrimp on lettuce and top with sauce. May also be used as a dip for shrimp or crawfish. Serves 4 to 6.

Crawfish Cardinal

2 tablespoons brown roux

2 cups fish stock, or water

1 pound crawfish tails

2 tablespoons finely chopped green onions

1 tablespoon chopped parsley

2 teaspoons paprika

Salt and black pepper to taste

Cayenne and black pepper to taste

Chef Hans' Hot Sauce to taste

1 ounce brandy

1 ounce heavy cream

Cook roux and stock 10 minutes. Add other ingredients except cream. Mix thoroughly. Add cream. Serve with rice. Serves 2 to 4.

Veal "New Orleans"

24 ounces veal, sliced thin

1 tablespoon flour

2 tablespoons butter or margarine

4 artichoke hearts or bottoms, drained and quartered

½ pound mushrooms, sliced

2 tablespoons chopped green onions

1 tablespoon chopped parsley

1 ounce white wine

½ cup half-and-half

Cayenne pepper to taste

Salt and coarsely ground black pepper to taste

Mix veal and flour. Melt butter in hot skillet. Add veal, stir, and brown lightly. Add artichokes and mushrooms. Simmer 1 minute. Reduce heat to low and add green onions, parsley, and wine. Mix well. Remove from heat. Add cream. Do not cook after cream is added or ingredients will separate. Season to taste with cayenne, salt, and pepper. Serves 4.

Wild Rice Pilaf with Oysters and Shrimp Creole

1 package Chef Hans Wild Rice Mix

2¼ cups water

½ stick butter

1 pint oysters

½ pound shrimp, peeled and deveined

1 (10¾-ounce) can mushroom soup

½ cup chopped green onions

1 tablespoon Worcestershire sauce

1 cup half-and-half, may substitute milk

Chef Hans Creole Seasoning to taste

Preheat oven to 300°. Cook the wild rice mix in water according to directions and set aside. Melt butter in a saucepan and sauté the oysters and shrimp over medium heat for 3 minutes, stirring constantly. Add the mushroom soup, green onions, Worcestershire, and half-and-half. Bring to a simmer and fold in the cooled rice blend. Season to taste. Place in a baking dish and bake for 20 minutes. Serves 4.

Chianti Restaurant

6535 Line Avenue
Shreveport, LA 71106
(318) 868-8866

Enrico Giacalone
Chef/Proprietor

Enrico and Nino Giacalone, Italian-born brothers, transcend family culture and traditions with training in fine dining. They opened Chianti Restaurant in the fall of 1987, during which period the local economy could only support a red-and-white checkered tablecloth-style restaurant. With great success, Chianti featured a vast menu that included the most popular Regional Italian fare. As the years went by, the local economy improved and Enrico and Nino slowly evolved the restaurant to fine dining by redecorating, and offering the much more sophisticated and renowned northern Italian cuisine. With continued success in maintaining a clientele with the most discriminating taste, Enrico introduced signature dishes that have become popular among the locals and he would like to share a few with you. He hopes you enjoy them!

Scaloppini di Vitello Alle Noci e More
• • • • • • Veal Scaloppini with Nuts and Berries • • • • • • • • • •

6 (1-ounce) scaloppini white veal, pounded lightly

2 tablespoons unsalted butter

6 medium-size mushrooms, sliced

2 dozen large blackberries, washed and patted dry

1½ tablespoons roasted slivered almonds

1 medium-size shallot, chopped

2 ounces blackberry brandy

1 ounce dry white wine

1 pint heavy whipping cream

Salt and pepper to taste

In a large skillet, sauté veal with butter at medium heat for a minute on each side. Remove the veal (medium rare), set it on a plate, and cover it. Turn the heat source to high, and in the same skillet, add more butter if needed, then add mushrooms, blackberries, almonds, and shallot; sauté the ingredients for 1 minute. Add brandy and carefully make it flame with a match. Add wine and let all the liquid reduce by half. Add the cream and cook the sauce until you have it reduced to a medium-thick consistency. Add the scaloppini to the sauce to reheat for a minute, place 3 each on 2 plates, pour the sauce over, and serve immediately. Makes 2 entrées.

Country Place Restaurant

1302 Country Club Circle
Minden, LA 71055
(318) 377-8398

Tom McFarland
Chef/Proprietor

Tom McFarland has twenty-seven years experience in cooking and catering services. He trained with a Greek chef as well as two chefs specializing in New Orleans cooking.

When you visit Country Place Restaurant in Minden, you're in for a treat. Chef/owner Tom McFarland is known throughout the area for the quality and presentation of the food he serves.

Southwest Chicken Breast

. . . .

5 (5-ounce) boneless, skinless
  chicken breasts
1 onion, chopped
1 bell pepper, chopped
2 medium tomatoes, chopped
1 (8-ounce) package mushrooms
Cheddar and Monterey Jack
  cheeses, shredded

Season chicken breasts to taste. Brown on each side until just done. Combine and sauté onion, bell pepper, tomatoes, and mushrooms. Place breasts in oven-proof pan and add sautéed mushroom mixture. Top with cheeses. Put in warm oven until cheeses melt. Serve warm. Serves 5.

Hot Water Cornbread

. . . .

3 cups self-rising white cornmeal
3 eggs, beaten
Vegetable oil

Add enough boiling water to cornmeal to make it moist, not wet. Add eggs and blend until smooth. Spoon into hot 350° oil in a heavy skillet, and cook until golden brown on both sides. Serves 10.

Banana Blueberry Pie

1 (8-ounce) package cream cheese, softened

2 cups sugar

2 eggs

1 (16-ounce) package frozen Cool Whip topping, thawed

3 bananas, sliced, divided

2 graham crust pie shells

1 (21-ounce) can blueberry pie filling, divided

Extra Cool Whip for garnish

Blend together cream cheese, sugar, eggs, and Cool Whip. Slice ½ the bananas into each pie shell. Spread each pie with ½ the cheese mixture and ½ blueberry pie filling. Refrigerate until ready to serve. Top each pie with extra Cool Whip. Makes 2 pies.

Dominic's Italian Restaurant

1409 East 70th Street
Shreveport, LA 71105
(318) 797-2782

Dominic's of Natchitoches
805 Washington Street
Natchitoches, LA 71457
(318) 354-7767

Dominic Cordaro
Chef/Proprietor

Dominic Cordaro has worked for over forty years in the restaurant business. His father and mother Mr. and Mrs. Joseph B. Cordaro (deceased) raised eleven children. His mother was an excellent chef and he attributes his love for cooking to her. He also trained under the legendary chef and personality, Ernest Palmisano, Sr. Both of these people had an impact on his career by giving him a wide variety of culinary experiences and different avenues to explore in the food industry.

Chef Cordaro has also had the opportunity to serve such celebrities as Bill Clinton, Tom Landry, Tommy Lasorda, Terry Bradshaw, Archie and Eli Manning, Hal Sutton, David Toms, former Shreveport mayor Keith Hightower, Mr. and Mrs. John Manno, Sr., and various other state and local officials.

The Italian Salad

Our pride! From the beginning, this salad has been our signature. We have always felt that a salad of this nature should set the tone for a meal.

SALAD:

Iceberg, Boston, and romaine lettuce

Fresh basil, herbs, and spices

Cherry tomatoes

Chopped olives

Provolone cheese

Wedge of lemon

This particular salad starts out with three kinds of lettuce—iceberg, Boston, and romaine—blended with fresh basil, cherry tomatoes, herbs, and spices, and mixed with our Italian Salad Dressing. The salad is then topped with a variety of chopped olives and provolone cheese, and accented with a wedge of lemon.

ITALIAN SALAD DRESSING:

¼ cup pure virgin olive oil

2 tablespoons red wine vinegar

Hint of sugar

Squeeze of lemon

Chopped basil

Salt and pepper to taste

Mix and serve with Salad.

Mama Lou's Spingees
Italian Donuts

2 cups all-purpose flour

2 teaspoons baking powder

1 teaspoon salt

3 eggs

1 tablespoon sugar

Cinnamon to taste

1 cup milk

Vegetable oil for frying

Mix ingredients in large bowl until you have a semi-liquid batter. Pour vegetable oil in a deep skillet for frying the donuts. Heat oil until hot, but not boiling. Drop donut mixture by the spoonful into hot oil and cook until golden brown. Remove donuts from the oil. These donuts may be served with confectioners' sugar. Serve hot.

Angel Hair Pasta with Crawfish Tails

• •

1 pound angel hair pasta

¼ cup olive oil

1 pound peeled crawfish tails

1 medium tomato wedge

1 cup chopped fresh zucchini

1 cup chopped fresh yellow squash

1 tablespoon freshly minced garlic

Pinch of oregano

6 basil leaves

¼ cup chopped fresh parsley

Dash of lemon pepper

Squeeze of lemon juice

Romano cheese for topping

Cook pasta and set aside. Pour olive oil in a large skillet. Combine remaining ingredients, except lemon pepper and lemon juice, in skillet. Sauté for about 8 minutes. While sautéing, add lemon pepper and lemon juice. Stir ingredients gently. Put individual servings of pasta on plates and top with sauté mix. Sprinkle with Romano cheese. Serve hot. Makes 6 servings.

Enoch's Café and Pub

507 Louisville Avenue
Monroe, LA 71201
(318) 388-ENOC (3662)
www.enochsirishpub.com

Doyle and Yvette Jeter
Owners

An Irish Pub with a Louisiana Attitude

Enoch's was first established on St. Patrick's Day in 1980. Since then Enoch's has achieved legendary status in north Louisiana as a café, pub, and live music venue. Everyone from Jerry Jeff Walker and Leon Russell to Zachary Richard have played Enoch's many stages. The newest and grandest Enoch's, their fourth location, is very much the Irish pub. Visitors from County Mayo and Cork have exclaimed they feel right at home. The Guinness doesn't hurt! These days you may very well find a trio from Ireland or a Scottish piper filling the pub with Celtic sounds. Frequent musicians playing Enoch's include the Celtic Star, Beth Patterson, Sligo John Hennessey, or the Conly's Irish Band. We never forget our Louisiana roots, so be prepared to hear some Cajun, country, and rockabilly as well. Enoch's grill still turns out some of the best pub grub found anywhere, and they still offer a wide variety of vegetarian sandwiches. On special nights you will find a crowd enjoying big bowls of Irish stew, jambalaya, corned beef and cabbage, or gumbo. It depends on the mood and the music.

Enoch's Guinness Gravy

½ cup vegetable oil

1 small onion, chopped

½ small green bell pepper, chopped

1 (8-ounce) can mushrooms, drained, chopped

½ stalk celery, chopped

2 cups fresh beef stock

¼ cup shredded roast beef

⅓ cup chopped fresh parsley

1 bay leaf

Oregano

Basil

Powdered thyme

Garlic powder

Salt to taste

Black pepper to taste

Cayenne pepper

2 pints Guinness Irish Stout

½ cup brown sugar

½ cup roux

In a saucepot, heat oil and sauté onion, bell pepper, mushrooms, and celery until soft. Add beef stock and shredded roast beef. Add all herbs and spices to taste. (A pinch of each will do with a triple pinch of garlic powder). Add Guinness and brown sugar. Whisk all ingredients together and bring to a boil. Add roux, a small amount at a time, and whisk well. Simmer for 30 minutes. The gravy can be served on just about anything and can be used as a base for a great stew!

Fertitta's 6301 Restaurant

6301 Line Avenue
Shreveport, LA 71100
(318) 865-6301

Joe Fertitta
Owner

This four-star American restaurant serves good food and fine wines in an elegant atmosphere. Ferititta's has been awarded the Wine Spectator Award of Excellence.

Crab-Topped Portobello au Gratin

· ·

POMMERY CREAM SAUCE:

1 cup white wine

½ shallot, minced

1 cups heavy cream

1 tablespoon Creole grain mustard

1 teaspoon Old Bay Seasoning

Kosher salt as needed

In a medium-size saucepan, combine white wine and shallot. Bring to a boil and reduce by half. Whisk heavy cream into wine reduction and lower heat to medium high. Let the sauce reduce by half. Once it has reduced, it will be thick enough to coat a spoon. Remove from heat. At this point, whisk in mustard and Old Bay. Adjust seasoning with kosher salt. Chill the sauce until needed. Makes 2 cups.

MARINATED AND GRILLED PORTOBELLOS:

5 portobello mushrooms, stems removed

½ cup extra virgin olive oil

¼ cup balsamic vinegar

¼ cup lite soy sauce

2 cloves garlic, minced

Kosher salt to taste

Fresh-cracked black pepper to taste

Remove the stems of the portobellos with paring knife. Using a spoon, scrape away the undercarriage (dark brown fronds) from under the cap. In a small mixing bowl, whisk together the oil, vinegar, soy sauce, garlic, salt, and pepper. Set the cleaned portobellos in a medium-size pan. Pour the marinade over the mushrooms and coat evenly. Let marinate approximately 10 minutes. (Do not let the mushrooms marinate too long otherwise the flavor of the marinade will overpower the overall taste of the dish.) Once the mushrooms have marinated, grill over a medium-high flame. Grill on each side approximately 2 to 3 minutes or until a grill mark is made. Be careful not to over-

(continued)

(Crab-Topped Portobello au Gratin continued)

cook. (The final cooking process is completed once they are assembled.) Once grilled, set aside until they have cooled to room temperature.

CRAB MIXTURE:

2 pounds jumbo lump crabmeat

3 ounces Pommery Cream Sauce

5 marinated and grilled portobellos

5 slices baby Swiss cheese

1 bunch scallions, sliced

1 roasted pepper, peeled and julienned

½ cup shredded Parmesan cheese

Preheat oven to 400°. Using a medium-size mixing bowl, gently toss the jumbo lump crabmeat and Pommery Cream Sauce together. Set aside. Arrange the portobellos, cap side down, on a nonstick sheet pan. Evenly distribute the Crab Mixture onto the center of each cap. Place one slice of the Swiss cheese on top of each assembled portobello. Sprinkle the scallions and arrange the roasted peppers on top of the Swiss cheese. Evenly distribute the Parmesan on top of the portobellos. Bake approximately 25 minutes or until golden brown on top. Serve immediately. Makes 5 servings.

Chopped Salad

. . . .

SMOKED TOMATO DRESSING:

4 Roma tomatoes, halved and smoked

1 ounce pecan shells

6 ounces tomato purée

1 cup sour cream

1 cup mayonnaise

1 tablespoon minced garlic

3 dashes Worcestershire sauce

3 dashes Tabasco sauce

Kosher salt to taste

Fresh ground black pepper to taste

Cut tomatoes in half lengthwise and place in a range top smoker with pecan shells. Set smoker over a medium-high flame on a gas range. Smoke for approximately 10 minutes. Remove tomatoes from smoker and cool to room temperature.

In medium-size mixing bowl, combine all other ingredients and whisk together until thoroughly combined and creamy. Place cooled tomatoes in food processor and purée. Add smoked tomato purée to dressing mixture and whisk together. Adjust seasoning with salt and pepper. Refrigerate until needed.

SAUCE:

1 head Romaine lettuce, shaved

1 vine ripe tomato, small dice

½ red onion, small dice

2 hard-cooked eggs, chopped

5 pieces bacon, cooked and chopped

1 potato, julienned and fried, or 2 (4-ounce) cans shoestring potatoes for garnish

8 ounces Smoked Tomato Dressing

Combine all ingredients except potatoes in a medium mixing bowl. Gently toss until thoroughly combined. Shape the salad in a compact tower on chilled plates. Top each salad with potatoes for garnish. Serve immediately. Serves 5.

Note: If you do not have a range top smoker, replace the smoked Roma tomatoes with 1 cup ketchup and 2 dashes liquid smoke.

Lemon Crunch Pie

PIE CRUST:

1 cup sugar

1½ cups graham cracker crumbs

3 cups shredded coconut

1 cup all-purpose flour

1 cup butter, melted

Preheat oven to 325°. In a medium mixing bowl, combine all dry ingredients. Form a well in the center of the dry ingredients and pour the melted butter into it. Mix together until well combined. Use half of the crust mixture to line a nonstick 9-inch pie pan. Reserve remaining crust to top the pie.

LEMON FILLING:

3 (15-ounce) cans sweetened condensed milk

½ teaspoon lemon extract

1 cup fresh lemon juice

3 eggs, beaten

Whisk all ingredients together until well blended. Pour filling mixture into lined pie shell. Evenly distribute the remaining Pie Crust on top of the pie. Bake for 25 minutes, or until top is firm to the touch and toasted brown. Once the pie has baked, let cool on a baker's rack until it has reached room temperature; refrigerate overnight (or for 24 hours) to let it set. Serve with whipped cream and fresh raspberries. Makes 1 (9-inch) pie.

Follette Pottery

2401 S. Service Road West
Ruston, LA 71270
(318) 513-9121
www.follettepottery.com

Kent and Libby Follette

Owners

Follette Pottery is nestled in the wooded hills of north Louisiana where spring water flows from the ground and wildlife abounds. Libby and Kent Follette have been making pottery to cook in, serve in, and entertain with for more than thirty years. Their pottery makes life a celebration.

Included with each piece of pottery is one of their unique Louisiana recipes. The family recipes, representing the cuisine of north and south Louisiana are available in *The Follette Pottery Cookbook.*

Kent and Libby have been guest chefs from Santa Barbara, California to Cambridge Springs, Pennsylvania. The Follettes have been featured in *Southern Living* and *Louisiana Life* magazines and have appeared on QVC and on PBS's *A Taste of Louisiana.*

Follette Pottery can be found throughout the United States in the finest galleries and craft shops, but visiting the establishment is a real experience. Kent's fine Louisiana humor and Libby's warm southern charm make for a memorable visit.

Crawfish Dip

1 cup finely chopped onion

1 cup finely chopped celery

1 cup finely chopped bell pepper

1 jalapeño, finely chopped

½ cup finely chopped parsley

½ cup finely chopped green onions

¼ cup butter

½ pound crawfish tails, chopped

½ pound crawfish tails, whole

1 (10¾-ounce) can cream of mushroom soup

Salt and pepper to taste

Crackers or chips

Sauté chopped onion, celery, bell pepper, jalapeño pepper, parsley, and green onions in butter for 10 minutes. Add crawfish tails and soup. Cook 10 minutes, stirring frequently. Add salt and pepper to taste. Serve with crackers or chips in a Follette Pottery chip and dip set! Serves 12.

Spinach Laura

½ stick butter, melted

3 tablespoons flour

1 (10-ounce) package spinach, thawed

3 eggs, slightly beaten

½ pint cottage cheese

1 teaspoon Creole seasoning

½ cup feta cheese, crumbled

Mix melted butter and flour over low heat. Add all ingredients except feta cheese and mix thoroughly. Fold into greased Follette Pottery baking dish. Sprinkle cheese over entire mixture. Place in cool oven. Bake at 350° for 45 minutes. Makes 6 servings.

Catfish Almondine

4 large catfish fillets, or other suitable fish

½ cup all-purpose flour

1 teaspoon Creole seasoning

⅓ cup cooking oil

¼ cup butter

⅔ cup slivered almonds

Lemon slices

2 tablespoons chopped parsley

Rinse fish and pat dry. Grease 4 Follette Pottery individual fish bakers. Dredge fillets in flour. Sprinkle with Creole seasoning. Pan-fry in cooking oil until fish is golden brown and flaky. Place in fish baker and put in warm (225°) oven to keep warm while preparing almonds. Pour off remaining oil from skillet and melt butter in same skillet. Add almonds and sauté 2 to 3 minutes, until crunchy. Pour almonds over fillets; garnish with lemon slices and parsley. Makes 4 servings.

Dumb Bunnies Peach Cobbler

2 cups all-purpose flour

4 teaspoons baking powder

1 teaspoon salt

2 cups sugar

2 teaspoons vanilla

1½ cups famous Ruston peaches

2½ cups milk

1 (8-ounce) container nondairy whipped topping

1½ sticks butter, melted

Combine flour, baking powder, salt, sugar, vanilla, milk, and butter. Pour into greased Follette Pottery giant pie dish. Cover with peaches. Place in a cold oven and bake 45 minutes at 350°. Serve warm topped with nondairy topping. Makes 6 servings.

Gerald Savoie's

2400 East 70th Street
Shreveport, LA 71105
(318) 797-3010
www.geraldsavoie.com

Shreveport's Real Cajun Restaurant

Many years ago, Gerald Savoie opened a restaurant on East 70th Street in Shreveport. The surroundings have changed, the city of Shreveport grew up around it, but one thing has remained consistent—the Savoie family's delicious Cajun Cuisine and high standards.

The popularity of the Savoie's traditional Cajun recipes made it necessary to expand several times over the years . . . and today, Savoie's serves hundreds of people a day! Gerald built his reputation on attention to quality and by making customers feel at home. That family tradition continues today, making this a rare family owned and operated business for many years.

The restaurant is open seven days a week and offers patio dining. Catering is available.

Red Snapper à la Gerald

. . . .

1 (8-ounce) red snapper fillet per person

Red pepper, garlic powder, butter, and salt to taste

6 ounces jumbo lump crabmeat per person

Season the snapper with red pepper, garlic powder, and a little salt. (Too much salt will make the snapper chewy.) Cook snapper in an old iron skillet with real butter, seasoning prior to cooking. After flipping the snapper, place the crabmeat in the same skillet with the same seasoning and butter. Do not burn the butter. When the snapper is done (about 5 minutes), place the crabmeat on the snapper. Serve immediately.

The Glenwood Village Tearoom

3310 Line Avenue
Shreveport, LA 71104
(318) 868-3652

. . . .

Sharon Gale McCullar
Proprietress

Specialists in Victorian Tea Luncheons

Nestled in amidst fine English antiques and china, gourmet teas, and ladies accessories, The Glenwood Tearoom has been featured in *Southern Living* magazine, *Weekend Getaways* in Louisiana and Mississippi, and *Destinations* magazine. Tearoom specialties include a Victorian Era Shepherd's Pie with Nutmeg Potato Crust, Purée a la Frankfort Soup, Lemon Blueberry Scones, Sticky Toffee Pudding with Caramel Sauce, handmade Champagne Truffles, and Victoria's Trifle. Guests may choose traditional afternoon tea medleys or select from the à la carte luncheon menu.

Mandarin Chicken and Almond Tea Finger Sandwiches

¾ cup cooked and finely chopped chicken breast

½ cup canned Mandarin oranges, drained (reserve liquid)

¼ cup sliced, darkly toasted almonds

1 (3-ounce) package cream cheese, softened

¼ cup heavy cream

2 tablespoons reserved Mandarin juice

6 slices white sandwich bread, very thin

Combine chicken, Mandarin oranges, and almonds; set aside. With electric mixer, whip cream cheese until light and fluffy; add heavy cream and Mandarin juice. Continue beating until very light in texture. Fold in chicken mixture. To assemble sandwiches, spread ½ cup mixture on each of 3 slices of bread. Top with remaining bread. With electric knife, trim crusts and cut each sandwich into 4 triangles. Refrigerate, covered with damp paper towels, until ready to serve. Makes 12 tea sandwiches.

Hazelnut Scones with Lathering Cream and Lemon Honey

. . . .

2 cups all-purpose flour

2 teaspoons baking powder

¼ teaspoon salt

½ cup sugar

¼ cup unsalted butter

½ cup chopped hazelnuts

2 large eggs, lightly beaten

½ cup heavy cream

1½ tablespoons Frangelico liqueur

1 tablespoon sugar for garnish

18 whole hazelnuts for garnish

Preheat oven to 350°. Sift dry ingredients together in a bowl. Add butter and work into dry ingredients until crumbly. Stir in chopped hazelnuts. Combine eggs, cream, and liqueur; add to dry ingredients, stirring just until moistened. Roll dough to ¾ inch thick on a lightly floured surface. Cut with a 2½-inch daisy or heart shape cutter, and place on lightly greased baking sheets. Sprinkle tops generously with sugar and place a hazelnut in each center. Bake for 15 minutes. Serve with Hazelnut Lathering Cream and Lemon Honey. Makes 1 dozen scones.

LATHERING CREAM:

1 cup heavy cream

¼ cup powdered sugar, sifted

1 tablespoon Frangelico liqueur

½ to 1 teaspoon grated lemon rind

Beat cream at medium speed until foamy; gradually add powdered sugar, beating at high speed until stiff peaks form. Gently fold in liqueur and lemon rind. Makes 2 cups.

LEMON HONEY:

4 large eggs

2 egg yolks

2 cups sugar

1 tablespoon grated lemon rind

½ cup freshly squeezed lemon juice

¼ cup unsalted butter

Combine all ingredients except butter in double boiler; cook, stirring regularly, until as thick as honey. Add butter and allow to melt into lemon honey. Cool. Makes 2½ cups.

Jesse's Steak and Seafood

3942 Front Street
Winnsboro, LA 71295
(318) 435-9948

Nell Book
Owner

Jesse's Steak and Seafood offers a casual atmosphere featuring great steaks, succulent seafood, and legendary po-boys.

Pee Wee's Crawfish Casserole

1 (16-ounce) package spaghetti noodles

2 cups chopped green onions

4 cups chopped bell peppers

4 cups chopped celery

1 pound margarine

2 (49½-ounce) cans of mushroom soup

1 (#10-can) Cheddar cheese sauce

5 pounds crawfish tails

Boil noodles; drain. Sauté onions, bell peppers, and celery in margarine until tender. Add mushroom soup and cheese. Bring to a slow boil. Then add boiled noodles and crawfish. Season to taste. Put in large pan and bake for 15 minutes at 350°. Serves 25 to 30 people.

Bread Pudding

PUDDING:

2 loaves bread, white or honey wheat

6 cups milk

6 cups sugar

4 tablespoons vanilla flavoring

6 eggs

Cinnamon to taste (optional)

Preheat oven to 350°. Cover bread with milk. Mix the sugar, vanilla, eggs, and, if desired, cinnamon together with the milk and bread. Pour into a buttered 12x20-inch pan and bake 45 minutes (for golden brown crust).

SAUCE:

½ pound (2 sticks) butter

2 cups sugar

6 whole eggs, whipped

3 tablespoons amaretto or rum (optional)

In saucepan, combine butter and sugar until melted, stirring frequently. Remove from heat, stir in whipped eggs until mixture thickens. Add Amaretto or rum, if desired. Pour Sauce over baked Pudding. Serves 20 to 25 people.

Ms. Lucy's Classic Cajun

Culture and Cooking
17362 Zaunbrecher Road
Jones, LA 71250
(318) 823-2842

Lucy Henry
Zaunbrecher
Chef

Born in the southwest Louisiana town of Gueydan, Lucy grew up on her parent's rice farm. At a young age, Lucy's mother Mary Eloise Richard Henry taught her how to use the rice, poultry, beef, pork, vegetables, and seafood indigenous to Louisiana to create simple, yet delicious Cajun meals. In an effort to preserve her family's great recipes, Lucy compiled a cookbook called *Classic Cajun Culture and Cooking* in 1994. Her friends encouraged her to start selling the cookbook on local television and the result was a half-hour cooking show, *Ms. Lucy's Classic Cajun Culture and Cooking*. After two years on commercial TV, Lucy joined the Louisiana Public Broadcasting family of great cooks. The program was syndicated through the National Educational Telecommunications Association (NETA) to public television stations around the country.

Shrimp Casserole

1 pound peeled shrimp
¼ cup margarine
½ cup chopped onion
½ cup chopped green pepper
½ cup chopped celery
¼ cup margarine
1 (10¾-ounce) can cream of mushroom soup
½ (10¾-ounce) can Cheddar cheese soup
2½ cups cooked long-grain rice
½ cup chopped green onions

Preheat oven to 350°. Sauté shrimp in margarine. Sauté onion, green pepper, and celery in margarine. Add mushroom and Cheddar cheese soups, and shrimp; mix. Add rice and green onions. Mix thoroughly. Pour into 9x13-inch casserole pan that has been sprayed with vegetable spray. Bake for 30 to 40 minutes. Serve hot. Serves 8.

Note: Smoked sausage (½ pound), sliced thin, may be added to casserole before baking.

Crabmeat au Gratin

⅔ cup chopped onion
¼ cup chopped bell pepper
½ cup margarine or butter
3 tablespoons flour
1 (5-ounce) can evaporated milk
Salt and pepper to taste
3 cups lump crabmeat
¼ cup chopped or minced parsley
½ cup grated cheese
2 tablespoons paprika

Sauté onion and bell pepper in margarine or butter. Slowly stir in flour, stirring constantly. Slowly stir in evaporated milk, stirring constantly. Add salt and pepper to taste, crabmeat, and parsley. Pour into 6 individual foil crab shells or a casserole dish that has been sprayed with nonstick cooking spray. Sprinkle cheese and paprika over top of casserole. Bake until hot and bubbly, about 20 minutes. Serves 6.

Blueberry Pie

· ·

PIE CRUST:

1⅓ cups plain flour

½ teaspoon salt

½ cup all vegetable shortening

3 tablespoons cold water

½ cup pecan pieces

Preheat oven to 350°. Sift flour and salt. Add vegetable shortening and cut in with a pastry cutter or 2 knives for pea-size consistency. Add water. Work in together. Roll out on lightly floured pastry board and put in a 9-inch pie pan. Bake for about 10 minutes, then sprinkle pecan pieces over the bottom of crust and continue to bake until the crust turns golden brown. Cool completely before adding Filling.

FILLING:

1 (8-ounce) package cream cheese, softened

1 cup granulated sugar

1 (8-ounce) carton frozen Cool Whip, thawed

1 pint raw fresh blueberries

Cream together cream cheese and sugar. Add Cool Whip and mix well. Add blueberries and fold into cream cheese mixture. Pour mixture into baked pie shell and refrigerate overnight.

Note: Strawberries or peaches may be used as a substitute for the blueberries.

Olive Street Bistro

1027 Olive Street
Shreveport, LA 71101
(318) 221-4517

Giuseppe Brucia
Executive Chef/Proprietor

Giuseppe Basciano
Chef de Cuisine

Olive Street Bistro offers fresh Italian and Mediterranean food in a great atmosphere. From hand-tossed gourmet pizzas to homemade bread, this locally-owned restaurant provides dishes for the whole family to enjoy.

Carpaccio di Filetto di Bue Bistro

• •

10 ounces filet of beef

¼ lemon

Black pepper to taste

2 tablespoons shredded Parmigiano per person

BASIL SAUCE:

1 bunch basil

1 clove garlic

2 tablespoons pine nuts

Kosher salt to taste

2 tablespoons extra virgin olive oil

Pepper to taste

Place the beef in a freezer for 3 hours, or long enough to be lightly frozen.

Cut the uncooked meat into fine slices and arrange on 4 individual plates. Pour Basil Sauce, peppers, and lemon juice over the beef slices. Add Parmigiano to each plate. Serve with toast or country bread. Serves 4.

Wash the basil and allow to drain. Pat dry and chop in blender with the garlic, pine nuts, and kosher salt. Slowly add the oil to the blender until the mixture is creamy.

Insalata di Finocchi e Arance

2 large ripe oranges

2 fennel (anise) bulbs

Juice from ½ lemon

2 tablespoons honey

2 tablespoons Grand Marnier

1 tablespoon chopped tarragon

2 tablespoons chopped walnuts or pecans

3 tablespoons extra virgin olive oil

Kosher salt to taste

Black pepper

Peel oranges and remove all white pith from the flesh; save juice. Cut oranges into segments. Thinly slice fennel. Put in bowl with orange segments. Add all other ingredients and mix well. Put mixture in the refrigerator for 10 minutes. Serve in individual bowls.

Spaghetti à la Peppino

4 tablespoons water

8 anchovies

4 tablespoons extra virgin olive oil

4 garlic cloves, chopped

3 tablespoons chopped Italian parsley

1 jalapeño, chopped

6 tomatoes, blanched, skinned, diced, and deseeded

2 tablespoons capers

¾ cup pitted black olives

1 (16-ounce) package Italian spaghetti

Kosher salt to taste

Put water in small pot, add anchovies until dissolved on low heat, and sieve; set aside. In a skillet, sauté the oil, garlic, parsley, and jalapeño, and cook until light brown. Add tomatoes, capers, olives, and anchovies; simmer for 15 minutes. Cook spaghetti al dente in boiling, salted water; drain and add to skillet. Mix and serve.

Slayden's Bar-B-Q

1401 N. Washington
Bastrop, LA 71220
(318) 281-3926

Johnye Armistead
Owner

Established by Dan and Helen Slayden in 1962, Slayden's Bar-B-Q takes pride in being the oldest established family-owned restaurant in Morehouse Parish. Their menu is simple and distinctive. Everything is homemade with top quality products. Their barbeque is original and unusual. Their beans, potato salads, and pies are made from scratch.

Slayden's Coconut Cream Pie

16 ounces milk

3 egg yolks

⅓ cup sugar

1 teaspoon vanilla

3 tablespoons cornstarch

¼ cup butter

¾ cup flaked coconut

1 (10-inch) pie shell, baked

Heat milk. Beat egg yolks, sugar, vanilla, and cornstarch together. Add hot milk and butter and cook until thick. Add coconut and pour into pie shell.

MERINGUE:

3 egg whites

5 tablespoons sugar

Pinch of salt

¼ teaspoon cream of tartar

1 teaspoon cornstarch

Beat whites until foamy. Add sugar, salt, cream of tartar, and cornstarch. Continue to beat until stiff. Spread the Meringue over the pie and bake at 350° until brown.

Superior Grill

**6123 Line Avenue
Shreveport, LA 71106
(318) 869-3243**

**3636 St. Charles Avenue
New Orleans, LA 70115
(504) 899-4200**

**5435 Government Street
Baton Rouge, LA 70806
(225) 927-2022**

Superior Grill was founded in 1983 by Phil Barbaree and Robert Kirchoff in Shreveport. Since its opening, the Superior Grill name has become synonymous with fine Mexican dining. Travelers all across the country have enjoyed the great food and festive atmosphere at "The Grill." Superior has been voted by the locals in the Shreveport area as the best place to hang out and for the best margaritas in town. With different generations of customers moving out of town to different parts of Louisiana, it became important to The Grill to move forward, too. In 1991, the Baton Rouge location was opened, then in 1997, New Orleans came about. Now the great food of The Grill is available statewide!

Grilled Fish or Shrimp Tacos

TACO SAUCE:

½ cup mayonnaise
½ cup plain yogurt
½ red onion, chopped
¼ teaspoon white pepper
1 ounce Chardonnay wine
½ tablespoon minced garlic
½ teaspoon chicken base
¼ teaspoon horseradish
1 tablespoon Creole mustard

In a metal mixing bowl, add all ingredients; mix and refrigerate until needed.

PICO DE GALLO:

½ onion, diced
2 bell peppers, diced
3 fresh tomatoes, diced
1 jalapeño, diced
1 ounce olive oil
1 ounce chopped cilantro
1 ounce garlic powder
½ teaspoon black pepper
¼ teaspoon salt

Mix all ingredients in a large mixing bowl and refrigerate until needed.

SEAFOOD:

Tilapia or trout, or 26/30-count shrimp
Corn tortillas

Grill fresh fish fillets or shrimp, you should grill them using a lemon pepper sauce and a little butter. emove and place on tray. Take corn tortillas and heat on skillet for 10 seconds on each side, then form tortilla into taco shape in your hand. Ladle about 1 ounce of Taco Sauce in the bottom of each shell. Place 4 ounces of fish or grilled shrimp in the shell and cover with finely shredded lettuce and a little finely shredded red cabbage. Top with Pico de Gallo and serve.

Crawfish Enchiladas

1 jumbo yellow onion, diced

½ cup chopped fresh jalapeño peppers

1½ cups diced fresh tomatoes

2 ounces white Zinfandel

1 teaspoon ground cumin

1 teaspoon garlic powder

1 teaspoon ground black pepper

1½ pounds crawfish tails

1 package corn tortillas

Cheddar cheese

Sauté the onions and jalapeños in a saucepan until onions are transparent. Add the tomatoes, wine, seasoning, and crawfish and sauté for an additional 3 minutes. Remove from heat. Heat tortillas in an ungreased skillet for 10 seconds each. Take heated tortillas and spoon in 3 ounces of the crawfish mixture and roll. Place in a greased 9x13-inch oven pan. Top enchiladas with sauce. Cover with Cheddar cheese and heat in oven until cheese is melted. Serve hot.

Chicken Tortilla Soup

½ gallon water

1 (16-ounce) can whole peeled tomatoes

2 (8- to 10-ounce) skinless chicken breasts, uncooked

1 (16-ounce) can tomato juice

1 tablespoon black pepper

1 tablespoon cumin

1 tablespoon garlic powder

3 jalapeños, finely chopped

1½ ounces chicken base

1 potato, peeled and cubed

1 yellow squash, cubed

¼ head cabbage, chopped

⅓ cup rice

1 zucchini, cubed

4 ribs celery, chopped

1 carrot, chopped

1 onion, chopped

1 tablespoon garlic powder

In a large stockpot, combine water, tomatoes, chicken, tomato juice, spices, jalapeños, and chicken base. Bring to a boil, then add remaining ingredients; lower temperature to let simmer for 10 to 15 minutes. After it has simmered, use a potato masher to stir contents until all chicken has been broken up and spread throughout the soup. It is then ready to serve.

Uncle Earl's Pea Patch Café

109 Abel Street
Winnfield, LA 71483
(318) 628-3560
www.peapatchgallery.com

Gail Shelton
Owner

Laurie Malone
Chef

The Pea Patch Café is located inside the Pea Patch Art Gallery and Antique Mall in historic downtown Winnfield, the home of three of Louisiana's governors. Chef Laurie Malone specializes in southern cooking, including black-eyed peas and cornbread, a sure favorite of their hometown governor, Earl Long. It is his farm, the Pea Patch, that gives the unique business its name. They also serve sandwiches, salads, and desserts. Dine in for a delightful hometown atmosphere amidst beautiful antiques and artwork by owner Gail Shelton. They are open for lunch Monday through Friday from 11:00 a.m. to 2:00 p.m.

Black-Eyed Peas and Buttermilk Cornbread

4 cups dry peas

2 tablespoons salt

1 teaspoon garlic powder

1 teaspoon Tony Chachere's seasoning

½ teaspoon pepper

Rinse dry peas and place in crockpot; cover with water. Add seasonings and cook on HIGH 6 hours or LOW about 12 hours. These can also be cooked on the stove, boiling them for about 30 to 45 minutes, or until tender. Serves 8 to 10. The peas are high in fiber and low in fat. They are best served over rice, with Buttermilk Cornbread, and fresh coleslaw.

BUTTERMILK CORNBREAD:

2 tablespoons vegetable oil

1 cup white or yellow cornmeal

½ cup flour

2 tablespoons baking powder

1 teaspoon salt

½ teaspoon baking soda

1 egg

1 cup buttermilk

Preheat oven to 400°. Heat oil in baking pan or iron skillet in oven. Mix dry ingredients. Add egg and buttermilk. Pour in pan when hot; bake for 15 minutes.

Sawdust Pie

1½ cups sugar

1 cup buttermilk

1 teaspoon vanilla

½ teaspoon cinnamon

½ teaspoon nutmeg

3 eggs

3 tablespoons margarine, melted

3 tablespoons flour

1 graham cracker pie crust

Preheat oven to 350°. Mix all ingredients and pour into crust. Bake for 45 to 50 minutes. Serve with whipped cream and graham cracker crumb topping. Makes 1 pie.

The Village Restaurant

8334 Old Highway 171
Grand Cane, LA 71032
(318) 858-3368

Andrew and Kathryn
Bing
Owners

Andy and Kathryn's restaurant has been serving some of the best home-style cooking since November 1995. The restaurant is located in historic Grand Cane in Desoto Parish. They boast that they have the best fried catfish in Louisiana! Customers are greeted each morning with the savory smell of prime rib, Cajun gumbos, and ètouf-fée.

Lemon Meringue Pie

. . . .

1 (9-inch) pie shell, unbaked

1½ cups sugar

⅓ cup plus 1 tablespoon corn-starch

1½ cups water

3 egg yolks, slightly beaten

3 tablespoon margarine

½ cup lemon juice

2 drops yellow food color

Preheat to 400°. Bake pie shell; set aside to cool. Mix sugar and cornstarch in a medium saucepan. Gradually stir in water. Cook over medium heat, stirring constantly, until the mixture thickens and boils. Boil and stir for 1 minute. Gradually stir at least half the hot mixture into the egg yolks; blend into the hot mixture in the saucepan. Boil and stir for 1 minute. Remove from heat and stir in margarine, lemon juice, and food color. Immediately pour into pie shell. Heap the Meringue onto the hot pie filling and spread over the filling carefully sealing the meringue to the edge of the crust to prevent shrinking or weeping. Bake about 10 minutes or until golden brown. Makes 1 pie.

MERINGUE:

3 egg whites

¼ teaspoon cream of tartar

6 tablespoons sugar

½ teaspoon vanilla

Beat egg whites and cream of tartar until foamy. Beat in sugar, 1 tablespoon at a time, and continue beating until stiff and glossy. Do not underbeat! Beat in vanilla.

Pecan Pie

1 cup dark Karo syrup
1 tablespoon margarine
½ cup sugar
3 eggs
Pinch of salt
1 cup chopped pecans
1 teaspoon vanilla

Preheat oven to 400°. Heat syrup and margarine together over medium heat until margarine melts. Stir sugar and eggs together in bowl. Stir in salt. When margarine has melted, add syrup mixture to bowl. Stir in pecans and vanilla. Pour into unbaked pie shell. Place in oven for 10 minutes; then turn oven temperature down to 300° for 45 minutes. Makes 1 pie.

Fudge Pie

1 cup sugar
3 tablespoons cocoa
¼ cup margarine, melted
2 eggs
⅔ cup evaporated milk
1 tablespoon vanilla
1 (9-inch) pie shell, unbaked
Cool Whip topping

Preheat oven to 425°. Mix all of the ingredients except pie shell and Cool Whip with an electric mixer. Place mixture in shell and bake for 12 minutes, turn down to 350° and bake about 30 minutes more. Serve with Cool Whip topping. Makes 1 pie.

Waterfront Grill

5201 DeSiard
Monroe, LA 71203
(318) 345-0064
www.waterfrontgrill.com

Sam and Don Weems
Chefs/Proprietors

The Waterfront Grill overlooks the beautiful Bayou DeSiard. The restaurant opened in February 1997 to rave reviews! The popular restaurant features catfish, shrimp, oysters, beef, and chicken and all types of seafood—"none of it fried." Waterfront Grill was featured in *Southern Living* magazine in 2001. Don Weems was selected as 2002 Restaurateur of the Year by the Louisiana Restaurant Association!

Wine and Herb Baked Catfish with Wild Rice

⅓ cup diced garlic

2 cups butter, melted

½ cup white wine

½ cup olive oil

¼ cup oregano

¼ cup parsley flakes

2 tablespoons crushed red pepper

1 tablespoon salt

12 (3- to 5-ounce) catfish fillets

Tony Chachere's seasoning

1 (7-ounce) box Uncle Ben's long-grain wild rice, cooked according to directions

Preheat oven to 500°. Sauté garlic in melted butter. Add wine, olive oil, oregano, parsley flakes, red pepper, and salt. Lightly season catfish with Tony Chachere's seasoning. Bake in a baking dish for approximately 15 minutes, or until done. Whisk butter mixture until blended and pour over catfish and bake until mixture bubbles around edges. Serve over bed of wild rice. Spoon juice over the catfish and rice. Serves 8 to10.

Grilled Chicken and Tomato Basil Cream Sauce over Bowtie Pasta

1 (14-ounce) can crushed tomatoes

1 (14-ounce) can diced tomatoes

1 cup water

½ cup dried basil

⅓ cup oregano

Salt to taste

Crushed red pepper to taste

⅓ cup white wine

1 quart heavy whipping cream

⅓ cup diced garlic

⅓ cup butter

1 cup grated Parmesan cheese

6 boneless, skinless chicken breasts, grilled and diced

6 cups cooked bowtie pasta

Simmer tomatoes with water over low heat 1½ hours. While simmering, add basil, oregano, salt, red pepper, and white wine. Add heavy whipping cream and set over low heat. Roast garlic in skillet with butter for 1 to 2 minutes; do not let it brown. Add garlic to tomato sauce. Remove from heat. Add Parmesan cheese. Add layer of chicken over pasta. Top with sauce. Serves 6 to 8.

Glossary

aïoli ~ A garlic mayonnaise from France usually served with seafood.

al dente ~ An Italian phrase used to describe pasta or vegetables cooked just until firm, not soft or overdone.

ancho ~ A fairly mild red chile pepper.

andouille ~ A thick Acadian sausage of lean smoked pork, ranging from bland to very peppery.

anise ~ An herb that tastes like licorice. It is often used in pastries, cheeses, etc.

antipasto ~ An appetizer that is generally served before pasta.

appareil ~ A mixture of ingredients already prepared for use in a recipe.

Arborio rice ~ An Italian medium-grain rice that is used frequently for risotto.

arugula ~ A leafy salad herb that has an aromatic peppery flavor.

baguette ~ A long, thin loaf of French bread.

bain-marie ~ (Water bath) A technique where a container of food is placed over a large shallow pan of warm water to gently cook the food, without overcooking. Can be in an oven or on top of a range.

balsamic vinegar ~ A very fine, aged vinegar made in Modena, Italy, from white Trebbiano grape juice.

basil ~ An aromatic herb widely used in Mediterranean and Italian cooking.

basmati rice ~ A long-grain rice with a nutty flavor.

bay leaf ~ This aromatic herb comes from the evergreen bay laurel tree, native to the Mediterranean. Dried bay leaves are used frequently in poultry, fish, and meat dishes as well as stocks and soups.

béarnaise ~ One of the classic French sauces. It is made with emulsified egg yolks, butter, fresh herbs, and shallots. It is often served with meat, grilled fish, and vegetables.

béchamel ~ One of the basic French sauces. It is a sauce made from white roux, milk or cream, onions, and seasonings.

beignet ~ A French word for batter-dipped, fried fritters, usually sweet like a doughnut, and dusted with confectioners' sugar.

beurre blanc ~ A white butter sauce made from shallots, white wine vinegar, and white wine that has been reduced and thickened with heavy cream and unsalted butter.

beurre manié ~ A paste of flour and butter used to thicken sauces.

bisque ~ A thick, rich soup usually made from puréed seafood (oysters, shrimp, or lobster) and thickened with cream.

blanch ~ To plunge fruits and vegetables into boiling water briefly, then into cold water to stop the cooking process.

bon appétit ~ Literally, "good appetite" or "enjoy your meal."

boudin blanc ~ A peppery, pale-brown link of pork meat, liver, onions, and other seasonings. Rice is usually what binds the fillings of this richly seasoned sausage.

braise ~ The slow cooking of food in a tightly covered container with a flavoring liquid equal to about half the amount of the main ingredient.

Brie ~ A soft cows' milk cheese made in the French region of Brie.

brûlée ~ A French word for "burnt" and refers to a caramelized coating of sugar, such as a topping for crème brûlée.

brunoise ~ Vegetables that have been finely diced or shredded, then cooked slowly in butter.

bruschetta ~ Toasted bread slices rubbed with garlic and drizzled with extra virgin olive oil.

café au lait ~ Coffee and chicory blend with milk; usually a half-and-half mixture of hot coffee and hot milk.

Cajun ~ Slang for Acadians, the French-speaking people who migrated to south Louisiana from Nova Scotia in the 18th century. Cajuns were happily removed from city life, preferring a rustic life along the bayous. The term now applies to the people, the culture, and the cooking.

cannelloni ~ Large, round tubular-shaped pasta, typically stuffed then baked with a sauce.

caper ~ The pickled bud of a flowering caper plant. It is found on the Mediterranean coast. Capers are often used as a condiment in salads, in making tartar sauce, and as a seasoning in broiling fish.

capon ~ A castrated young male chicken, fed a fattening diet and brought to market before it is ten months old.

caramel ~ Sugar that has been cooked until it melts and becomes a golden brown color.

cardamom ~ A member of the ginger family. It has a spicy flavor and is used in Indian and Middle Eastern dishes.

caul fat ~ Considered superior, this thin fatty membrane that lines the abdominal cavity is usually taken from pigs or sheep, and resembles a lacy net.

cayenne pepper ~ Red chile pepper that is dried and ground fine for home use.

chaurice ~ A highly spiced pork or beef sausage used in Cajun cooking.

chervil ~ An herb belonging to the parsley family. It is best used fresh because of its delicate flavor.

chicory ~ An herb, the roots of which are dried, ground, and roasted and used to flavor coffee.

chiffonade ~ Leafy vegetables (such as spinach and lettuce) cut into thin strips.

Chinese five-spice powder ~ Used extensively in Chinese cooking, this pungent mixture of 5 ground spices usually consists of equal parts of cinnamon, cloves, fennel seed, star anise, and Szechuan peppercorns.

chipotle ~ A brownish-red chile pepper that has been dried and smoked and sometimes canned. This chile pepper has a smoky flavor and is very hot.

chives ~ A member of the onion family used in flavoring foods.

chutney ~ A sweet and/or sour seasoning that can be made from fruits and vegetables and flavored with many kinds of spices.

ciabatta ~ Italian bread named for its slipper shape.

cilantro ~ A fresh coriander leaf.

clarified butter ~ Butter that has been heated to remove the impurities.

clarify ~ To remove all impurities.

concassé ~ Any mixture that has been ground or coarsely chopped, such as a tomato concassé.

condiment ~ Any seasoning, spice, sauce, relish, etc., used to enhance food at the table.

consommé ~ A clear strained stock, usually clarified, made from poultry, fish, meat, or game and flavored with vegetables.

coriander ~ A member of the carrot family. Fresh coriander is also called cilantro. This herb is prized for its dried seeds and fresh leaves and is used in similar ways to parsley.

coulis ~ A thick sauce or purée made from cooked vegetables, fruits, etc.

court-bouillon ~ A rich, spicy soup, or stew, made with fish fillets, tomatoes, onions, and sometimes mixed vegetables.

couscous ~ Traditional couscous is generally made from coarsely ground semolina, a wheat flour used for pasta. It is popular in the Mediterranean areas of Morocco and Algeria. It is often served over vegetables or meats along with sauces.

crème brûlée ~ A custard made from eggs and covered with a "burnt" layer of sugar that has caramelized in the oven.

crème fraîche ~ Made from unpasteurized cream with an additive such as yogurt that gives it a distinctive flavor.

Creole ~ The word originally described those people of mixed French and Spanish blood who migrated from Europe or were born in southeast Louisiana. The term has expanded and now embraces a type of cuisine and a style of architecture.

crevette ~ The French word for "shrimp."

cumin ~ A spice from the seeds of the cumin plant. It is often used in making pickles, chutneys, and especially curries.

currant ~ A fruit used to make jams and jellies. It is also used as a glaze for meats. The red variety is widely used.

curry powder ~ A mixture of spices widely used in preparing and cooking meats and vegetables. It is often used in Indian cooking.

daikon ~ A large radish.

deglaze ~ A process of dissolving cooking juices left in a pan where meats or poultry have been cooked. This is achieved by adding liquids such as stock or wines to the sediment and then reducing it to half the volume. The sauce is then strained and seasoned.

demi-glace ~ A brown sauce boiled and reduced by half.

Dijon mustard ~ Mustard made from a white wine base.

dill ~ An herb used with vinegar to pickle cucumbers. It is also used to flavor foods.

dirty rice ~ Pan-fried, leftover cooked rice sautéed with green peppers, onions, celery, stock, liver, giblets, and many other ingredients.

dredge ~ To coat food with a dry ingredient such as bread crumbs, cornmeal, or flour.

Dungeness crab ~ A large rock crab found in the Pacific Northwest.

espagnole sauce ~ A rich, reduced brown stock containing herbs, tomato purée or fresh tomatoes, and a mixture of browned vegetables, all thickened by brown roux.

étouffée ~ A succulent Cajun dish made from a spicy roux and crawfish or shrimp along with vegetables (usually celery, bell peppers, and onions). Usually served over rice.

fagioli ~ The Italian word for "beans."

fais do-do ~ The name for a lively party where traditional Cajun dance is performed.

farfalle ~ Butterfly-shaped pasta.

fennel ~ A vegetable bulb or herb with a spicy flavor. It is often used in soups and salads.

feta cheese ~ A soft and crumbly goat's milk cheese often used in salads and Greek dishes.

filé powder ~ Sassafras leaves that have been dried and used in the final stages to thicken and flavor gumbo. Okra can also be used to thicken gumbo instead of filé powder.

filo; phyllo ~ A very thin dough that contains little fat and is used for strudel, baklava, and other pastries.

flan ~ An open custard tart made in a mold. Caramel cream custard is a popular flan dessert.

foie gras ~ The enlarged liver of a fattened or force-fed goose.

frais, fraîche ~ Fresh.

fraise ~ French for "strawberry."

free-range ~ Poultry or animals allowed to roam and feed without confinement, as opposed to commercially bred animals, which are caged.

fumet ~ Liquid that gives flavor and body to sauces and stocks. Fish fumet is used to poach fish fillets. It is made from dry white wine, fish stock, and bouquet garni.

garde manger ~ Pantry area where a cold buffet can be prepared.

garnish ~ A small amount of a flavorful, edible ingredient added as trimmings to complement the main dish and enhance its appearance.

ginger ~ A spice from a rhizome of a plant native to China. It is used fresh in Chinese cooking, but can also be used dried or ground.

glace ~ French for ice cream.

glaze ~ It is used as a coating to give a shiny appearance to roasts, poultry, custards, jams, and jellies.

lutinous rice ~ Sticky rice used by the Japanese to make sushi and rice cakes.

Gorgonzola ~ A strong Italian blue cheese.

gratons ~ The Acadian-French word for fatty pork skins fried in lard (also known as cracklings).

Glossary

grillades ~ Squares of braised beef or veal. Grillades and grits is a popular local breakfast.

guava ~ A sweet, fragrant tropical fruit. It makes delicious jellies.

gumbo ~ A Cajun or Creole soup thickened with okra or filé powder. Gumbo is an African word for "okra."

habanero ~ An extremely hot chile pepper, oval-shaped and smaller than the jalapeño. The color changes from green to orange and red upon ripening. It is used in stews and sauces.

haddock ~ Closely related to a cod but smaller and thin-skinned. It is excellent broiled in butter.

halibut ~ The largest member of the flounder family. It can be smoked, broiled, or grilled.

haricot vert ~ French for "green string beans."

herbs de Provence ~ A mixture of assorted dried herbs that commonly contains basil, fennel seed, lavender, marjoram, rosemary, sage, summer savory, and thyme.

Herbsaint ~ An anise-flavored liqueur that tastes like licorice.

hoisin sauce ~ A thick brown sauce made from soybeans, garlic, sugar, and salt that is used in Chinese cooking to flavor sauces and marinades.

hollandaise ~ One of the classic sauces in French cooking. It is made from an emulsion of hot clarified butter and eggs lightly heated until it begins to have the consistency of a smooth custard. It also contains lemons and shallots.

infuse ~ To soak spices, herbs, or vegetables in a liquid to extract their flavor.

jalapeño ~ A very hot green chile pepper generally used fresh, but also available canned.

jambalaya ~ A Cajun dish of rice, shrimp, crawfish, sausage, chicken, and beans, seasoned with Creole spices.

julienne ~ Vegetables cut into thin strips.

kalamata olive ~ Large, black Greek olive.

kale ~ A frilly, leafy vegetable of the cabbage family.

King Cake ~ A ring-shaped pastry decorated with colored sugar in the traditional Mardi Gras colors (purple, green, and gold) that represent justice, faith, and power. A small plastic baby is hidden inside the cake and the person who finds it must provide the next King Cake.

lagniappe ~ This word is Cajun for "something extra," like the extra doughnut in a baker's dozen. An unexpected nice surprise.

leek ~ A member of the onion family that is used in soups, casseroles, etc.

loganberry ~ Similar to a blackberry and raspberry, it can be served with cream as a dessert, a filling for tarts, or as a cream pudding.

mandoline ~ A tool used to cut vegetables evenly into thick or thin slices.

mango ~ A delicious, sweet tropical fruit often served alone as a dessert or used in cooking preserves and chutneys.

marinade ~ A liquid, including seasonings, to flavor and tenderize fish, meat, and poultry before cooking.

marinara ~ A tomato sauce flavored with herbs and garlic, usually served with pasta.

Merlot ~ A red-wine grape that produces a fruity flavor.

mesclun ~ A mixture of wild salad leaves and herbs. They are generally served with dressing containing walnut or olive oil and wine vinegar.

mirepoix ~ A mixture of cut vegetables—usually carrot, onion, celery, and sometimes ham or bacon—used to flavor sauces and as a bed on which to braise meat.

mirin ~ A sweet and syrupy Japanese rice wine used for cooking.

mirliton ~ A hard-shelled squash.

miso ~ A soybean paste.

Mornay Sauce ~ A classic French sauce; béchamel sauce to which egg yolks, cream, and cheese are added.

muffuletta ~ This huge sandwich is made up of thick layers of several different types of Italian meats and cheeses and a layer of olive salad. Served on special muffuletta bread.

oregano ~ Oregano is an herb very similar to marjoram but more pungent. It is widely used in Greek and Italian cooking.

orzo ~ Rice-shaped pasta.

panache ~ French to describe something mixed or multicolored such as salads, fruit, or ice cream.

panéed ~ Breaded and pan-fried.

pancetta ~ Italian bacon that is sometimes rolled into a solid round.

paprika ~ A variety of red bell pepper that has been dried and powdered and made into a cooking spice. It is used in making Hungarian goulash, etc.

penne ~ Tube-shaped pasta cut on the diagonal.

peperonata ~ An Italian dish of bell peppers, tomatoes, onions, and garlic cooked in olive oil. It can be served hot or cold.

pepperoncini; peperoncini ~ A hot red chile pepper served fresh or dried.

pepperoni ~ An Italian salami of pork and beef seasoned with hot red peppers.

phyllo ~ See filo.

picante sauce; piccante sauce ~ Hot spicy tomato-based sauce.

piccata ~ Veal scallop.

plantain ~ A tropical fruit similar to the banana.

po-boy ~ A type of sandwich that started out as an inexpensive meal. There are fried oyster po-boys, shrimp po-boys, and others. All are served on French bread.

poisson ~ French for "fish."

poivre ~ French for "pepper."

omodoro ~ Italian for "tomato."

orcini ~ Italian for "wild mushrooms."

portobello mushroom ~ A large cultivated field mushroom that has a firm texture and is ideal for grilling and as a meat substitute.

praline ~ A sweet candy patty. The main ingredients are sugar, water, and pecans.

prawn ~ A large shrimp.

prosciutto ~ Italian ham cured by salting and air drying.

purée ~ Food that is pounded, finely chopped, or processed through a blender or strained through a sieve to achieve a smooth consistency.

quiche ~ A custard-filled tart with a savory flavor.

radicchio ~ A reddish member of the chicory family used as a garnish or for salad.

ratatouille ~ A mixture of tomatoes, eggplants, zucchini, bell peppers, and onions cooked in olive oil. It can be served hot or cold.

red beans and rice ~ Red beans cooked in seasonings and spices and usually with chunks of sausage and ham—served over a bed of rice.

reduce ~ To boil down a liquid to thicken its consistency and concentrate its flavor.

relleno ~ The Spanish work for "stuffed."

rémoulade ~ One of the classic French sauces. It is made from mayonnaise seasoned with chopped eggs and gherkins, parsley, capers, tarragon, and shallots. It is served with shellfish, vegetables, and cold meats.

rice wine ~ Distilled from fermented rice.

ricotta ~ The Italian word meaning "recooked." It is a soft cheese made from whey and has a slight sweet taste.

rigatoni ~ Italian macaroni.

riso ~ Italian for "rice." A rice-shaped pasta; used to make risotto, an Italian rice dish.

risotto ~ An Italian arborio rice dish simmered slowly.

roghan josh ~ A spicy lamb dish from India, red in color and served with rice.

rosemary ~ A shrub with aromatic needle-like leaves. It is used fresh or dried as an herb, especially with lamb, pork, and veal.

rouille ~ A spicy red pepper and garlic mayonnaise.

roulade ~ French for a rolled slice of meat or piece of fish filled with a savory stuffing.

roux ~ A mixture of flour and fat (usually butter or shortening) cooked together slowly to form a thickening agent for sauces, gumbos, and other soups.

sec ~ French for "dry."

scaloppine, scaloppina ~ An Italian term for a thin scallop of meat. The meat is dredged in flour, then sautéed and served variously.

shallot ~ A sweet member of the onion family. It has a more delicate flavor than regular onions. It is used extensively in French cooking.

shiitake ~ A dark brown mushroom with a meaty flavor. It is available both fresh and dried. It was originally from Japan but is now cultivated in both America and Europe.

slurry ~ A thin paste of water and flour (or cornstarch), which is stirred into hot preparations (such as soups, stews, and sauces) as a thickener. After the slurry is added, the mixture should be stirred and cooked for several minutes in order for the flour to lose its raw taste.

sommelier ~ Wine steward.

sorrel ~ A leafy plant often used in salads, soups, omelets, purées, and sauces. It has a distinct lemon taste.

sweat ~ To cook in a little fat (in a covered pot) over very low heat, so that the food exudes some of its juice without browning: Used especially with vegetables.

tamari ~ Similar to but thicker than soy sauce, tamari is also a dark sauce made from soybeans.

tapenade ~ A thick paste made from capers, anchovies, ripe olives, olive oil, lemon juice, seasonings, and sometimes small pieces of tuna.

tartar sauce ~ A sauce made with mayonnaise, egg yolks, chopped onions, capers, and chives. It is often served with fish, meat, and poultry.

tasso ~ A highly seasoned Cajun sausage made from pork.

thyme ~ An herb with a pungent smell that belongs to the same family as mint. It is used in soups, stocks, casseroles, and stews.

timbale ~ Metal mold shaped like a drum.

tofu ~ A white Japanese bean curd made from minced soybeans boiled in water then strained and coagulated with sea water. It is soft and easily digested.

tomatillo ~ Mexican fruit related to the tomato. It is often used in salsa, salads, sauces, etc.

tournedo ~ A trimmed cut of beef or veal filet.

U10 or U12 jumbo shrimp ~ Ten or twelve shrimp to a pound.

veal ~ The meat of milk-fed baby calves.

vermicelli ~ A thin Italian pasta.

vinaigrette ~ A basic dressing of oil and vinegar with salt, pepper, herbs, and sometimes mustard.

white sauce ~ Béchamel or velouté sauce, both made from roux.

yuca ~ (Cassava) A root that ranges from six to twelve inches long and two to three inches in diameter. Peeled, grated white flesh can be used to make cassareep (a West Indian condiment found in Caribbean markets) and tapioca.

zabaglione ~ A rich Italian custard made of egg yolks beaten with Marsala wine and sugar until very thick.

zest ~ The outer skin of citrus where the important oils have accumulated.

Recipe Index

A

A French Cake 140

Abbeville Pork 216

Acadiana Creamy Crab Cakes 236

Alligator:

    Alligator Ragout with Chipotle Creole Tomato Sauce 96

    Bayou Stir-Fry 304

    Szechuan Spicy Alligator 135

Anchovies with Basil Bruschetta and Stewed Vidalia Onions, Marinated 70

Andouille-Crusted Fish with Cayenne Butter Sauce 80

Angel Hair Pasta with Crawfish Tails 318

Angels on Horseback 201

Appetizers:

    Angels on Horseback 201

    Crawfish Dip 327

    Greek Spread 224

    Korean BBQ Oysters 298

    Oysters Pujo 252

Apples:

    Apple Loaf 223

    Arugula Salad with Apples, Ricotta Salata, and Poppy Seeds 83

    English Apple Pie 225

Artichokes:

    Artichoke and Oyster Soup 214

    Crab Sardou 46

    Lafayette's Crawfish and Artichoke Bisque 229

    Veal Delmonico 180

Arugula Salad with Apples, Ricotta Salata, and Poppy Seeds 83

B

Bacon, Lettuce, and Tomato Soup 163

Bailey's Crawfish Cake with Jack Daniel's Corn Sauce 286

Baked Chicken and Rice 275

Baked Stuffed Red Snapper 261

Baklava – Steve Doucas' Original 244

Bananas:

    Banana Bliss 62

    Banana Blueberry Pie 315

    Banana Cream Pie with Caramel Drizzles and Chocolate Sauce 42

    Bananas Foster French Toast 168

    Mashed Sweet Potatoes with Bananas, Bourbon, and Vanilla 53

Barbecue:

    Barbequed Oyster Po-Boys 90

    Bar-B-Que Shrimp 210

    Korean BBQ Oysters 298

    Mr. B's New Orleans Barbequed Shrimp 74

    Ron's Bar-B-Que Shrimp 143

    Saffron Barbecue Sauce 120

Basil Purée 70

Bavarian Potato Soup 129

Bayou Pearls 149

Bayou Stir-Fry 304

Beef:

    Beef Stew Crockpot 274

    Cajun Rice Mix 268

    Carpaccio di Filetto di Bue Bistro 340

    Easy Beef Brisket 274

    Edgar's Cajun au Jus Beef 143

    Enoch's Guinness Gravy 320

    Filet Mignon au Poive 235

    House Filet 32

    Prime Beef Tenderloin 31

    Scaloppini di Vitello Alle Noci e More 312

    Steak Cubed with Mushrooms in Cabernet Wine Sauce 17

Veal Delmonico 180

Veal Marcelle 40

Veal New Orleans 309

Veal Primo 173

Beets with Goat Cheese and Walnuts, Grilled 71

Bell Peppers:

Cajun Frittata with Tomato Horseradish and Boiled Shrimp 104

Chicken and Andouille Smoked Sausage Gumbo 58

Crawfish and Andouille Stuffed Pork Loin with Hot Pepper Jelly Demi-Glace 131

Mr. B's Gumbo Ya Ya 73

Pee Wee's Crawfish Casserole 335

Roasted Red Pepper and Wild Mushroom Bisque with Crabmeat 194

Roasted Red Pepper Cream Soup 116

Shrimp and Andouille Pasta, The 169

Shrimp-Stuffed Bell Peppers 160

Smoked Pork Fettuccini 217

Stuffed Tomatoes with Crab and Corn Coulis 150

Vegetables in a Sweet Potato Cream with Pasta 61

Bisques:

Corn and Crabmeat Bisque 113

Corn Fest Bailey Bisque 283

Crawfish Bisque 201

Lafayette's Crawfish and Artichoke Bisque 229

Mirliton, Shrimp, and Crab Bisque 65

Roasted Red Pepper and Wild Mushroom Bisque with Crabmeat 194

Shrimp and Corn Bisque 241

Shrimp Bisque 56

Blackened Catfish 231

Black-Eyed Peas and Buttermilk Cornbread 349

Blueberries:

Banana Blueberry Pie 315

Blueberry Pie 338

Bon Ton Bread Pudding with Whiskey Sauce 18

Bon Ton Homemade Turtle Soup 14

Bon Ton Shrimp Rémoulade Salad 15

Bouillabaisse 103

Bread Pudding:

Bon Ton Bread Pudding with Whiskey Sauce 18

Bread Pudding 166, 227, 335

Bread Pudding with Bourbon Sauce 114

Bread Pudding with Jack Daniel's Sauce 249

Bread Pudding with Rum Sauce 146

Chocolate Bread Pudding 92, 256

Mr. B's Bread Pudding with Irish Whiskey Sauce 75

Praline Bread Pudding 171

White Chocolate Bread Pudding 77

White Chocolate Bread Pudding Soufflé 235

White Chocolate Bread Pudding with Frangelico Cream Sauce 206

Breads:

Apple Loaf 223

Buttermilk Cornbread 349

Crawfish Cornbread 219

Crespelle 199

Date Nut Bread 223

Hazelnut Scones with Lathering Cream and Lemon Honey 333

Hot Water Cornbread 314

Mama Lou's Spingees 317

Sweet Potato Muffins 233

Broccoli Soup, Kitty Kimball's 161

Brownies, Mocha 302

Cabbage:

Pot Stickers 133

Tuna Pasteur 94

Vegetables in a Sweet Potato Cream with Pasta 61

Cajun Frittata with Tomato Horseradish and Boiled Shrimp 104

Cajun Hot Bites 215

Cajun Rice Mix 268

Cakes:

Cheesecake 221

Recipe Index

Cream Cheese Cake 123
French Cake, A 140
Gateau Sirop 187
Holiday Pumpkin Cheesecake 264
Carpaccio di Filetto di Bue Bistro 340
Catfish:
Blackened Catfish 231
Catfish Almondine 328
Miss Mayme's Seafood Gumbo 291
Sweet Potato Catfish with Andouille Cream
Drizzle 91
Cedar Plank Fish with Citrus Horseradish Crust 38
Cheese:
Cheese Salad with Basil Olive Vinaigrette 287
Cheesy Chicken and Spaghetti 301
Chef Floyd Clavelle's Snapper and Garlic
Cream Sauce 263
Cream of Brie Cheese with Lump Crabmeat
Soup 158
Creole Cream Cheese 78
Creole Onion Soup 34
Dakota's Lump Crabmeat and Brie Soup 119
Cheesecakes:
Cheesecake 221
Crabmeat Cheesecake with Pecan Crust 78
Cream Cheese Cake 123
Holiday Pumpkin Cheesecake 264
Shrimp and Crabmeat Cheesecake 22
Chef Floyd Clavelle's Snapper and Garlic Cream
Sauce 263
Chef Hans' Crawfish in Heaven 307
Chef Hans' Shrimp Rémoulade 308
Chef Roy's Frog Wellington 192
Chef Tory's Seared Redfish and Chili Glazed
Shrimp Salad 29
Chicken:
Baked Chicken and Rice 275
Bayou Stir-Fry 304

Cajun Hot Bites 215
Cheesy Chicken and Spaghetti 301
Chicken and Andouille Gumbo 169
Chicken and Andouille Smoked Sausage
Gumbo 58
Chicken and Sausage Gumbo 247
Chicken Braciuolini 238
Chicken Clemençeau 36
Chicken Clemençeau with Brabant Potatoes
48
Chicken Tortilla Soup 347
Grilled Chicken and Tomato Basil Cream
Sauce over Bowtie Pasta 355
Mandarin Chicken and Almond Tea Finger
Sandwiches 332
Miss Mayme's Seafood Gumbo 291
Mr. B's Gumbo Ya Ya 73
Southern Pecan Chicken Champignon 211
Southwest Chicken Breast 314
Chilled Champagne-Strawberry Soup with Mint
Ice Cream 85
Chocolate:
Chocolate Bread Pudding 92, 256
Chocolate Pecan Pie 220
Chocolate Sauce 44
Ile Flottante au Chocolate et au Rhum 126
Mocha Brownies 302
Orange Chocolate Crème Brûlée 151
White Chocolate Bread Pudding 77
White Chocolate Bread Pudding with
Frangelico Cream Sauce 206
White Chocolate Bread Pudding Soufflé 235
White Chocolate/Macadamia Crème Brûlée
299
Chopped Salad 324
Classic Crème Brûlée 68
Cobblers:
Dumb Bunnies Peach Cobbler 328

Peach Cobbler 123

Warm Strawberry Cobbler with Vanilla Ice Cream 99

Corn:

Alligator Ragout with Chipotle Creole Tomato Sauce 96

Corn and Crabmeat Bisque 113

Corn Fest Bailey Bisque 283

Corn Salad 281

Crawfish, Corn, and Potato Chowder 179

Crawfish Cornbread 219

Roasted Corn and Poblano Chowder 272

Shrimp and Corn Bisque 241

Stuffed Tomatoes with Crab and Corn Coulis 150

Cornbread:

Buttermilk Cornbread 349

Cornbread Dressing – Louisiana Style 124

Crawfish Cornbread 219

Hot Water Cornbread 314

Crab:

Acadiana Creamy Crab Cakes 236

Bayou Pearls 149

Corn and Crabmeat Bisque 113

Corn Fest Bailey Bisque 283

Crab Sardou 46

Crabmeat à la Landry 203

Crabmeat au Gratin 144, 337

Crabmeat Broussard 20

Crabmeat Cheesecake with Pecan Crust 78

Crabmeat Imperial 15

Crab-Topped Portobello au Gratin 322

Cream of Brie Cheese with Lump Crabmeat Soup 158

Dakota's Lump Crabmeat and Brie Soup 119

Eggs New Orleans 36

Fried Green Tomatoes with Crabmeat Rémoulade 197

Gnocchi with Crab and Truffle 100

Joe's Stuffed Eggplant 147

Louisiana Crab Cakes 67

Mirliton, Shrimp, and Crab Bisque 65

Miss Mayme's Seafood Gumbo 291

Mustard and Cornmeal-Crusted Salmon with Lump Crabmeat and Lemon Butter 157

Pan-Fried Louisiana Soft-Shell Crab, Sautéed Crawfish Tails, and Meunière Sauce 27

Pan-Grilled Grouper with a Crabmeat and Curry Coconut Cream Sauce 184

Ralph and Kacoo's Seafood Gumbo 176

Ralph and Kacoo's Stuffed Crabs 177

Red Snapper à la Gerald 330

Roasted Red Pepper and Wild Mushroom Bisque with Crabmeat 194

Seafood au Gratin 212

Seafood Gumbo 289

Shrimp and Crabmeat Cheesecake 22

Snapper Pontchartrain 293

Soft-Shell Crab Dorè 21

Soup Jacqueline 153

Spaghetti Fruitte de Mare 198

Stuffed Portobello Mushrooms 174

Stuffed Tomatoes with Crab and Corn Coulis 150

Very Best Seafood Gumbo, The 284

Crawfish:

Angel Hair Pasta with Crawfish Tails 318

Bailey's Crawfish Cake with Jack Daniel's Corn Sauce 286

Chef Hans' Crawfish in Heaven 307

Crawfish and Andouille Stuffed Pork Loin with Hot Pepper Jelly Demi-Glace 131

Crawfish, Corn, and Potato Chowder 179

Crawfish Bisque 201

Crawfish Cardinal 309

Crawfish Casserole 227

Crawfish Chowder 301

Crawfish Cornbread 219

Crawfish Dip 327

Crawfish Enchiladas 346

Crawfish Étouffée 231, 250, 254, 277

Crawfish Fettuccini 203

Crawfish with Spicy Lobster Sauce 136

Creamy Cajun Crawfish and Tasso Sauce 208

Recipe Index

Fried Eggplant with Crawfish Monica Sauce 170

Hallelujah Crab 149

Lafayette's Crawfish and Artichoke Bisque 229

Pee Wee's Crawfish Casserole 335

Sautéed Crawfish Tails 27

Seafood au Gratin 212

Seafood Gumbo 289

Snapper Pontchartrain 293

Spaghetti Fruitte di Mare 198

Stuffed Mushrooms with Crawfish 153

Tunk's Crawfish Étouffée 292

Very Best Seafood Gumbo, The 284

Cream Cheese Cake 123

Cream of Brie Cheese with Lump Crabmeat Soup 158

Creamy Cajun Crawfish and Tasso Sauce 208

Crème Brûlée:

Classic Crème Brûlée 68

Orange Chocolate Crème Brûlée 151

Passion Fruit Crème Brûleé 95

White Chocolate/Macadamia Crème Brûlée 299

Creole Onion Soup 34

Creole Tomato, Cucumber, and Vidalia Onion Salad 51

Crêpes Broussard 23

Crespelle 199

Dakota's Lump Crabmeat and Brie Soup 119

Date Nut Bread 223

Desserts:

Baklava – Steve Doucas' Original 244

Banana Bliss 62

Banana Blueberry Pie 315

Banana Cream Pie with Caramel Drizzles and Chocolate Sauce 42

Blueberry Pie 338

Bon Ton Bread Pudding with Whiskey Sauce 18

Bread Pudding 166, 227, 335

Bread Pudding with Bourbon Sauce 114

Bread Pudding with Jack Daniel's Sauce 249

Bread Pudding with Rum Sauce 146

Cheesecake 221

Chilled Champagne-Strawberry Soup with Mint Ice Cream 85

Chocolate Bread Pudding 92, 256

Chocolate Pecan Pie 220

Classic Crème Brûlée 68

Cream Cheese Cake 123

Crêpes Broussard 23

Dumb Bunnies Peach Cobbler 328

English Apple Pie 225

Flaming Almonds Amaretto for Two 180

French Cake, A 140

Fresh Berry Pie 294

Fudge Pie 352

Gateau Sirop 187

Ile Flottante au Chocolate et au Rhum 126

Lemon Crunch Pie 325

Lemon Ice Box Pie 26

Lemon Meringue Pie 351

Mama Lou's Spingees 317

Mocha Brownies 302

Mr. B's Bread Pudding with Irish Whiskey Sauce 75

Mrs. Carmen's Lemon Meringue Pie 287

Orange Chocolate Crème Brûlée 151

Passion Fruit Crème Brûleé 95

Peach Cobbler 123

Pecan Pie 352

Pineapple Sherbet 140

Praline Bread Pudding 171

Sabayon Glacé 155

Sawdust Pie 349

Slayden's Coconut Cream Pie 343

Strawberry Pie 123

Sweet Potato Pie 280

Warm Strawberry Cobbler with Vanilla Ice Cream 99

White Chocolate Bread Pudding 77

White Chocolate Bread Pudding Soufflé 235

White Chocolate Bread Pudding with Frangelico Cream Sauce 206

White Chocolate/Macadamia Crème Brûlée 299

Dressing – Louisiana Style, Cornbread 124

Duck Confit Wild Mushroom Potato Hash 105

Dumb Bunnies Peach Cobbler 328

Easy Beef Brisket 274

Edgar's Cajun au Jus Beef 143

Eggplant:

Eggplant Dupuy 205

Fried Eggplant with Crawfish Monica Sauce 170

Grilled Eggplant, Tomato, Fresh Mozzarella, Portobello Mushrooms, and Fresh Basil Salad 240

Joe's Stuffed Eggplant 147

Eggs:

Cajun Frittata with Tomato Horseradish and Boiled Shrimp 104

Classic Crème Brûlée 68

Egg Soufflé 233

Eggs New Orleans 36

Orange Chocolate Crème Brûlée 151

Passion Fruit Crème Brûleé 95

White Chocolate/Macadamia Crème Brûlée 299

Enchiladas, Crawfish 346

English Apple Pie 225

Enoch's Guinness Gravy 320

Escargot Casserole 127

Étouffée, Crawfish 231, 250, 254, 277

Étouffée, Tunk's Crawfish 292

Fettuccine con Tartufi Nero 88

Filet Mignon au Poive 235

Fish:

Andouille-Crusted Fish with Cayenne Butter Sauce 81

Baked Stuffed Red Snapper 261

Blackened Catfish 231

Catfish Almondine 328

Cedar Plank Fish with Citrus Horseradish Crust 38

Chef Floyd Clavelle's Snapper and Garlic Cream Sauce 263

Chef Tory's Seared Redfish and Chili Glazed Shrimp Salad 29

Grilled Fish or Shrimp Tacos 345

Horseradish Crusted Drum 52

J.E.'s Salmon Confit 305

Miss Mayme's Seafood Gumbo 291

Mustard and Cornmeal-Crusted Salmon with Lump Crabmeat and Lemon Butter 157

Pan-Grilled Grouper with a Crabmeat and Curry Coconut Cream Sauce 184

Pan-Roasted Seafood Bouillabaisse with a Tomato-Saffron Broth and Garlic Creamed Potatoes 103

Pompano Napoleon 24

Red Snapper à la Gerald 330

Red Snapper with Roasted Garlic and Tomato Provençal 117

Redfish Pontchartrain 271

Seared Wild Striped Bass, Potato Porcini, Risotto Fried Leeks, Tomato, Cognac Fumé 102

Sesame Crusted Yellow-Fin with Asian Vinaigrette 121

Snapper Pontchartrain 293

Sweet Potato Catfish with Andouille Cream Drizzle 91

Tuna au Poivre 195

Tuna Pasteur 94

Wine and Herb Baked Catfish with Wild Rice 354

Recipe Index

Flaming Almonds Amaretto for Two 180

Francese 198

French Bread:

    Bananas Foster French Toast 168

    Bon Ton Bread Pudding 18

    Bread Pudding 227

    Bread Pudding with Bourbon Sauce 114

    Bread Pudding with Rum Sauce 146

    Chocolate Bread Pudding 256

    Louisiana Crab Cakes 67

    Mr. B's Bread Pudding with Irish Whiskey Sauce 75

    Praline Bread Pudding 171

    White Chocolate Bread Pudding 77

    White Chocolate Bread Pudding Soufflé 235

French Toast, Bananas Foster 168

Fresh Berry Pie 294

Fresh Ricotta and Maine Lobster Ravioli 108

Fried Eggplant with Crawfish Monica Sauce 170

Fried Green Tomatoes with Crabmeat Rémoulade 197

Frog Wellington, Chef Roy's 192

Fruit:

    Apple Loaf 223

    Banana Bliss 62

    Banana Blueberry Pie 315

    Banana Cream Pie with Caramel Drizzles and Chocolate Sauce 42

    Bananas Foster French Toast 168

    Blueberry Pie 338

    Chilled Champagne-Strawberry Soup with Mint Ice Cream 85

    Crêpes Broussard 23

    Date Nut Bread 223

    Dumb Bunnies Peach Cobbler 328

    English Apple Pie 225

    Fresh Berry Pie 294

    Insalata di Finocchi e Arance 341

Lemon Crunch Pie 325

Lemon Ice Box Pie 26

Lemon Meringue Pie 351

Mango Lime Vinaigrette 63

Mashed Sweet Potatoes with Bananas, Bourbon, and Vanilla 53

Mrs. Carmen's Lemon Meringue Pie 287

Passion Fruit Crème Brûleé 95

Peach Cobbler 123

Peach Marmalade 224

Peach or Kumquat Sauce 220

Pineapple Sherbet 140

Sabayon Glacé 155

Strawberry Pie 123

Warm Strawberry Cobbler with Vanilla Ice Cream 99

Fudge Pie 352

G

Ganache, White Chocolate 155

Garam Masala (Mixture of Ground Spices) 107

Garlic Beurre Blanc Sauce 269

Gateau Sirop 187

German Potato Salad 129

Gnocchi with Crab and Truffle 100

Gravy, Enoch's Guinness 320

Greek Spread 224

Green Chile Grits 55

Green Shrimp Salad 283

Grilled Beets with Goat's Cheese and Walnuts 71

Grilled Chicken and Tomato Basil Cream Sauce over Bowtie Pasta 355

Grilled Eggplant, Tomato, Fresh Mozzarella, Portobello Mushrooms, and Fresh Basil Salad 240

Grilled Fish or Shrimp Tacos 345

Grits, Green Chile 55

Gumbo:
    Chicken and Andouille Gumbo 169
    Chicken and Andouille Smoked Sausage
        Gumbo 58
    Chicken and Sausage Gumbo 247
    Miss Mayme's Seafood Gumbo 291
    Mr. B's Gumbo Ya Ya 73
    Ralph and Kacoo's Seafood Gumbo 176
    Seafood Gumbo 247, 289
    Very Best Seafood Gumbo, The 284

Hallelujah Crab 149
Hazelnut Scones with Lathering Cream and
    Lemon Honey 333
Holiday Pumpkin Cheesecake 264
Horseradish Crusted Drum 52
Hot and Sour Soup 134
Hot Water Cornbread 314
House Filet 32

I

Ile Flottante au Chocolate et au Rhum 126
Insalata di Finocchi e Arance 341
Italian Salad, The 317

J

J.E.'s Salmon Confit 305
JJ's Meaux Jeaux Pork Medallions 165
Joe's Stuffed Eggplant 147
Johnny Jambalaya's Beat the "Summertime
    Blues" Pasta Salad 163

K

Kim Chee Cabbage 94
Kitty Kimball's Broccoli Soup 161
Korean BBQ Oysters 298

L

Lafayette's Crawfish and Artichoke Bisque 229
Lasyone's Red Beans and Sausage 278
Lemon Grass Soup 259

Lemons:
    Lemon Crunch Pie 325
    Lemon Ice Box Pie 26
    Lemon Meringue Pie 351
    Mrs. Carmen's Lemon Meringue Pie 287
Lobster Ravioli, Fresh Ricotta and Maine 108
Louisiana Crab Cakes 67

M

Mama Lou's Spingees 317
Mandarin Chicken and Almond Tea Finger
    Sandwiches 332
Mandy's Cheese-Stuffed Mushrooms 164
Mango Lime Vinaigrette 63
Marinated Anchovies with Basil Bruschetta and
    Stewed Vidalia Onions 70
Mashed Sweet Potatoes with Bananas, Bourbon,
    and Vanilla 53
Meringue 227, 343, 351
Mirliton, Shrimp, and Crab Bisque 65
Miss Mayme's Seafood Gumbo 291
Mocha Brownies 302
Mr. B's Bread Pudding with Irish Whiskey Sauce
    75
Mr. B's Gumbo Ya Ya 73
Mr. B's New Orleans Barbequed Shrimp 74
Mrs. Carmen's Lemon Meringue Pie 287
Muffins, Sweet Potato 233
Mushrooms:
    Chicken Clemençeau with Brabant Potatoes
        48
    Crab-Topped Portobello au Gratin 322
    Duck Confit Wild Mushroom Potato Hash 105
    Mandy's Cheese-Stuffed Mushrooms 164
    Marinated and Grilled Portobellos 322
    Meunière Sauce with Mushrooms 79
    Pasta Primavera 60
    Roasted Red Pepper and Wild Mushroom
        Bisque with Crabmeat 194
    Steak Cubed with Mushrooms in Cabernet
        Wine Sauce 17
    Stuffed Mushrooms with Crawfish 153
    Stuffed Portobello Mushrooms 174

Tempura Cèpe 98

Veal Marcelle 40

Mustard and Cornmeal-Crusted Salmon with Lump Crabmeat and Lemon Butter 157

My Good Friend Bob's Tomato Curry Purée with Cumin Grilled Shrimp 107

New Potatoes with Cream Sauce 281

Onions:

Creole Onion Soup 34

Creole Tomato, Cucumber, and Vidalia Onion Salad 51

Marinated Anchovies with Basil Bruschetta and Stewed Vidalia Onions 70

Potato, Leek and Onion Soup 269

Orange Chocolate Crème Brûlée 151

Oysters:

Angels on Horseback 201

Artichoke and Oyster Soup 214

Barbequed Oyster Po-Boys 90

Korean BBQ Oysters 298

Oyster Stew 141

Oysters Alvin with Bouillon Rice 16

Oysters Pujo 252

Poached Oysters in a Saffron-Tomato Coulis 84

Potato and Parmesan Crusted Oysters with Saffron Barbecue Sauce 120

Ralph and Kacoo's Seafood Gumbo 176

Seafood Gumbo 247, 284

Wild Rice Pilaf with Oysters and Shrimp Creole 310

Pad Thai 258

Pan-Fried Louisiana Soft-Shell Crab, Sautéed Crawfish Tails, and Meunière Sauce 27

Pan-Grilled Grouper with a Crabmeat and Curry Coconut Cream Sauce 184

Pan-Roasted Seafood Bouillabaisse with a Tomato-Saffron Broth and Garlic Creamed Potatoes 103

Parsnips, Crispy Fried 53

Passion Fruit Crème Brûleé 95

Pasta:

Angel Hair Pasta with Crawfish Tails 318

Bayou Pearls 149

Cheesy Chicken and Spaghetti 301

Crawfish Fettuccini 203

Fettuccine con Tartufi Nero 88

Fresh Ricotta and Maine Lobster Ravioli 108

Grilled Chicken and Tomato Basil Cream Sauce over Bowtie Pasta 355

Johnny Jambalaya's Beat the "Summertime Blues" Pasta Salad 163

Pasta Primavera 60

Pee Wee's Crawfish Casserole 335

Prime Beef Tenderloin 31

Shrimp and Andouille Pasta, The 169

Shrimp and Tasso Pasta 229

Shrimp Saint Charles 190

Smoked Pork Fettuccini 217

Spaghetti à la Peppino 341

Spaghetti Fruitte di Mare 198

Vegetables in a Sweet Potato Cream with Pasta 61

Peaches:

Dumb Bunnies Peach Cobbler 328

Peach Cobbler 123

Peach Marmalade 224

Peach or Kumquat Sauce 220

Pecans:

Baklava – Steve Doucas' Original 244

Chocolate Pecan Pie 220
Pecan Butter 211
Pecan Crust 78
Pecan Filling 244
Pecan Mixture 23
Pecan Pie 352
Southern Pecan Chicken Champignon 211
Spiced Pecans 304
Pee Wee's Crawfish Casserole 335

Pies:
Banana Blueberry Pie 315
Banana Cream Pie with Caramel Drizzles and
    Chocolate Sauce 42
Blueberry Pie 338
Chocolate Pecan Pie 220
Dumb Bunnies Peach Cobbler 328
English Apple Pie 225
Fresh Berry Pie 294
Fudge Pie 352
Lemon Crunch Pie 325
Lemon Ice Box Pie 26
Lemon Meringue Pie 351
Mrs. Carmen's Lemon Meringue Pie 287
Peach Cobbler 123
Pecan Pie 352
Sawdust Pie 349
Slayden's Coconut Cream Pie 343
Strawberry Pie 123
Sweet Potato Pie 280
Warm Strawberry Cobbler with Vanilla Ice
    Cream 99
Pineapple Sherbet 140
Poached Oysters in a Saffron-Tomato Coulis 84
Po-Boys, Barbequed Oyster 90
Pompano Napoleon 24
Pork: *see also* Sausage
Abbeville Pork 216
Crawfish and Andouille Stuffed Pork Loin with
    Hot Pepper Jelly Demi-Glace 131
JJ's Meaux Jeaux Pork Medallions 165
Pork Chops and Potato Bake 275

Rosemary and Garlic Marinated Pork
    Tenderloin 87
Smoked Pork Fettuccini 217
Pot Stickers 133
Potatoes:
Bavarian Potato Soup 129
Beef Stew Crockpot 274
Chicken Clemençeau with Brabant Potatoes
    48
Crawfish, Corn, and Potato Chowder 179
Garlic Mashed Potatoes 88
German Potato Salad 129
Gnocchi with Crab and Truffle 100
New Potatoes with Cream Sauce 281
Pontalba Potatoes 33
Pork Chops and Potato Bake 275
Potato, Leek, and Onion Soup 269
Potato and Parmesan Crusted Oysters with
    Saffron Barbecue Sauce 120
Roasted Corn and Poblano Chowder 272
Seared Wild Striped Bass, Potato Porcini,
    Risotto Fried Leeks, Tomato, Cognac
    Fumé 102
Traditional Potato Salad 59
Truffled Potato Sauce 52
Praline Bread Pudding 171
Praline Yams 219
Prime Beef Tenderloin 31
Pumpkin Cheesecake, Holiday 264

Rabbit à la Creole 126
Ralph and Kacoo's Seafood Gumbo 176
Ralph and Kacoo's Stuffed Crabs 177
Red Beans and Sausage, Lasyone's 278
Red Curry 259
Red Snapper:
Baked Stuffed Red Snapper 261
Chef Floyd Clavelle's Snapper and Garlic
    Cream Sauce 263
Red Snapper à la Gerald 330
Red Snapper with Roasted Garlic and Tomato
    Provençal 117

Recipe Index

Redfish Pontchartrain 271

Rémoulade, Shrimp 49, 308

Rémoulade Sauce 147

Rice:

    Baked Chicken and Rice 275

    Bayou Stir-Fry 304

    Bouillon Rice 16

    Cajun Rice Mix 268

    Crawfish Casserole 227

    Lasyone's Red Beans and Sausage 278

    Shrimp Casserole 337

    Wild Rice Pilaf with Oysters and Shrimp Creole 310

    Wine and Herb Baked Catfish with Wild Rice 354

Roasted Corn and Poblano Chowder 272

Roasted Red Pepper and Wild Mushroom Bisque with Crabmeat 194

Roasted Red Pepper Cream Soup 116

Ron's Bar-B-Que Shrimp 143

Rosemary and Garlic Marinated Pork Tenderloin 87

Sabayon Glacé 155

Salad Dressing:

    Asian Vinaigrette 121

    Basil-Kalamata Olive Vinaigrette Dressing 287

    Blue Cheese Dressing 90

    Dried Cherry Vinaigrette 98

    Italian Salad Dressing 317

    Mango Lime Vinaigrette 63

    Mango Vinaigrette 29

    Poppy Seed Dressing 83

    Sherry Vinaigrette 51

    Smoked Tomato Dressing 324

    Spinach Salad Dressing 21

    Toasted Garlic Dressing 66

    Vinaigrette 71, 95

    Vinaigrette Dressing 186

Salads:

    Arugula Salad with Apples, Ricotta Salata, and Poppy Seeds 83

    Bon Ton Shrimp Rémoulade Salad 15

    Cheese Salad with Basil Olive Vinaigrette 287

    Chef Tory's Seared Redfish and Chili Glazed Shrimp Salad 29

    Chopped Salad 324

    Corn Salad 281

    Creole Tomato, Cucumber, and Vidalia Onion Salad 51

    Francese 198

    German Potato Salad 129

    Green Shrimp Salad 283

    Grilled Beets with Goat's Cheese and Walnuts 71

    Grilled Eggplant, Tomato, Fresh Mozzarella, Portobello Mushrooms, and Fresh Basil Salad 240

    Italian Salad, The 317

    Johnny Jambalaya's Beat the "Summertime Blues" Pasta Salad 163

    Salad of Dandelions, Crispy Seared Foie Gras, and Tempura Cèpes 98

    Traditional Potato Salad 59

Salmon Confit, J.E.'s 305

Salmon with Lump Crabmeat and Lemon Butter, Mustard and Cornmeal-Crusted 157

Sandwiches, Mandarin Chicken and Almond Tea Finger 332

Sauces:

    Alligator Ragout with Chipotle Creole Tomato Sauce 96

    Andouille Cream Drizzle 91

    Au Poive Sauce 235

    Banana Bliss 62

    Bananas Foster Syrup 168

Basil Purée 70
Basil Sauce 340
BBQ Oyster Sauce 90
Béchamel Sauce 32, 46
Béarnaise Sauce 32
Bourbon Sauce 114
Brandy Cream Sauce 31
Cabernet Wine Sauce 17
Cane Syrup Glaze 216
Caramel Sauce 44
Cayenne Butter Sauce 80
Cheese Sauce 293
Chef Hans' Shrimp Rémoulade 308
Chocolate Sauce 44
Crawfish Monica Sauce 170
Creamy Cajun Crawfish and Tasso Sauce 208
Curry Coconut Cream Sauce 184
Frangelico Cream Sauce 206
Garlic Beurre Blanc Sauce 269
Garlic Cream Sauce 263
Glaze for Cajun Hot Bites 215
Hollandaise 271
Hollandaise Sauce 47, 173
Hot Pepper Jelly Demi-Glace 131
Irish Whiskey Sauce 75
Jack Daniel's Corn Sauce 286
Jack Daniel's Sauce 249
Meunière Sauce 27, 173
Meunière Sauce with Mushrooms 79
Peach or Kumquat Sauce 220
Pico de Gallo 345
Pimento Sauce 22
Pommery Cream Sauce 322
Praline Sauce 171
Red Curry 259
Rémoulade Sauce 147
Rouille 94
Rum Sauce 146, 166
Saffron Barbecue Sauce 120
Sauce Doré 21

Sauce for JJ's Meaux Jeaux Pork
    Medallions 165
Shrimp Diablo Sauce 255
Soy-Vinegar Sauce 133
Spicy Lobster Sauce 136
Sweet and Sour Prune Sauce 87
Taco Sauce 345
Tasso Cream Sauce 55
Tomato Basil Cream Sauce 355
Truffled Potato Sauce 52
Whiskey Sauce 18

Sausage:
Andouille Cream Drizzle 91
Andouille-Crusted Fish with Cayenne Butter
    Sauce 80
Chicken and Andouille Gumbo 169
Chicken and Andouille Smoked Sausage
    Gumbo 58
Chicken and Sausage Gumbo 247
Crawfish and Andouille Stuffed Pork Loin with
    Hot Pepper Jelly Demi-Glacé 131
Lasyone's Red Beans and Sausage 278
Mr. B's Gumbo Ya Ya 73
Shrimp and Andouille Pasta, The 169
Shrimp and Tasso Pasta 229
Spinach and Andouille Stuffing 188
White Chocolate Ganache 77
Sawdust Pie 349
Scaloppini di Vitello Alle Noci e More 312

Scallops:
Pan-Roasted Seafood Bouillabaisse with a
    Tomato-Saffron Broth and Garlic Creamed
    Potatoes 103
Pompano Napoleon 24
Spaghetti Fruitte di Mare 198

Seafood: *see also specific seafood*
Miss Mayme's Seafood Gumbo 291
Pan-Roasted Seafood Bouillabaisse with a
    Tomato-Saffron Broth and Garlic Creamed
    Potatoes 103
Ralph and Kacoo's Seafood Gumbo 176
Seafood au Gratin 212
Seafood Gumbo 247, 284, 289

Recipe Index

Very Best Seafood Gumbo, The 284

Seared Wild Striped Bass, Potato Porcini, Risotto Fried Leeks, Tomato, Cognac Fumé 102

Sesame Crusted Yellow-Fin with Asian Vinaigrette 121

Sherbet, Pineapple 140

Shrimp:

Bar-B-Que Shrimp 210

Bon Ton Shrimp Remoulade Salad 15

Cajun Frittata with Tomato Horseradish and Boiled Shrimp 104

Chef Hans' Shrimp Rémoulade 308

Chef Tory's Seared Redfish and Chili Glazed Shrimp Salad 29

Green Shrimp Salad 283

Grilled Fish or Shrimp Tacos 345

Joe's Stuffed Eggplant 147

Mirliton, Shrimp, and Crab Bisque 65

Miss Mayme's Seafood Gumbo 291

Mr. B's New Orleans Barbequed Shrimp 74

Pompano Napoleon 24

Ralph and Kacoo's Seafood Gumbo 176

Ron's Bar-B-Que Shrimp 143

Sauce Doré 21

Seafood au Gratin 212

Seafood Gumbo 284, 289

Shrimp and Andouille Pasta, The 169

Shrimp and Corn Bisque 241

Shrimp and Crabmeat Cheesecake 22

Shrimp and Green Chile Grits with Tasso Cream Sauce 55

Shrimp and Tasso Pasta 229

Shrimp and White Beans 239

Shrimp Baton Rouge 154

Shrimp Bisque 56

Shrimp Butter 177

Shrimp Casserole 337

Shrimp Diablo 255

Shrimp Pie 141

Shrimp Rémoulade 49

Shrimp Saint Charles 190

Shrimp-Stuffed Bell Peppers 160

Snapper Pontchartrain 293

Spaghetti Fruitte de Mare 198

Very Best Seafood Gumbo, The 285

Wild Rice Pilaf with Oysters and Shrimp Creole 310

Slayden's Coconut Cream Pie 343

Smoked Pork Fettuccini 217

Snapper Pontchartrain 293

Soft-Shell Crab Dorè 21

Soups:

Artichoke and Oyster Soup 214

Bacon, Lettuce, and Tomato Soup 163

Bavarian Potato Soup 129

Beef Stew Crockpot 274

Bon Ton Homemade Turtle Soup 14

Chicken Tortilla Soup 347

Chilled Champagne-Strawberry Soup with Mint Ice Cream 85

Corn and Crabmeat Bisque 113

Corn Fest Bailey Bisque 283

Crawfish, Corn, and Potato Chowder 179

Crawfish Bisque 201

Crawfish Chowder 301

Cream of Brie Cheese with Lump Crabmeat Soup 158

Creole Onion Soup 34

Dakota's Lump Crabmeat and Brie Soup 119

Hot and Sour Soup 134

Kitty Kimball's Broccoli Soup 161

Lafayette's Crawfish and Artichoke Bisque 229

Lemon Grass Soup 259

Mirliton, Shrimp, and Crab Bisque 65

My Good Friend Bob's Tomato Curry Purée with Cumin Grilled Shrimp 107

Oyster Stew 141

Pan-Roasted Seafood Bouillabaisse with a Tomato-Saffron Broth and Garlic Creamed Potatoes 103

Potato, Leek and Onion Soup 269

Roasted Corn and Poblano Chowder 272

Roasted Red Pepper and Wild Mushroom Bisque with Crabmeat 194

Roasted Red Pepper Cream Soup 116

Shrimp and Corn Bisque 241

Shrimp Bisque 56

Soup Jacqueline 153

Spinach Laura 327

Tina's Vegetable Soup 243

Turtle Soup 112

Southern Pecan Chicken Champignon 211

Southwest Chicken Breast 314

Spaghetti:

Cheesy Chicken Spaghetti 301

Spaghetti à la Peppino 341

Spaghetti Fruitte di Mare 198

Spinach:

Creamed Spinach 32, 47

Fried Baby Spinach 53

Oysters Pujo 252

Spinach and Andouille Stuffing 188

Spinach Laura 327

Spinach Salad Dressing 21

Spring Roll 94

Steaks:

Filet Mignon au Poive 235

House Filet 33

Steak Cubed with Mushrooms in Cabernet Wine Sauce 17

Strawberries:

Chilled Champagne-Strawberry Soup with Mint Ice Cream 85

Crêpes Broussard 23

Fresh Berry Pie 294

Sabayon Glacé 155

Strawberry Pie 123

Warm Strawberry Cobbler with Vanilla Ice Cream 99

Stuffed Mushrooms with Crawfish 153

Stuffed Portobello Mushrooms 174

Stuffed Tomatoes with Crab and Corn Coulis 150

Sweet Potatoes:

Mashed Sweet Potatoes with Bananas, Bourbon, and Vanilla 53

Praline Yams 219

Sweet Potato Catfish with Andouille Cream Drizzle 91

Sweet Potato Muffins 233

Sweet Potato Pie 280

Vegetables in a Sweet Potato Cream with Pasta 61

Szechuan Spicy Alligator 135

Tina's Vegetable Soup 243

Toasted Garlic Dressing 66

Tomatoes:

Alligator Ragout with Chipotle Creole Tomato Sauce 96

Bacon, Lettuce, and Tomato Soup 163

Corn Salad 281

Creole Tomato, Cucumber, and Vidalia Onion Salad 51

Fried Green Tomatoes with Crabmeat Rémoulade 197

My Good Friend Bob's Tomato Curry Purée with Cumin Grilled Shrimp 107

Poached Oysters in a Saffron-Tomato Coulis 84

Red Snapper with Roasted Garlic and Tomato Provencal 117

Smoked Tomato Dressing 324

Stuffed Tomatoes with Crab and Corn Coulis 150

Traditional Potato Salad 59

Tuna:

Sesame Crusted Yellow-Fin with Asian Vinaigrette 121

Tuna au Poivre 195

Recipe Index

Tuna Pasteur 94

Tunk's Crawfish Étouffée 292

Turtle Soup 112

Turtle Soup, Bon Ton Homemade 14

Veal:

Scaloppini di Vitello Alle Noci e More 312

Veal Delmonico 180

Veal Marcelle 40

Veal "New Orleans" 309

Veal Primo 173

Vegetables: *see also specific vegetables*

Black-Eyed Peas and Buttermilk Cornbread 349

Fried Eggplant with Crawfish Monica Sauce 170

Pasta Primavera 60

Shrimp and White Beans 239

Shrimp-Stuffed Bell Peppers 160

Tina's Vegetable Soup 243

Vegetables in a Sweet Potato Cream with Pasta 61

Very Best Seafood Gumbo, The 284

Vinaigrette Dressing 186

Warm Strawberry Cobbler with Vanilla Ice Cream 99

White Chocolate Bread Pudding 77

White Chocolate Bread Pudding Soufflé 235

White Chocolate Bread Pudding with Frangelico Cream Sauce 206

White Chocolate Ganache 77

White Chocolate/Macadamia Crème Brûlée 299

Wild Rice Pilaf with Oysters and Shrimp Creole 310

Wine and Herb Baked Catfish with Wild Rice 354

Zucchini:

Angel Hair Pasta with Crawfish Tails 318

Pasta Primavera 60

Vegetables in a Sweet Potato Cream with Pasta 61

Restaurant Index

Bealer's Restaurant 111

Bella Fresca Restaurant 297

Bella Rose Food and Spirits 115

Blue Dog Café 183

Bon Ton Café 13

Bountiful Foods Catering 300

Brec's Magnolia Mound Plantation 139

The Brandy House Restaurant 303

Broussard's 19

Café Des Amis 185

Cajun Injector, Inc. 142

Cajun Landing 267

Catahoula's 189

Chef Hans' Gourmet Foods 306

Chef Roy's Frog City Café 191

Chianti Restaurant 311

Clancy's 25

Clementine Dining and Spirits 193

Commander's Palace 28

Country Place Restaurant 313

Cristiano's Ristorante 196

Cypress Bend 270

D.I.'s Cajun Food & Music 200

The Dakota Restaurant 118

Dickie Brennan's Steakhouse 30

Dominic's Italian Restaurant 316

Don's Seafood and Steakhouse 202

Dooky Chase's 35

Dupuy's Oyster Shop 204

Emeril Lagasse's NOLA 37

Emeril's Delmonico 39

Emeril's Restaurant 41

Enoch's Café and Pub 319

Fertitta's 6301 Restaurant 321

Fezzo's 207

Flanagan's 209

Follette Pottery 326

Fremin's 213

Galatoire's Restaurant 45

Gerald Savoie's 329

The Glenwood Village Tearoom 331

The Grapevine Café and Gallery 218

GW Fins 50

Hanson House 222

Harbor Seafood Restaurant 226

Herbsaint 54

Jesse's Steak and Seafood 334

Joe's Dreyfus Store Restaurant 145

Juban's Restaurant & Catering 148

K-Paul's Louisiana Kitchen 57

Lafayette's 228

Restaurant Index

The Landing Restaurant 273
Landry's Restaurant 230
Lasyone's Meat Pie Kitchen 276
Le Parvenu 64
Lea's Lunch Room 279
Lilette Restaurant 69
The Magnolia Room 282
Main Street Restaurant 122
Maison Daboval 232
Maison Lacour 152
Mansur's on the Boulevard 156
Mariner's 288
Michabelle Inn and Restaurant 125
Morel's 159
Mr. B's Bistro 72
Mr. Lester's Steakhouse 234
Ms. Lucy's Classic Cajun 336
Nash's Restaurant 237
Nottoway Plantation 162
Oak Alley Plantation 167
Olive Street Bistro 339
The Palace Café 242
Palace Café 76
Pat's of Henderson 246
Peristyle 82
Prejean's Restaurant 248
Primo's 172

Pujo St. Café 251
Ralph and Kacoo's 175
Ralph Brennan's BACCO 86
Ralph Brennan's Red Fish Grill 89
René Bistrot 93
Restaurant August 97
Restaurant Cuvée 101
Saia's Oaks Plantation 178
Slayden's Bar-B-Q 342
SNO'S Seafood and Steakhouse 253
Stella! 106
Superior Grill 344
A Taste of Bavaria 128
Thai Cuisine 257
Tope Lá! 130
Trey Yuen 132
Tunk's Cypress Inn 290
Uncle Earl's Pea Patch Café 348
The Village Restaurant 350
Walker's Cajun Dining 260
Waterfront Grill 353
Yellow Bowl Restaurant 262

Other Cookbooks in the
BEST RESTAURANT RECIPES SERIES

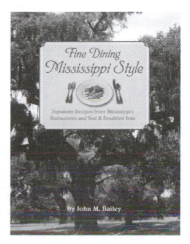

**Fine Dining
Georgia Style**

978-1-893062-66-5
1-893062-66-X
8⅜x10⅞ • Hardbound
Full-color photographs
Illustrated • 136 pages • $24.95

**Fine Dining
Tennessee Style**

978-1-893062-59-7
1-893062-59-7
8⅜x10⅞ • Hardbound
Full-color photographs
Illustrated • 200 pages • $24.95

**Fine Dining
Mississippi Style**

978-1-893062-55-9
1-893062-55-4
8⅜x10⅞ • Hardbound
Full-color photographs
Illustrated • 168 pages • $24.95

Buy the entire set at a 60% discount—
that's all 3 cookbooks for only $29.95!

The cookbooks shown above all contain the most popular, signature recipes from the leading restaurants in each state. The cookbooks sell for $24.95 each, but can be purchased as a three-book set for the special price of $29.95! (That's a 60% discount off the total list price of $74.85.) This is a great opportunity to collect exceptionally tasteful recipes that have been superbly developed and perfected by the leading chefs of these states.

QUAIL RIDGE PRESS

Preserving America's Food Heritage

P. O. Box 123 • Brandon, MS 39043 • 1-800-343-1583 • www.quailridge.com

Other Popular Louisiana Cookbooks from Quail Ridge Press

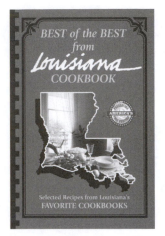

These cookbooks each contain over 300 classic recipes selected from Louisiana's leading cookbooks. Of all the cookbooks in the acclaimed BEST OF THE BEST STATE COOKBOOK SERIES, the Louisiana editions are the most popular!

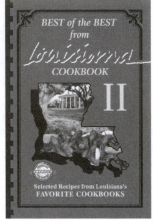

Best of the Best from Louisiana Cookbook

978-0-937552-13-1 • 0-937552-13-5
6x9 • 288 pages • Comb-bound • Illustrations
Photographs • Index • $16.95

Best of the Best from Louisiana Cookbook II

978-0-937552-83-4 • 0-937552-83-6
6x9 • 288 pages • Comb-bound • Illustrations
Photographs • Index • $16.95

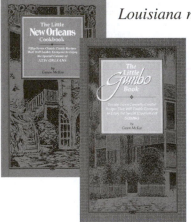

Louisiana native Gwen McKee created these two classic cookbooks!

The Little New Orleans Cookbook

Features fifty-seven select recipes that capture the famous New Orleans tradition of incredible food.

978-0-937552-42-1 • 0-937552-42-9
4⅞ x 8¼ • 80 pages • Hardbound • $9.95

The Little Gumbo Book

Specializes in one dish and provides a step-by-step guide to preparing twenty-seven varieties of this Louisiana tradition.

978-0-937552-17-9 • 0-937552-17-8
4⅞ x 8¼ • 64 pages • Hardbound • $9.95

Louisiana Alphabet is a celebration of what makes the Pelican State special . . . from A to Z. Fun-to-read rhymed verse and whimsical collage illustrations present a delightful alphabetical account of the people, places, and things that give Louisiana its unique charm. Both children and adults will be entertained and informed by exploring the state letter by letter.

Louisiana Alphabet

978-1-893062-31-3 • 1-893062-31-7
10x8½ • 32 pages • Hardbound • Full-color illustrations • $15.95

Order Form

QTY	TITLE	PRICE	AMOUNT
	Lousiana's Best Restaurant Recipes	$19.95	
	Fine Dining Georgia Style	$24.95	
	Fine Dining Mississippi Style	$24.95	
	Fine Dining Tennessee Style	$24.95	
	SPECIAL! Fine Dining 3-Book Set	$29.95	
	Best of the Best from Louisiana Cookbook	$16.95	
	Best of the Best from Louisiana Cookbook II	$16.95	
	The Little New Orleans Cookbook	$9.95	
	The Little Gumbo Book	$9.95	
	Louisiana Alphabet	$15.95	
	SUBTOTAL		
	7% Tax for MS residents		
	Postage ($4.00 any number of books)		+ 4.00
	TOTAL		

Name _____

Address _____

City/State/Zip _____

Email Address _____ Phone _____

❏ Check or money order enclosed

Charge to: ❏ Visa ❏ MasterCard ❏ American Express ❏ Discover

Card # _____

Signature _____ Exp. Date _____

Use this convenient order form and send with payment to:

ⓠ QUAIL RIDGE PRESS
P. O. Box 123 • Brandon, MS 39043
or call toll-free **1-800-343-1583** or visit **www.quailridge.com**.